Library of
Davidson College

THE GARLAND LIBRARY OF LATIN POETRY

selected by
Steele Commager
Columbia University

RES METRICA

WILLIAM ROSS HARDIE

GARLAND PUBLISHING, INC.

NEW YORK & LONDON
1979

The volumes in this series have been printed on
acid-free, 250-year-life paper.

486
H262w

Library of Congress Cataloging in Publication Data

Hardie, William Ross, 1862-1916.
  Res metrica.

  (The Garland library of Latin poetry)
  Reprint of the 1920 ed. published at the Clarendon
Press, Oxford.
  1. Classical languages--Metrics and rhythmics.
I. Title. II. Series.
PA186.H3 1979   486   77-70821
ISBN 0-8240-2970-4

Printed in the United States of America

RES METRICA

BY

W. R. HARDIE

RES METRICA

AN INTRODUCTION TO THE

STUDY OF GREEK & ROMAN

VERSIFICATION

BY THE LATE

WILLIAM ROSS HARDIE
M.A. LL.D.

*Professor of Humanity
in the University of Edinburgh
Formerly Fellow and Tutor of Balliol College*

OXFORD
AT THE CLARENDON PRESS
1920

OXFORD UNIVERSITY PRESS
LONDON   EDINBURGH   GLASGOW   NEW YORK
   TORONTO   MELBOURNE   CAPE TOWN   BOMBAY
HUMPHREY MILFORD
PUBLISHER TO THE UNIVERSITY

PREFACE

I AM reluctant to trouble the reader with what is more or less personal, but it seems necessary to explain how this book came to exist. In the spring of 1912 I was asked to review Schröder's *Horazens Versmasse, für Anfänger erklärt*, and I did not find that it solved the problem; it was not a thing which, if translated, would be helpful to 'beginners' in this country. In the summer it occurred to me to try the experiment of writing an account of Horace's lyric metres myself, and I wrote it, merely as an experiment and without the slightest intention of publishing it. Shortly after this I learned from Professor Lindsay that he was interested in getting something done towards making metrical knowledge more accessible to students; what he had in mind was finding somebody to translate Bickel's section on Metre in Gercke and Norden's *Einleitung in die Alterthumswissenschaft*. But Bickel's treatment, he agreed, was not satisfactory for our purpose; like Schröder's it was too technical and too condensed for the ordinary reader. I showed him my experimental account of Horace's metres, and chiefly through his instigation and encouragement I wrote in the following summer accounts of some of the more familiar metres such as the Hexameter and Iambic Trimeter. These I now thought of as chapters in a possible, though still hardly probable, book. The experiment which I made with most reluctance was that of writing a chapter on Greek lyric verse, but this also was done, in September 1913. The conditions of teaching in this country are not like those of Germany, and few teaching posts allow much time for writing or research; so it was only at rather long intervals that I could take this metrical business in hand. I say this not in the least as regretting or resenting the conditions, and not at all as an apology for the deficiencies of the book. I am not sure that with more time to give to it I should have made it any better; it might even have been, for practical purposes and for the ordinary reader, worse. Such as it is, it owes its existence largely to Professor Lindsay's encouragement. For its defects he is not responsible; he removed some of them, and he has contributed valuable advice and suggestions. He is in no way responsible for what is said about Saturnian verse in the chapter on 'Metre at Rome'. It was at one time a part of the design that he should contribute a chapter on the metre of the Roman Drama. But it now seems best to refer the reader to his account of Plautine metre in the Introduction to the larger edition of the *Captivi* (Methuen and Co., 1900).

The method of the book will be thought unscientific, but it seemed best to avoid any attempt at deductive, exhaustive, and systematic exposition. To begin with what is highly abstract and general—as with definitions of Rhythm and Metre—is to run a risk of being involved at once in what is disputable and speculative, or what can scarcely be clear and significant to the reader until he has already become familiar with numerous particular facts. To avoid what is controversial, to remain on what is fairly firm ground, has been one of the main objects kept in view. Controversial matter has been segregated as far as possible by relegation to an Excursus. It is hoped that some general notions of rhythm and metre will gradually become clearer to the reader as he proceeds, and a Glossary of metrical terms has been appended in order to enable him to ascertain whether an idea which he gathers from the text of the book was meant to underlie it or not.

It has been a further aim to treat metre in a rather more historical way than has sometimes been done, and to keep it in closer contact with literary study and literary interests. But a strictly historical method would have been as difficult to carry out as a deductive and theoretical method. The Chronological Table is intended to supply the defects of the text in this matter of sequence in time or consecutiveness.

A strictly deductive or a strictly historical method would have made each chapter more dependent on what preceded it. It seemed desirable to make each chapter a thing which would be fairly intelligible if read separately. This results in a certain amount of repetition, which would be a fault in a work of literary art. In a text-book utility may be allowed to prevail over artistic considerations. The main business of the writer of a text-book is to devise ways of putting things which will make them clear, forms of statement which are not misleading or complicated or abstruse: the grouping of facts is also part of his business, the arranging of them so that they will support one another and their connexion will appear. It is not his business to devise new theories. But neither is it his business to accept theories, whatever their present

PREFACE

vogue, without criticism. Even the writer of a text-book must take up some position, and he may perhaps usefully in a Preface try to state briefly what he has been doing when he has not been occupied solely with what I have defined as his main business.

In regard to the history of the Hexameter and especially of its caesura, the writer of this book disagrees with some current methods and is inclined to dispute, or 'disable' as evidence, a good deal of recent statistics.

In regard to Iambic and Trochaic Verse, evidence is offered—statistics, I think, too simple to be disputable—that the peculiarly Roman line (with spondees in what for a Greek were the wrong places) did not die out gradually, but gained ground, from Ennius to Accius, and then was ejected by a reaction or new movement. An outline of the history of metre at Rome has been attempted (pt. II, chap. ii) which is intended to show briefly what the Romans were trying to do at different periods and what were the difficulties they had to contend with.

The tragedies of Seneca have been kept in view, as throwing light both on Horace's metrical ideas and on Roman metrical practice of the imperial age.

As to Greek lyric verse, the writer is aware that he will be regarded by Mr. White and others as $Κρονίων$ $ὄζων\ καὶ\ βεκκεσέληνος$, when he expresses doubts about the quadrisyllabic structure of Aeolic verse and about Choriambo-Ionic structure of the 'Enoplius'. This, however, is quite deliberate, and, though it does not rest on complete knowledge of the evidence, it does not rest on complete ignorance of it either. In an Excursus (after chap. i of pt. II) will be found an attempt to show that three passages which have been quoted as important do not prove what they are supposed to prove (i.e. that the Choriambo-Ionic arrangement is as old as the fifth century B.C.). To revert to dactylic scansion and to suggest that 'anacrusis', though unsupported by tradition, is a more useful idea than 'hypercatalexis' is a proceeding likely to evoke the objection, 'So you think that modern metricians may know more about Greek verse than the Greeks did'; and to reply 'That is exactly what I do think' will perhaps elicit still more severe condemnation, if the holders of the now prevalent views condescend to notice it at all. I have suggested a comparison with Ptolemaic and Copernican astronomy, but this of course may be disallowed. 'The Greeks', it will be said, 'did not construct the stars; they did construct their own verse, and must have known what it was.' To this I should reply 'Do we accept their grammar, or their critical treatment of texts?' They spoke their language and wrote the texts, but is it not the case that the arts of analysis and interpretation lagged far behind creation, and were developed surprisingly late? Do we believe Quintilian when he says of the 'Historical Infinitive': '*stupere gaudio Graecus*: simul enim auditur *coepit*'; or when he takes Virgil to have written 'qui non risere parentes' in the sense of 'who have not smiled upon or to a parent'—a plural resumed by a singular *hunc* in the next line? Is it a happy description of the shorter gen. pl. in Latin (*deum*) to say that it is the acc. sing. used for the gen. pl.? Do we think it, I do not say true, but possible, that Homer wrote μετὰ δ' οὔ σφι πατὴρ κίε δάκρυα λείβων (the father in question being by this time dead—killed in an earlier book)? And what would Bentley have said of a critic who gravely discussed τῶν ἐν τοῖς ὀφθαλμοῖς παρθένων as a phrase for the pupil of the eye (κόρη)—this not in a dithyramb, but in a plain prose treatise—as the writer *De Sublimitate* does? Examples like these could easily be multiplied. Why should the Greek treatment of metre be supposed to be infallible? Besides, I am not at all sure that we know what the Greek treatment really was in the sixth or fifth centuries. Still less do we know what metre was before Sappho, or in Indo-European times. Further, one might point out that writers on English metre have again and again assumed that poets wrote something that is *not* best described as they themselves would have described it; e.g. that Milton did not really write a line of five iambi in *Paradise Lost*. But I do not lay great stress on this last argument; I should lay more stress on it, if I had more belief in the theories about English verse which these writers have propounded. There is also the case of French verse. How much agreement is there about that, although metricians would have the advantage of being able to interrogate contemporary poets who are writing it? Greek verse was much more complicated and varied: what is the probability that Hephaestion would be able to give a true account of lyric forms which had for long ceased to be composed?

For these reasons it does not seem to me at all illegitimate to inquire what is the best way of describing verse-forms rather than what is the way supported by tradition.

CONTENTS

PART I

THE SIMPLER AND MORE FAMILIAR FORMS OF VERSE

CHAPTER	PAGE
I. THE HEROIC HEXAMETER:	
(i) Origin and General Structure	1
(ii) Subordinate Divisions	14

Excursus:

(a) Hexameters in the Lyric and Tragic poets 26
(b) Statistics relating to Virgil's verse . 27

II. THE COLLOCATION OF WORDS IN EPIC VERSE (ELISION, HIATUS, ETC.) . 30

III. THE ELEGIAC COUPLET . . . 49

IV. ANAPAESTS 56

V. IAMBIC VERSE:
(i) The Iambic Trimeter and 'Senarius' 68

Excursus:

(a) 'Choriambic substitution' . . 86
(b) The Roman disregard for 'Porson's Canon' 87

CHAPTER		PAGE
	(c) The nature and history of the old spondaic 'Senarius' at Rome	88
	(d) The length of the first syllable in an impure or heavy iambus	91
	(ii) The Iambic Tetrameter Catalectic	92
VI.	THE SCAZON OR CHOLIAMBUS	98
VII.	THE TROCHAIC TETRAMETER AND 'SEPTENARIUS'	103
VIII.	HENDECASYLLABICS OR PHALAECEI	114

PART II

I.	GREEK LYRIC VERSE:	
	(i) Archilochus, Alcman, and Sappho	118
	Excursus (a) 'Aeolic' Verse	136
	(ii) Simple or Homogeneous Metres (μονο-ειδῆ)	143
	(iii) Pindar and the Dramatic Poets	165
	Excursus (b) On the quadrisyllabic scansion of 'Dactylo-epitrite' verse, on 'Iambic Syncopation', and on 'Ictus'	177
II.	THE HISTORY OF METRE AT ROME	196
III.	LYRIC METRES OF HORACE	223

APPENDIX

(A)	GLOSSARY OF SOME METRICAL TERMS	261
(B)	CHRONOLOGICAL TABLE	270

PART I

CHAPTER I

THE HEROIC HEXAMETER

I. Origin and General Structure

It is a singular fact about Greek literature that it begins with poems of great power and splendour, which exercised a vast influence in later times and in their greatest parts were hardly, if ever, surpassed by the work of later poets. But of course it is only for us that Greek literature begins in this way. There is nothing extant that we can certainly or convincingly describe as pre-Homeric. That much did exist is certain. It has long been recognized that the Homeric poems are not really very early or primitive, but the crown and consummation of a long period of poetic effort and experiment. This is no less clear in their form and versification, with which we are here concerned, than in their diction and style and contents. Hexameters are often spoken of as sung, and we hear of a musical accompaniment, but it is probable that what was really sung was a more primitive form of ballad in shorter lines, such as conjecture or imagination can sometimes reconstruct out of Homeric lines. Thus

> ἠράμεθα μέγα κῦδος,
> ἐπέφνομεν Ἕκτορα δῖον

sounds like a primitive song of triumph, and

> οἶδ' ἐπὶ δεξιά,
> οἶδ' ἐπ' ἀριστερὰ
> νωμῆσαι βῶν

has the air of being an ancient *tripudium* or threefold dance of an armed warrior. The longer hexameter indicates a transition from singing to recitation. Perhaps it was the work mainly of Ionians. At all events it belongs to a dialect whose uncontracted forms lent themselves to dactylic verse (μυθέομαι, χάλκεα, ἐρέω, ἀργυρέοιο), and, further, forms of words have been adapted to dactylic verse by successive minstrels (e.g. ἀθάνατος, ἀκάματος, with the first syllable lengthened). Much of the diction has been cast into shapes which readily make up a hexameter. There are a great many complete lines that are recurrent or conventional (κυκλικοὶ στίχοι, e.g. αὐτὰρ ἐπεὶ πόσιος καὶ ἐδητύος ἐξ ἔρον ἕντο), there are parts of lines that recur in the same way, and various names or epithets for gods and heroes lay to the poet's hand (κυανοχαίτης, ἐννοσίγαιος, ἀγελείη τριτογένεια, ἑκατηβελέταο ἄνακτος). This 'stock-in-trade' seems to imply that at some time the minstrel improvised his song, though constructions like the *Iliad* and *Odyssey* are not the result of improvisation. Advance and improvement were probably made in a half-conscious way, by the poet's sense of euphony and feeling for rhythm. Very exact laws can be laid down for Homeric hexameters, but we must beware of thinking that they resemble the principles or methods of Virgil, Horace, and Ovid.

The verse itself, the 'Dactylic Hexameter', may be constructed theoretically as follows:—It belongs to what the Greeks called the γένος ἴσον in rhythm, the dactyl is a foot which falls into two equal parts ($- = \cup\cup$) and its length is that of four short syllables or unit-times[1]. Constructing the verse, then, out of its elements, we start with

$\cup\cup\cup\cup$ | $\cup\cup\cup\cup$ | $\cup\cup\cup\cup$ | $\cup\cup\cup\cup$ | ....

---

[1] χρόνος πρῶτος is a convenient term of ῥυθμική, meaning the time which is made audible, in verse, by a normal short syllable. It may be made audible in music by a short note, ♪; or made perceptible by a movement of the body, as in dancing.

HEXAMETER

an indefinite string of groups of four short sounds. But the perpendicular lines which we have drawn to separate them into groups have no real existence. The groups are made perceptible as groups by an *ictus* on the first of each (in dactylic verse—anapaests belong to the same γένος, but we are not now considering them):

ύ υ υ υ ύ υ υ υ ύ υ υ υ &c.

Next, the grouping can be made still more obvious by putting a long for the first two shorts. This gives us an indefinite string of 'dactyls', and it must be cut into 'lengths' to give us verse. 'Lengths cut off' is Aristotle's phrase (τομὴ ῥυθμοῦ, τμητά). A hexameter is a 'length' of six μέτρα, feet or units, a tetrameter a 'length' of four. But if these lengths are to be perceived as separate groups, they must have some sort of structure, the beginning or end must be made perceptible. In the hexameter the end is made perceptible by decreeing that the last foot shall always be of two syllables. But the effect of this closing cadence would be obscured unless the preceding foot were the normal one. Therefore a hexameter ends in a dactyl and spondee, or at all events in a dactyl and a disyllabic foot. There is another possibility or alternative (it is found in Homer and was fancied in a later age by Alexandrian poets and their imitators at Rome)—the last *two* feet may consist of long syllables, or the line may end in three long syllables and a doubtful syllable (ἑκηβόλου Ἀπόλλωνος). In this case the *fourth* foot will usually be a dactyl.

This theoretic construction, the construction of a hexameter *in vacuo*, leaves us with two problems to consider, a smaller and a larger one.

The smaller question is about the nature of the last foot or last two syllables of a line. Such effects as Virgil's

                        Turres ét tecta Latinor'(-um)
ardua cernebant iuvenes

suggest that our statement ought to have been 'the end of the group of six is marked by making the last foot a spondee'. If so, in an ending like *attigit arvă*, the short syllable will be a *syllaba anceps* in the sense that it can count as a long. It is at the end of a line or group, not thrust up, as it were, against a following syllable whose beginning ends it. A short pause or silence completes the time, like a short rest in music, the pause for which the Greek symbol was ∧ ; so that the last foot is $-\cup\wedge$. That seems the most reasonable way of contemplating the matter. The objection to it is that it does not accord with ancient theory, and that there are a few lines—but very few—which it does not explain. The last foot was thought of by the ancients not as a dactyl which combined its two short syllables into one long, but as a dactyl which dropped its last syllable, $-\cup(\cup)$. On this view the last syllable is *anceps* in the sense that if actually long it may count as short.

Against this ancient theory a reader of Virgil may raise the objection: 'but there are lines which end with a real and unmistakable spondee, for the last syllable is not the last syllable of a word; there is "elision":

Turres et tecta Latinor(um)
ardua cernebant iuvenes.'

'And, again', he may proceed, 'are not lines which end in almost equally unmistakable spondees (like *primus ab oris*) far more numerous?' But elision at the end of a hexameter is not certainly older than Callimachus.[1] And it is chiefly in

[1] Ἡμισύ μοι ψυχῆς ἔτι τὸ πνέον, ἥμισυ δ' οὐκ οἶδ'
εἴτ' Ἔρος εἴτ' Ἀίδης ἥρπασε, πλὴν ἀφανές.

It has been suggested that Ennius introduced this effect in Latin by writing 'altisonum cael(um)' at the end of a line. Ennius is credited with inventing monosyllabic forms *cael* and *gau* for *caelum* and *gaudium*, on the analogy of Homer's κρῖ and δῶ. Elision would not explain *gau* so readily as it does *cael*. But it may be doubted whether Ennius ever

Latin that spondees are in an overwhelming majority. In Homer one line in five (or if we nowhere write a ν ἐφελκυστικόν, one line in four) ends in a short vowel not closed by a consonant (as in νῆᾰ, ᾿Ατρείδαο, ἔθηκε). In Ovid, *Met.* vii, the proportion is 1 in 12; in Virgil, *Ecl.* 1 in 14·3, *Georg.* 1 in 11, *Aen.* i. 1–500, 1 in 17·2. The Romans had a liking for making a last syllable long when it could legitimately be done, as is seen in Horace's Sapphics and Alcaics. So, perhaps, the ancient theory of a trochaic ending is to some extent justified by the history of the verse. The lines which the other theory does not explain are chiefly these two in Virgil:

> inseritur vero et fetu nucis arbutus horrid(a)
> et steriles platani,   (*Georg.* ii. 69.)

and

> et spumas miscent argenti vivaque sulpur(a)
> Idaeasque pices.   (*Georg.* iii. 449.)

But the text of neither passage is above suspicion. Much earlier we find in an epigram of Simonides:

> ἦ μέγ' ᾿Αθηναίοισι φόως γένεθ', ἡνίκ' ᾿Αριστογείτων ῞Ιππαρχον κτεῖνε καὶ ῾Αρμόδιος.

But it is not safe to infer that either the hyperbaton or the trochee belonged to recognized metrical practice. When a proper name had to be put into a metrical inscription the rigidity of metrical laws had to yield a little. There are inscriptions extant in which metre has to submit to much harsher treatment than this.

The second question is much more important. In cutting

really wrote such lines at all. They may have been fictitious examples of solecisms or eccentricities. We know (from Pompeius, 289. 10 K.) that Lucilius not merely *said* that there were 100 kinds of solecism, each with its own appropriate name, but actually described them: e.g. Tmesis: 'as if we were to write', 'as if Ennius wrote "Massili—portabant iuvenes ad litora—tanas."'

off a 'length' of six dactyls we cut off what was too long, what cannot really be delivered in one breath, without a pause or break, as a single whole. Aristoxenus laid it down that for feet of this γένος (τετράσημοι or τετράχρονοι πόδες, of the γένος ἴσον) the maximum length of a phrase or κῶλον is four feet. This may or may not be an absolute and final law of rhythm. But it seems sound, and at all events the hexameter as we know it is not one continuous whole, but a whole made up of two parts. Mere theory will not enable us to divide it. Mere theory might suggest 3+3, and give us a line like:

ὦ Διὸς ἁδυεπὲς φάτι, τίς ποτε τᾶς πολυχρύσου.
(*Oed. Tyr.* 151.)

This is part of a lyric system, it is not an epic line. We must go back from theory to history and recall

ἠράμεθα μέγα κῦδος | ἐπέφνομεν Ἕκτορα δῖον.

To history, but not to accessible history. Pre-Homeric facts and conditions, not now recoverable with certainty, and very unlikely to be recovered by direct evidence, resulted in the hexameter being a line which might be divided in one of three ways. What is common to them is that they divide it into *unequal* parts. That is the vital fact about a hexameter. It is not 3+3, but 2½+3½, *or* (much less frequently, in Homer) 3½+2½, *or*, very frequently in Homer, 11+13[1] (measured in short syllables).

(a) μῆνιν ἄειδε, θεά, | Πηληϊάδεω Ἀχιλῆος.

(b) διογενὲς Λαερτιάδη | πολυμήχαν' Ὀδυσσεῦ.

(c) ἄνδρα μοι ἔννεπε, Μοῦσα, | πολύτροπον, ὃς μάλα πολλά.

The two parts are not set down clumsily side by side, as were the parts of the primitive 'Saturnian' line in Italy. They are

[1] 11+12 if we adopt the ancient theory, mentioned above, that the last foot is trochaic.

linked together in a subtle way, by the fact that rhetorical division or division in sense does not coincide with the middle of the line. The elegiac pentameter, we may say, shows the artistic and deliberate use of the method of juxtaposition from which the Saturnian never emerged.

Of the three forms (a) and (c) prevail in Homer. In the first 100 lines of the *Iliad* (c) occurs no fewer than 48 times. (b) is certainly infrequent in Homer, though not so infrequent as is sometimes supposed. Its occurrence was investigated by Lehrs (*De Aristarchi Studiis Homericis*², p. 394 f.), who found that lines indubitably of the type (b) occur in the *Iliad* with a frequency which varies in different books from 1 in 100 to 1 in 50, while in the *Odyssey* they are less frequent still, from about 1 in 100 to 1 in 200. This result may be true for lines like

διογενὲς Λαερτιάδη, πολυμήχαν' 'Οδυσσεῦ,

which *cannot* be anything but hephthemimeral. But (like many recent statistics for Virgil) it is rather a curiosity of enumeration than an important fact. It does not represent the metrical art of the poet. A hephthemimeral effect is not so rare as that. There are many lines in which there is no doubt the end of a word at the penthemimeral or trochaic division, but in which the hephthemimeral division is obviously dominant and gives the line its character:

Ἀτρείδης τε, ἄναξ ἀνδρῶν, | καὶ δῖος Ἀχιλλεύς (*Il.* i. 7)
νοῦσον ἀνὰ στρατὸν ὦρσε κακήν, | ὀλέκοντο δὲ λαοί (l. 10)
ἐκπέρσαι Πριάμοιο πόλιν, | εὖ δ' οἴκαδ' ἱκέσθαι (l. 19)
παῖδα δ' ἐμοὶ λύσαιτε φίλην, | τὰ δ' ἄποινα δέχεσθαι (l. 20)
ὣς ἔφατ', ἔδεισεν δ' ὁ γέρων | καὶ ἐπείθετο μύθῳ (l. 33)
μὴ δὴ οὕτως, ἀγαθός περ ἐών, | θεοείκελ' Ἀχιλλεῦ (l. 131)
ὅσσον φέρτερός εἰμι σέθεν, | στυγέῃ δὲ καὶ ἄλλος (l. 186).

Of hephthemimeral lines in this wider sense I find 9 in the first 100 lines of the *Iliad*, and 10 in lines 101–200, or one line in ten. (There are a few more lines which are doubtful, in which the penthemimeral or trochaic division competes in importance with the hephthemimeral.) If we do not proceed in this way our figures will not do justice to the metrical skill of Homer. His cadences will be much less varied. Lehrs practically eliminates a quite recognizable and effective type of line.

In Virgil (a) and (b) are very frequent. (a) is indeed dominant in Latin hexameters generally. Ennius, Lucretius, and Virgil agree in having this division in about 64 per cent. of their lines. (c) is very rare in Virgil and later poets, much rarer than is sometimes supposed. A line of the type (b) very often has a word-ending in the middle of the second foot, that is, a subordinate trihemimeral division:

Non comptae ⋮ mansere comae | sed pectus anhelum.

This is natural; for if a poet began his line with 'Italiam', it would happen very often that the next two words went together: 'fato profugus'. Further, it was natural that the syllables before (b) should very often be a word of iambic form, like 'comae'; so there would be the end of a word at (c), the Homeric or trochaic division. But lines like:

et quorum pars magna fui.   quis talia fando

or

accipe quae peragenda prius.   latet arbore opaca

are not 'Homeric' in effect, for the reader's ear. The strongly marked hephthemimeral pause throws the other pause into the shade. In Homer, too, there are many lines like:

νοῦσον ἀνὰ στρατὸν ὦρσε κακήν, ὀλέκοντο δὲ λαοί,

but it is not these lines that are characteristic of Homer. The line (*Aen.* v. 140):

haud mora, prosiluere suis, ferit aethera clamor

is not really like

litora deseruere, latet sub classibus aequor.

The second of these *is* 'Homeric', the first is not.[1] Lines of the type ' non comptae mansere comae ' are said to number 1,020 in the *Aeneid*: if they are to count as having ' trochaic ' division, it is obvious that the divergence between Homer and Virgil is considerably lessened. But the Homeric effect is not really found except in lines like:

> Iaside Palinure, ferunt ipsa aequora classem.
> fas omne est, Cytherea, meis te fidere regnis.
> Anchisa generate, deum certissima proles.

The poet seems to have had a liking for the effect with a vocative at the beginning of a speech. In Latin it meant that accent and ictus coincided ('generáte, Cytheréa'). Lines with unquestionable ' trochaic' division are more frequent in Ennius than in later poets, and sometimes a special effect of sound is intended:

> labitur uncta carina, volat super impetus undas.

But even in Ennius they are not very frequent; the proportion in which they occur is about 8 per cent.

It was first suggested by Bergk, and Usener later in his *Altgriechischer Versbau* endeavoured to base the view on various kinds of evidence, that the Homeric hexameter grew out of two shorter lines:

> νῆα μὲν οὖν πάμπρωτον
> (ϝ)ερύσσομεν εἰς ἅλα δῖαν

(neglect of the ϝ at this point, it was argued, was a tradition set up by the older form of the verse),

> εἷσε δέ μ' εἰσαγαγοῦσα
> ἐπὶ θρόνου ἀργυροήλου

---

[1] But they are put in the same class by Norden (*Aen.* vi, Appendix VII, p. 423), who regards *both* as having a 'weibliche Hauptcaesur', writing the first

> haud mora prosiluere ‖ suis | ferit aethera clamor

(where *hiatus* can be similarly explained). In recent years this contention has fallen into discredit, and it has been held that the hexameter perhaps originated in several different ways. There was the 'bucolic' hexameter, it was urged, with its marked division after the fourth foot:

ἕλκετο δ' ἐκ κολεοῖο μέγα ξίφος, | ἦλθε δ' Ἀθήνη.

Upon this it may be observed that separate lyric lines of four and two dactyls would not necessarily by uniting produce a hexameter. The line of four feet would not necessarily have a pause or division so placed that a hexameter with its vital and characteristic caesura would come into existence.[1]

But there are hexameters, both in Greek and Latin, which *do* seem to have a marked pause or division exactly in the middle of the line, after the third foot. It is desirable to consider these before proceeding further. But neither these nor other types of line can be considered profitably until we have determined what the words 'caesura' and 'pause' are to mean.

A *caesura* is a cutting or severance (τομή) between two parts of a line, a division which does not coincide with the end of a foot (for a division that does coincide with the end of a foot it is convenient to use another word, *diaeresis*). It

[1] It has been observed that certain lengthenings such as παρὰ δ' ἀνήρ and Κρονίων, found in the sixth foot, are also found in the fourth. But the fourth is almost the only foot where Κρονίων *could* be introduced, barring the second, where it would not be very euphonious (it may be an accident that no line beginning ᾧ τε Κρονίων ὄλβον ἐπικλώσῃ ... is found). The fourth foot, when it ends with the end of a word, shows little tendency to take the form − ∪; rather the opposite. Hermann and Wernicke (*lex Wernickiana*) observed that the foot is either a dactyl or ends with a naturally long vowel; mere lengthening by position is infrequent—ἅμα δ' ἄλλοι λαὸς ἕπέσθω is an exceptional line. In a few lines, e.g. βλοσυρῶπις ἐστεφάνωτο (*Il.* xi. 36), βοῦν ἧνιν εὐρυμέτωπον (x. 292), as in Ennius's *ponebāt ante salutem*, an original long quantity of the termination perhaps survives.

HEXAMETER

is often a 'pause', but it is not a pause of measurable or fixed duration.[1] It is not a metrical 'pause'; by that is meant an interval of silence which *can* be measured in terms of the duration of short syllables or χρόνοι πρῶτοι: e.g. when a group of three dactyls is 'catalectic' there is a pause at the end which is δίχρονος or δίσημος (arboribusque com|āē ⋏). It is a metrical division with which some sort of *rhetorical pause* or pause in the sense usually coincides. If it is doubtful where the metrical *caesura* occurs, the doubt must be set at rest by the sense or the rhetoric. Thus in the line:

> pascite ut ante boves, pueri ; submittite tauros,

if the punctuation is right which puts only a comma before *pueri* and a semicolon after it, the caesura is *after* 'pueri', it is ἐφθημιμερής (after the seventh half-foot, after 3½ feet), *semiseptenaria*, not πενθημιμερής, *semiquinaria*. There are some lines (but not so very many) where a word placed like *pueri* seems to have exactly the same sense-pause—a very slight one—after it as before it:

> Ascanius clari ⋮ condet ⋮ cognominis Albam

or

> Cecropidae iussi—miserum—septena quotannis.
> (*Aen.* vi. 21.)

Here we must be content to say that the line has either or both *caesuras*.

Lines which fall asunder or all but fall asunder in the middle, owing to a pause or the end of a word at the end of the third foot, are not very common. In *Il.* xv. 18

> ἦ οὐ μέμνῃ ὅτε τ' ἐκρέμω ὑψόθεν ἐκ δὲ ποδοῖιν

---

[1] In practice its length depends on the dramatic instinct of the reciter. In actually dramatic verse, iambic or trochaic, there must sometimes be a pause much *longer* than a metrical 'pause' would be.

emendation is almost certainly necessary, though some editors still retain ἐκρέμω. The line should run:

ἦ οὐ μέμνῃ ὅτε τε κρέμω ὑψόθεν.[1]

In *Od*. iii. 34 no such remedy is possible:

οἱ δ' ὡς οὖν ξείνους ἴδον, ἀθρόοι ἦλθον ἅπαντες.

Are we to say of this line 'bonus dormitavit Homerus'? It is certainly on the very verge of the legitimate. Virgil, too, comes near the verge in *Aen*. vii. 625:

 pars arduus altis
pulverulentus equis furit, omnes arma requirunt.

Here, as happens so often in Virgil where there is some strange or curious effect, there is a reminiscence of Ennius. The Homeric and the Virgilian line have this in common that the third foot is a dactyl; two short syllables precede the break, stimulating the reader (Christ suggests) to rapid onward movement. The division before ἴδον and *furit* is metrically so important that it can be felt in spite of the longer rhetorical pause after them.[2] We need not hesitate much about saying 'dormitavit Ennius', for Ennius did many things that cannot be defended.

 cui par imber et īgnīs | spiritus et gravis terra

is not a good hexameter. In the line

 spernitur orator bonus, horridus miles amatur,

---

[1] L. Müller mentions a similar correction required in Paulinus (21. 46): 'quaeque suis proprie egerit hic in finibus edam' (read *gerit* for *egerit*).

[2] Another Virgilian line with no very obvious caesura is *Aen*. xii. 144:
 magnanimi Iovis ingratum ascendere cubile.
Terentianus Maurus and Servius thought that it had none at all, but it is saved by the slight separation which was felt between the elements of a compound word, 'in-gratum', an effect required also to explain lines of Lucretius ('quid enim im-mortalibus atque beatis') and Lucilius ('Scipiadae magno im-probus obiciebat asellus').

the disruption of the line may be meant to emphasize the antithesis. Horace has a similar line (*Epp.* ii. 2. 75):

> hac rabiosa fugit canis, hac lutulenta ruit sus.

But the hexameter of Satire (or Epistle) is a different thing from the Epic hexameter, and should be treated separately, as a stream flowing in a channel of its own. Several Virgilian lines have a monosyllabic conjunction after the two short syllables, so that there is a possibility of a slight caesura on either side of the middle point:

> aut Ararim Parthus ⋮ bibet | aut ⋮ Germania Tigrim.
> (*Ecl.* i. 62.)

This is a euphonious line, very different in effect from what was perhaps Ennius's worst one:

> sparsis hastis longis campus splendet et horret.

With this we may further compare a line of Homer's which has a good deal of coincidence between word and foot and which did not escape criticism (*Il.* i. 214):

> ὕβριος εἵνεκα τῆσδε· σὺ δ' ἴσχεο, πείθεο δ' ἡμῖν.

This line, too, is quite euphonious, and its structure might be represented thus:

It has the 'trochaic' caesura, characteristic of Homer, and also the 'bucolic' diaeresis after the fourth foot, both of them well marked by a rhetorical pause.[1]

---

[1] Ancient metricians recognize as a type of hexameter the line that is divided in the middle, but think of it as having a comic effect. So Terentianus (who, as he usually does, reproduces in his own verse the effect he is speaking of):

> namque tome media est versu non apta severo . . .
> ipse etenim sonus indicat, | esse hoc lusibus aptum
> et ferme modus hic datur | a plerisque Priapo.

II. SUBORDINATE DIVISIONS

A caesura is a severance or cutting which divides a line or verse into two parts (phrases or κῶλα): two parts, that is, of which a line may legitimately consist. The three forms of caesura which we have now considered are vital to the existence of a hexameter. Any one of them may be *the* caesura of the line. The presence of any one of them prevents the verse from falling asunder and ceasing to be a hexameter.

But a caesura of course incidentally divides a *foot* also into two parts, and in this sense there may be caesurae in many places, not vital to the structure of the line. In πλάγχθη ἐπεὶ Τροίης the first foot is divided in the ratio 3 : 1 (the 'trochaic' caesura), and the second in the ratio 2 : 2. But it is the caesura after Τροίης that divides the line into its component parts.

Frequently there is a marked caesura, of this secondary or subsidiary kind, in the second foot:

οὐλομένην, ἣ μυρί᾽ Ἀχαιοῖς ἄλγε᾽ ἔθηκε.

Frequently also there is a marked diaeresis ('bucolic') after the fourth foot (*Il.* i. 247):

Ἀτρείδης δ᾽ ἑτέρωθεν ἐμήνιε. τοῖσι δὲ Νέστωρ.

A line might have either of these and yet be a very defective hexameter: *Il.* xix. 45, for example,

καὶ μὴν οἱ τότε γ᾽ εἰς ἀγορὴν ἴσαν, οὕνεκ᾽ Ἀχιλλεύς

seems just to escape disintegration, although it has a marked bucolic diaeresis—it escapes by means of a slight caesura after εἰς.[1] But in a great many lines—as in the two just quoted—

When it was 'given to Priapus', however, it was not as a hexameter, but as a combination of Glyconic and Pherecratean (*infra*, p. 176):

et ferme modus hic datŭr
a plerisque Priapo.

[1] Mr. J. W. White (*The Verse of Greek Comedy*, p. 152) discovers in Aristophanes a line which has *only* bucolic diaeresis: it is *Pax* 1111,

the strongest rhetorical pause in the line comes in the middle of the second foot or after the fourth, while in some lines there is a strong pause at both places. Such pauses may be so conspicuous as to characterize a line and distinguish it from other types. Yet these divisions are not on the same plane metrically with the three caesurae first discussed; for they must be accompanied by one of these three caesurae.

The mere ending of a word at one or other of these two places is not a fact of much importance. To be worth considering the division must be marked by a stronger rhetorical pause than occurs at the end of neighbouring words. Thus in ἐκπέρσαι Πριάμοιο πόλιν there is a caesura in the second foot, but it attracts little attention and cannot be said to mark off a section of the line. There is also a trochaic caesura in the next foot, a caesura capable of being the vital caesura; but it is the more marked break *after* πόλιν that counts as *the* caesura of the line (hephthemimeral). Similarly, in ἐλώρια τεῦχε κύνεσσι there is no bucolic diaeresis in any sense that it is worth while to contemplate. To reckon as a bucolic diaeresis any ending of a word at the end of the fourth foot will give misleading results. Gleditsch (*Metrik*, p. 119), following Hartel, says that 60 per cent. of Homer's lines have bucolic division, or 15,200 verses in all. This figure must be arrived at by counting lines like ἐλώρια τεῦχε κύνεσσιν or Ἀχαιοῖς ἄλγε᾽ ἔθηκεν. On this principle, *atque altae moenia*

' where the enclitic precludes penthemimeral caesura '. But the *rara avis* turns out to be only that common fowl, a *prava lectio*. The line is reported to be given by the MSS. thus:

Ἰε. οὐδεὶς προσδώσει μοι τῶν σπλάγχνων ; Τρ. οὐ γὰρ οἷόν τε—.

There is a syllable over, and it is clearly μοι that must be deleted (so Geldart and Hall, in the Oxford text). The line then runs:

οὐδεὶς προσδώσει | τῶν σπλάγχνων ;

It *has* a penthemimeral caesura; and, we may add, it would have to be read with a slight caesura there even if μοι were retained and τῶν ejected. But σπλάγχνων without the article is very unlikely.

Romae would be a bucolic ending in Latin, and Catullus's 'Peleus and Thetis' would be one of the most bucolic poems in the Latin language ('Peliaco quondam prognatae | vertice pinus'!). Lines in Homer in which a bucolic diaeresis attracts the reader's attention are not very frequent; lines which have any real claim to be 'bucolic' are not more than half as numerous as Hartel makes them. In Theocritus it is two lines out of three in some poems, every second line in others, and the term 'bucolic' is justified. On Hartel's method no clear distinction would be drawn between Homer[1] and Theocritus, and, further, the difference between Theocritus and the *Eclogues* would also be obscured. Virgil did *not* follow Theocritus in this feature of his verse, and this was recognized

---

[1] Apollonius has bucolic diaeresis much more frequently than Homer. Mr. Mooney (*Argon.*, Appendix, p. 415) says that it is found in 849 lines out of the 1,362 of the first book. That is about 62 per cent. But, like Hartel's figures for Homer, these figures are arrived at by including lines which have no real bucolic effect for the reader's ear. In the first 200 lines of Book I there are 41 in which the bucolic diaeresis is revealed by punctuation, i.e. there is at least a comma at the end of the fourth foot. Fifty-seven more lines I am prepared to regard as 'bucolic', though sometimes rather doubtfully. This results in a total of 98, or 49.5 per cent. In the first 100 lines of the *Iliad* I find six marked by punctuation (I take the Clarendon Press text for Homer, Mr. Mooney's for Apollonius), and 25 that can be called bucolic with some degree of plausibility (a total amounting to about half Hartel's percentage). In a line like

$$\chi\rho\acute{\upsilon}\sigma\epsilon\iota o\nu\ \mu\epsilon\tau\grave{a}\ \kappa\hat{\omega}as\ \epsilon\acute{\upsilon}\zeta\upsilon\gamma o\nu\ \mathring{\eta}\lambda a\sigma a\nu\ \text{'}A\rho\gamma\acute{\omega}\ (Arg.\ 4)$$

I am unable to see a bucolic division. There are two groups of three words each: the verb ἤλασαν has the accusative εὔζυγον Ἀργώ after it, and it is no more closely related to one of these two words than to the other. The divisions or pause before and after ἤλασαν are exactly equal, and neither of them is so marked as the division after κῶας. Again, in

$$oἰωνούς\ τ'\ ἀλέγειν\ ἠδ'\ ἔμπυρα\ σήματ'\ ἰδέσθαι\ (Arg.\ 145)$$

I am still less inclined to recognize a bucolic division. ἠδ' ἔμπυρα σήματ' ἰδέσθαι is a coherent group of words, with extremely slight divisions between them; the adjective ἔμπυρα must go very closely with σήματα.

HEXAMETER

by the ancients. Terentianus Maurus says that Theocritus has the effect in abundance:

> plurimus hoc pollet Siculae telluris alumnus,

but Virgil makes a sparing use of it:

> noster rarus eo pastor Maro, sed tamen inquit
> 'dic mihi, Damoeta, cuium pecus? an Meliboei?'

Atilius (c. 21) makes the same statement in prose: 'Theocritus hanc metri legem custodivit, Vergilius contempsit.' It seems clear that some at least of the ancient critics counted as bucolic only those lines in which there was a quite unmistakable or conspicuous break after the fourth foot.[1]

The bucolic line, with a diaeresis and not a caesura as its outstanding feature, stands by itself, and may almost be said to have a more definite character of its own than any one other type.

---

[1] There may be a comma at the end of the fourth foot without the lines being therefore bucolic, e.g.:

> sed tamen iste deus qui sit, da, Tityre, nobis.

This is a line with hephthemimeral caesura and the fifth foot slightly detached from its surroundings.

Virgil was too careful and subtle an artist to fail to put into his Pastorals some distinct suggestion of Theocritean rhythm. Bucolic lines are much more frequent than in the *Georgics* or *Aeneid*. Lines which any reader would feel to be bucolic come to about 10 per cent. In most of these the effect is marked by punctuation; lines in which there is at least a comma after the fourth foot come to $8\frac{1}{12}$ per cent. In the *Georgics* the lines of this stricter type come to $2\frac{1}{2}$ per cent.; the larger figure is $3-3\frac{1}{2}$ per cent. In the *Aeneid* bucolic lines are 1 to 2 per cent. Other Pastorals show a figure approaching that of the *Eclogues*: *Culex* about 7 per cent., *Dirae* about 7 per cent., Calpurnius's *Eclogues* about 7 per cent. (stricter type 5 per cent.). But, curiously, the *Lydia* and *Moretum* have only one bucolic line each, in 80 and 124 lines respectively (in the *Lydia* possibly two—there is another line which may be bucolic). The *Ciris* resembles the *Georgics*. Later epic closely resembles the *Aeneid* (Stat. *Thebais* i. $1\frac{1}{3}$ per cent., *Theb.* ii. $1\frac{1}{2}$ per cent., *Theb.* vi. 1–250 and *Ach.* i. 1–250 1 per cent., Val. Fl. *Argon.* i. $2\frac{1}{4}$ per cent.).

It shows some little tendency to occur in definable places. It is not unfrequent as the first line of a paragraph:

ἤτοι ὅ γ' ὣς εἰπὼν κατ' ἄρ' ἕζετο· τοῖσι δ' ἀνέστη
Μέντωρ ...

and it was still more clearly suited to be a penultimate line (*Od.* xi. 223–4):

ἀλλὰ φόωσδε τάχιστα λιλαίεο· | ταῦτα δὲ πάντα
ἴσθ', ἵνα καὶ μετόπισθε τεῇ εἴπῃσθα γυναικί.

Compare in the same book of the *Odyssey* ll. 136–7, 161–2, 202–3, 303–4, 340–1, 475–6. From epic poetry this effect passed into the elegiac epigram: the penultimate line was often a bucolic hexameter:

νῦν δ' ὁ μὲν εἰν ἁλί που φέρεται νέκυς, ἀντὶ δ' ἐκείνου
οὔνομα καὶ κενεὸν σῆμα παρερχόμεθα.

It is in Greek that this is found; Martial shows no liking for it.

It will have been observed that all the bucolic lines quoted above have a dactyl in the fourth place. This is all but universal, and it is easily understood. A spondee there (unless itself preceded by another spondee) would mean a cadence similar to that with which the whole line closes; the separation of the parts would be too great, the movement of the line too much arrested or retarded. Homer admits the effect very rarely (*Od.* x. 26):

ὄφρα φέροι νῆάς τε καὶ αὐτούς· οὐδ' ἄρ' ἔμελλεν.[1]

Christ, after explaining the principle and illustrating it by *Il.* vii. 212:

μειδιόων βλοσυροῖσι προσώπασι· νέρθε δὲ ποσσίν

(where the strange form προσώπασι seems to be due to avoidance of a spondee), adds that 'a similar preference for

---

[1] Lines of this type are not written by the Alexandrian poets or by Nonnus.

the dactyl in the fourth foot is not provable in Roman poets'. This is a mistake, if he is speaking of bucolic lines. Virgil's bucolic lines almost always have a dactyl in the fourth foot (*Ecl.* iii. 15 is one of the very rare exceptions [1]). The Romans had a strong liking for lines of the type:

molli paullatim | flavéscet cámpus arísta.

But we have seen that to count these as bucolic would result in inextricable confusion. If we count lines that are really 'bucolic', only one in thirteen has a spondee before the bucolic diaeresis.[2]

The two divisions which we have now considered, the trihemimeral caesura and the bucolic diaeresis, are the most important of the subordinate divisions. A marked pause nearer the beginning of the line, or nearer the end, is less frequent and less natural. In the hands of the Greeks the Epic hexameter showed no tendency to be hypermetric: each line has its cadence, its own close; there are no effects like Virgil's

turres et tecta Latinor|um
ardua cernebant iuvenes.

So a new sentence does not begin very near the end of the line. Sophocles' verse (*Trach.* 1010):

πάντων Ἑλλήνων ἀδικώτατοι ἀνέρες, οὓς δή

is un-Homeric, and rare in Virgil (*Aen.* ii. 458):

evado ad summi fastigia culminis, unde
tela manu miseri iactabant inrita Teucri.

The writers of the *Culex* and the *Aetna* show a liking for a very late division in the line:

[1] The precise facts are: In the *Eclogues*, out of 67 bucolic lines four have a spondee in the fourth foot; *Georgics*, 3 out of 59; Calpurnius, 3 out of 51; *Culex*, 3 out of 51 (*Aen.* vi., 3 in 15).

[2] This is based on a survey of over 9,000 lines in various poets.

THE HEROIC

> et mortem vitare monet per acumina. namque (*Culex* 184)
>
> et flammas et saeva quatit mihi verbera; pone Cerberus (219)
>
> heu quid ab officio digressa est gratia, cum te restitui superis (223)

(cf. *Aetna* 209, 216, 274, 514, 601).

Conversely, a division such as is marked by a full stop or a colon seldom occurs very near the beginning of the line. It is a rare and sometimes deliberate effect, as when Ovid ends a sentence with the end of the first dactyl, at the turning-point of the story of Midas (*Met.* xi. 118):

> vix spes ipse suas animo capit, aurea fingens
> omnia.   gaudenti mensas posuere ministri, etc.

Many minor variations and special effects are possible in the hexameter, most of them readily intelligible to the careful reader. One other question of some magnitude remains—the extent to which the 'trochaic' division of a dactyl is admitted ($-\cup\,|\,\cup$).

In Homer this division is very frequent in *the* caesura, in the vital caesura of the third foot. We have seen that this was perhaps the result of the construction of the verse out of two shorter lines. It is partly to this caesura that Homeric verse owes its greater ease and rapidity of movement, as compared with the verse of Virgil. Roman poets seldom have the 'trochaic' caesura; it may be that they were repelled by the inevitable coincidence of accent and ictus which it involved:

> O passi gravióra | .

Nonnus, on the other hand, cultivated it to excess, sometimes having it in half a dozen consecutive lines. The Homeric use of it gave facility and fluency to the verse; Nonnus's use of it justifies the term 'feminine' sometimes applied to it.

The 'trochaic' division might occur in feet other than the third, and in two or more consecutive feet. In the line:

αὖτις | ἔπειτα | πεδόνδε | κυλίνδετο λᾶας ἀναιδής

it is admitted three times, to give a special effect. So also in:

πολλὰ δ' ἄναντα κάταντα πάραντά τε δόχμιά τ' ἦλθον,

and in Ennius's line:

labitur uncta carina per aequora cana celocis.[1]

The Greek and the Latin hexameter differed in treatment of it. In Latin there was coincidence of ictus with accent—with an accent that was some sort of stress accent, not a musical accent or accent of pitch as in Greek.

The Greek hexameter disliked a trochaic division in the fourth foot (τομὴ κατὰ τέταρτον τροχαῖον). In the line last quoted πάραντά τε should be read as a group of four syllables. In *Il.* ix. 394:

Πηλεύς θήν μοι ἔπειτα γυναῖκα γαμέσσεται αὐτός

Aristarchus's γε μάσσεται is probably right and is adopted by many editors. In *Od.* i. 390:

καί κεν τοῦτ' ἐθέλοιμι | Διός γε | διδόντος ἀρέσθαι,

the words Διός γε διδόντος go closely together, with extremely slight pauses between them—a group of six syllables. *Il.* xxiii. 760:

ἄγχι μάλ', ὡς ὅτε τίς τε γυναικὸς ἐυζώνοιο

seems to be a real instance, with trochaic division of the third foot also. In *Il.* vi. 2:

πολλὰ δ' ἄρ' ἔνθα καὶ ἔνθ' ἴθυσε μάχη πεδίοιο,

there is trochaic division in the fourth foot, but not also in the third. This type of line is rare in Homer, and it is not found in Apollonius (Mooney, *Argon.*, Appendix, p. 415).

[1] Horace, in his letter to the future emperor, Tiberius, has a strange line of this type, without any obvious justification in the sense:

dignum ménte domóque legéntis honésta Neronis.

In Latin a trochaic division in the fourth foot is certainly not very frequent, but it does not seem to be disliked in the same degree. Ennius has a line—indefensible in structure— which has this division unsupported by any regular caesura:

corde capessere. semita nulla | pedem stabilibat.

Virgil has the division in such lines as:

tanto, nate, magis contende tenacia vincla,

and with a similar division in the fifth foot also:

sedimus impulimusque; ea lapsa repente ruinam

(where the sound imitates the sense). Ovid, *Met.* x. 95:

et platanus genialis acerque coloribus impar

is the only instance, quoted from any good writer, of the repetition of the effect in the third and fourth feet. The Latin hexameter also rejected a repetition of the effect in the *second* and third foot. Ovid and Lucan are said to have no line in which this occurs. It is found in pre-Augustan verse:

vos quoque signa | videtis | aquai dulcis alumnae,
cum clamore | paratis | inanes fundere voces.
                                           (Cicero, *Aratea*.)

The close of the line was subject to various restrictions. The heroic verse of the epic ran to its close with dignity and completeness. All the lines of Homer are separate; there is no continuity of scansion from one line to the next. In *Il.* xiv. 265 εὐρύοπα Ζῆν should no doubt be read, a monosyllabic accusative, not Ζῆν' with elision. Callimachus, in an elegiac couplet, ends a hexameter with οὐκ οἶδ', and Roman poets admitted this effect of hypermetron in epic verse, though even with them it is not very frequent (see above, p. 4). On the other hand, there are various points in which Homer shows greater freedom than later poets. A double spondee is most effective when a dactyl precedes, but Homer does not shrink from :

κακὸν ὣς δειδίσσεσθαι

or

ἐκ δίφρου γουνάζεσθον.

He ends a line with ἐπὶ δ' αἴγειον κνῆ τυρόν, but later poets were careful not to let the end of a word come at the end of the fifth foot. It is probable, however, that some of the endings in two spondaic words are not really Homer's, but due to the intrusion of later contracted forms (Λητόος υἱός and ἠόα δῖαν coming to be written Λητοῦς υἱός and ἠῶ δῖαν. Cf. ἐκ δίφροö in one of the passages quoted). Similarly, Ἀτρεΐδαο (– ⌣ ⌣ – ⌣) would come to be written Ἀτρείδαο. Thus 'Homer' gave more encouragement to the use of the σπονδειάζων than he himself perhaps intended. It was a piece of literary affectation with Alexandrian poets[1] and their Roman followers. Catullus has the ending in three consecutive lines (lxiv. 78 f.) :

electos iuvenes simul et decus innuptarum.

In Virgil it is more restricted, the ending rarely consisting of a Latin word—as in *magnum Iovis incrementum* in *Ecl.* iv, *intervallo* in *Aen.* v. 320 (after Lucretius)—more often of a Greek proper name ; or a spondaic ending is used to make the sound answer to the sense, as in :

aut leves ocreas lento ducunt argento.

After the Augustan age the σπονδειάζων went out of fashion. Manilius and Lucan have it very rarely. It vanishes also from late Greek epic: Nonnus does not admit it at all.

The Greek hexameter enjoyed great freedom in regard to the last word of the line. It might be a word of any number

---

[1] 'Every eleventh line in Callimachus, every sixth in Aratus, is a σπονδειάζων,' Gleditsch, *Metrik*, 2. 71.

of syllables from one up to seven (ὑπερηνορεόντων). In this, as in some other things, Ennius seems to have made the unsafe assumption that anything could be done in Latin that was possible in Greek. He also has various endings, from *exoritur sol* to *sapientipotentes*. But Latin later shows a strong preference for words of two, or three, syllables at the end of the line.[1] The result is that accent and ictus coincide in the last two feet, and Latin also had a liking for lines in which there was threefold coincidence:

incultisque rubens pendébit séntibus úva.

But whether this was the motive, or the only motive, for the rule is not quite certain. Accent and ictus coincide in a word like 'frúgiferéntes' (with a secondary accent on the first syllable). On the other hand, they were rather conspicuously separated in an ending like 'prétium dederitis'. Whether it was deliberately

[1] When Virgil does admit an ending in a word of one syllable it is sometimes for a picturesque effect in sound ('praeruptus aquae mons', *Aen.* i. 105; 'procumbit humi bos', v. 481; 'ruit Oceano nox', ii. 250; 'ruuntque equites et odora canum vis', iv. 132), more often it is a reminiscence of Ennius or Lucretius (which does not exclude its being at the same time a special sound-effect). Norden (*Aen.* vi, Appendix IX, p. 428) collects all the facts. Sometimes the monosyllable is an enclitic (' fides est, virum quem '), or there are two monosyllables ('hac stat, et cum, et dum'). Sometimes the archaic rhythm is meant to have a solemn or impressive effect ('deae mens, deum gens, et magnis dis'; the last a known reminiscence of Ennius, as *restituis rem* also is).

Endings in words of four or five syllables are mainly Greek, usually consisting of Greek words ('hymenaei, Noemonaqué Prytanimque, Erymanthi, Deidamia, Pirithoumque'). In the rare cases, where the word is Latin, there is usually a Greek metrical effect (e.g. hiatus, in *femineo ululatu*): *quadrupedantum* (*Aen.* xi. 614) seems to stand alone in Virgil. (Catullus has an extreme instance of Greek metrical devices with an ending in a Greek word, in *qua rex tempestate novo | auctús hymenaeo*. So Virgil has *gravidús autumno*. This dispondac ending, with a word of three long syllables, is of course to be classed with endings like *hymenaei*. Latin has no strong preference for a trisyllabic word of *that* shape.)

HEXAMETER

intended or not, the result came about that the Latin hexameter had its rhythm more obvious, and more clearly revealed by accent, at the end of the line. In the earlier part of the line, and especially in the middle of the line, divergence of ictus and accent was the rule. In iambic verse the opposite effect came about. In a Latin senarius there was divergence very often at the beginning and end of a line, and coincidence in the middle.

At the beginning of the line also there are differences between the Greek and the Latin hexameter. Homer has rather a liking, or at all events no dislike, for a spondee in the first place. Sometimes it is even a spondee isolated by a slight pause after it:

> τότε δ' οὔτι δυνήσεαι ἀχνύμενός περ
> χραισμεῖν, εὖτ' ἂν πολλοὶ κτλ.[1] (*Il.* i. 242.)

Latin preferred a dactylic beginning, and preferred it very strongly when the first foot was separated from the rest of the line by any kind of pause. This may be illustrated by one of the most groundless conjectures ever made in the text of a classical author, Bährens's *verbis* in Stat. *Silvae*, v. 3. 161. Statius there wrote of his father's prose version of Homer:

> tu par adsuetus Homero
> ferre iugum senosque pedes aequare solutis
> *versibus* et numquam passu breviore relinqui.

Versibus is perfectly sound and perfectly clear: lines of prose, lines released from metrical fetters. *Solvere verba* would mean to break them up into separate syllables or letters. But apart from that, Statius would never have begun a line with the rhythm 'verbis, et ...'. Latin has no dislike for a

---

[1] It is notable, and it was noted by ancient critics, that this effect resembles the 'Aeolic basis' found in certain types of Aeolian lyric verse.

slightly isolated dactyl, and even allows a full stop after a dactyl
(Ovid, *Met.* xi. 118):

>   . . . aurea fingens
> omnia. gaudenti mensas posuere ministri.

In Virgil almost the only instance in which two consonants
other than a mute and a liquid do not lengthen the syllable is
found in the line (*Aen.* xi. 309):

> ponite. spes sibi quisque, &c.

EXCURSUS

(*a*) *On Hexameters in the Lyric and Tragic poets.* Mention
has been made above of the line in Sophocles (*O.T.* 151), ὦ Διὸς
ἀδυεπὲς φάτι-, which has no caesura. The corresponding line in
the antistrophe:

> πρῶτά σε κεκλόμενος, θύγατερ Διός, ἄμβροτ' Ἀθάνα

might be mistaken for an ordinary hexameter.

Hexameters in lyric and tragic poets are apparent rather than
real. They are lyric groups of 4+2 or 3+3 dactyls. Their nature
may be realized by reading carefully the dactylic στάσιμον in the
Phoenissae (783 f.), or the hexameters which occur in the first
choric passage of the *Agamemnon* (104 f.), or in the *Andromache*
(103–141), or the hexameters in Pind. *Pyth.* ix and *Nem.* ix.
Differences are easily observed; a few of the more important are
the following:

(1) In none of these passages is there a single example of the
'trochaic' caesura, so frequent in Homer. It *is* found once or
twice in some rather conversational hexameters in the *Trach.*
and *Philoct.* of Sophocles (*Trach.* 1014, 1037—2 lines in 15 : *Phil.*
839). In the *Androm.* 105–16 are elegiac lines, but not ordinary
elegiac verse. In Xenophanes and in Theognis the trochaic caesura
is at least as frequent as in Homer, but it does not occur here.
There are also more dactyls than in normal elegiac verse.

(2) Trochaic division in the fourth foot is not avoided: *Phoen.*
786 οὐκ ἐπὶ καλλιχόροις στεφάνοισι | νεάνιδος ὥρας, 803 (antistr.)
μήποτε τὸν θανάτῳ προτεθέντα | λόχευμ' Ἰοκάστας.

(3) In Pindar, *Nem.* ix, many of the lines betray themselves by conspicuous lack of caesura: ἀνδροδάμαντ' Ἐριφύλαν, ὅρκιον ὡς ὅτε πιστόν. Horace's lyric hexameters in the *Odes*, as will be seen, are unlike epic hexameters; they do not, however, in any instance lack caesura. The Pindaric lines consist of two 'enoplii', which will be discussed later (pp. 177 f.).

Roman grammarians recognized a catalectic hexameter which they call *metrum angelicum*: it is 'celeritate nuntiis aptum'. 'Stesichorus invenit: unam enim syllabam detraxit hexametro, et fecit tale:

optima Calliope miranda poematibus.'

A verse of this form was called Χοιρίλειον or Διφίλιον by the Greeks. But it was not a heroic hexameter catalectic. It was written by Stesichorus (and verses like it have been written in English by Swinburne); and it occurred occasionally in other poets. It was a lyric verse of two κῶλα, which assumed the appearance of a hexameter if it had the hexameter's caesura, and if the third foot was a spondee and not a trochee; but it did not necessarily have either of these things: it might be

ἀενάοις ποταμοῖσἰν | ἄνθεσί τ' εἰαρινοῖς.

(*b*) *On Statistics relating to Virgil's verse*. The number 1,020 mentioned above, for lines in the *Aeneid* of the type:

non comptae mansere comae, sed pectus anhelum

(i.e. the type in which there is a word-ending in the middle of the second and fourth feet, and also after the first short syllable of a dactyl in the third foot) is given by Norden, as arrived at by La Roche. From it he proposes to deduct 105 cases, in which *que* precedes the trochaic break:

fataque fortunasque virum moresque manusque.

Such lines, he maintains, have really a penthemimeral caesura:

fataque fortunas‖que virum moresque manusque.

No doubt 'que' was slightly detached in pronunciation from 'fortunas'; but surely this would be a slighter pause than that which comes between two quite separate words, such as the pause *after* 'que'. Even that pause does not seem to me to have a good claim to be the chief caesura in the line. 'Virum' is a genitive going with 'fata' and 'fortunas', and the reader connects it with them, though no doubt it belongs to 'mores' and 'manus' also ('fates and fortunes of the heroes, and [their] characters and deeds'): so that this too would be a line with hephthemimeral caesura. A recent article in the *Classical Quarterly* (April, 1914) by Mr. W. G. D. Butcher seems to follow Norden in classifying as lines with trochaic caesura lines of the type 'non comptae mansere comae'—'sit mihi fas audita loqui, sit numine vestro' is the example given, where the hephthemimeral caesura again seems to me clearly the dominant one. The reasons given for the procedure are unconvincing. 'Ancient writers differ as to whether the trochaic or hephthemimeral caesura should take precedence. . . . Perhaps the best argument in favour of the trochaic caesura is that it is natural to accept the first available caesura in the verse. For instance, in a line beginning

infandum, regina

we have no certainty that another caesura will follow, so that we should naturally adopt the first caesura as the principal one, and consider any other that may follow as subsidiary.' This seems to me no argument at all. In a line like

et quorum pars magna fui. quis talia fando

a much more marked pause follows almost instantly. Why should a caesura be held to be dominant merely because it comes a little earlier in the line?

Mr. Butcher gives 1,037 as the number of lines in the *Aeneid*, which he calls 'normal trochaic' (i.e. lines like 'non comptae mansere comae'). Of hephthemimeral lines he finds only 371. But in the first 100 lines of the sixth book I find 20 (excluding lines of the type 'non comptae mansere comae', and excluding some in which the hephthemimeral pause is at least *equal* to the penthemimeral). The lines that I reckon as clearly hephthemimeral are: 3, 4, 7, 9, 12, 13, 18, 20, 24, 40, 44, 52, 59, 72, 73, 77, 88, 98, 99, 100. If I am right about these, and if these 100 lines are a fair sample of Virgil's verse, there should be about 2,000 hephthemimeral lines in the *Aeneid*; and to these I would, of course, add about 1,000 more, those of the type 'non comptae mansere comae'. Thus about a third of the lines of the *Aeneid* would be hephthemimeral, and about two-thirds penthemimeral. 'Trochaic' would be Mr. Butcher's 'abnormal trochaic'—119. But there are more than that, though not, I think, many more: lines to be added are those like Norden's

        litora deseruere, latet sub classibus aequor

(which would slightly reduce the total of 1,037 or 1,020 or whatever it is).

For these reasons I regard both Norden's statistics and Mr. Butcher's as unconvincing and unsatisfactory. If out of 9,878 lines in the *Aeneid* as many as 8,349 have penthemimeral caesura, Virgil's verse could no longer be extolled for its variety of cadence; it would, on the contrary, be exceedingly monotonous. And if there are 1,156 lines with trochaic caesura, it would be perceptibly less unlike Homer's verse than it is. The counting, it would seem, should be done over again. But would the result be worth the labour? Possibly; but it might result only in putting more accurately what can be roughly estimated by surveying a few hundred lines. In the first 100 lines of book i I do not get a result seriously different from that elicited from book vi: 22 hephthemimeral lines (excluding 'non comptae mansere comae'—one of these is 'posthabita coluisse Samo. || hic illius arma': could any caesura that is *not* the chief caesura justify the hiatus?).

Holding this view, I 'disable' or disqualify Mr. Butcher's conclusions about the authorship of *Opuscula*; that the *Culex* was written by Virgil is a conclusion that I am inclined to disagree with in any case.

What is said above in general terms about Virgil is confirmed by a survey of 1,000 lines of the *Aeneid* (viii.-ix. 269): lines with hephthemimeral division, 25·8 per cent.; lines in which it is difficult to decide between penthemimeral and hephthemimeral, but in which penthemimeral is certainly not predominant, 5·8 per cent.; these two together, 31·6 per cent.; trochaic division, 1·8 per cent.; lines in which it is difficult to decide between trochaic and hephthemimeral, 4·4 per cent.: total lines which are not penthemimeral, 37·8 per cent.

CHAPTER II

THE COLLOCATION OF WORDS IN EPIC VERSE, ELISION, HIATUS, ETC.

THE structure of a particular line has been represented above (p. 13) by a diagram in which the χρόνοι or syllables look like rectangular blocks of stone carefully fitted together. In order to realize the nature of ancient verse, as compared with the verse of English or German or other modern languages, it may be worth while to pursue this illustration a little further. The words in Greek and Latin verse are rather like rectangular pieces of marble built into a wall. They are exactly measured; ancient versification contemplates long and short syllables which in length are in the ratio 2 : 1. The long is twice the short, though in actual pronunciation it cannot have been precisely so. The second syllable in 'volŭcres' or πολύτροπος, when lengthened as it might be in formal and finished verse, can hardly have been really equal to the first syllable of σκῆπτρον. But for metre the syllables counted as equal. Further, words in ancient verse seem to come more into contact than words in the more or less accentual verse of a language like English. They fill up more completely the spaces provided for them by metre, and the end of a word is not unaffected by the beginning of the word that follows it. We may roughly represent this in a diagram as follows, drawing perpendicular lines to mark off the (dactylic) time-spaces provided by metre:

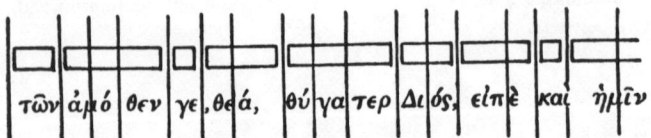

If we now take as an example of English verse, in its loosest and most accentual form, Longfellow's line

This is the forest primeval, the murmuring pines and the hemlocks,

we must represent this in a very different way—how, exactly, it is difficult to say. There must be quantitative spaces; all verse has quantity, it is not a series of momentary explosions of sound. But in English a strong stress accent may be said to usurp the place of quantity and to be confused with it. The diagram may be something like this:

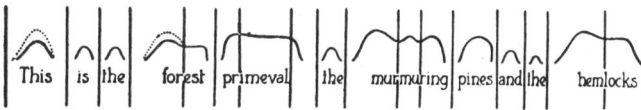

Here the dotted lines in the first two feet are meant to indicate the effect of the English stress accent. In the first foot the words 'is' and 'the' are about equally inconspicuous to the ordinary English ear. But in ancient verse the consonants *sth*, whether within the same word or in separate words, would mean a long syllable (κρατερὸς θεός). English verse differs in many features from the verse of Greece and Rome, and some of these it may be instructive to consider in dealing with iambic verse. Fŏrēst may be said to be an iambus, and some English writers have tried to use it so. But the English accent really forbids its use as a disyllabic foot of which the second syllable is the more important or conspicuous. The Latin accent of the classical period did not prevent the metrical use of 'dăbūnt' as an iambus, and it had no power to make 'pŏpulus' a dactyl. What we are concerned with at present is the comparative looseness with which English words are set down side by side. What is normal in Greek and Latin is rare in English. Elision: the definite article *the*

sometimes seems to suffer elision in verse, but hiatus is the rule. Length by 'position':

> and pulpit, drum ecclesiastic,
> was beat with fist instead of á stick—

the effect is intentionally comic, and the words 'a stick' are normally qualified to form the last foot of a purely iambic line, ă stíck.

In the *opus quadratum*, or *ex saxo quadrato*, of ancient verse, we have to consider three things: (1) 'length by 'position'; (2) elision (with its opposite aphaeresis, which is much less common; and with crasis, which is also comparatively infrequent); (3) the conditions under which hiatus *is* allowed.

1. The phrase 'length by position', as it is now used, means that a syllable is long owing to the 'position' of the vowel before two consonants.' Originally 'by position' θέσει was contrasted with φύσει in the sense of 'convention', deliberate or artificial agreement, συνθήκῃ; θέσει μακρά meant 'long by poetic convention'. It is more convenient to think of 'position' in the other sense.

When a short vowel is followed by one consonant within a word the consonant goes with the following syllable (μă-λă-κός), and no lengthening can occur. The consonant at the end of a word goes with the vowel before it, and a possibility of lengthening begins. But with only one consonant lengthening is infrequent. With two, if they are a mute and a liquid, it is frequent, but still optional. With two consonants that are not a mute followed by a liquid lengthening is the rule, and exceptions very few. So we can construct an ascending scale of lengthened syllables, beginning with what are licences and ending with what is all but compulsory.

(*a*) Lengthenings before one consonant within a word, which have no justification except metrical convenience: ἀκάματος, ἀθάνατος, ἀποπέσῃσι, Ζεφυρίη, σῠνεχές, πᾰρέχῃ, μέλανι, ἔμαθον (written μείλανι, ἔμμαθον). Later poets seldom ventured upon such changes except in the case of proper names (Ītalia, Sīdŏnius). These syllables are really θέσει μακραί in the original sense of θέσει, convention.

(*b*) Lengthening before one consonant, which is usually at the end of a word, but sometimes in the next word, μέροπες ἄνθρωποι. Here the condition is that the *ictus* of the verse falls upon the syllable; without it, lengthening is rare, and special explanations have to be looked for (πολλὰ λισσομένη, πυκνὰ ῥωγαλέην). With the consonant in the next word, the first word is often δέ (ὣς φάθ', ὁ δὲ τόξον, *Il.* xv. 478) or τε (as in χωλαί τε ῥυσαί τε, *Il.* ix. 503). Here the consonant is a liquid, as it is in Virgil's reproduction of the effect, 'liminaquē laurusque dei', *Aen.* iii. 91, but other poets have it with other consonants (Accius, 'metalliquē caculaeque': Grattius and Ovid have it with *p*, 'taxiquē pinusque, Othrysquē Pindusque').

Many apparent lengthenings before one consonant in Homer were accounted for when Bentley detected the original presence of the Digamma. In other cases the lengthened vowel was one that had once been long. But there are many cases to which neither of these explanations is applicable. Very frequently the lengthening is before a more or less marked *caesura*, and the ictus of the first foot had a similar effect (ἐπεὶ δή, τὰ περὶ καλά). Of Roman poets Ennius and Virgil sometimes did what Homer had done, but other poets were very sparing in their use of such things or, like Lucretius and Catullus, avoided them altogether. When Horace wrote 'ne quis humasse velīt Aiacem' he was deliberately reproducing an old quantity—it is a legal archaism in a king's interdict. Virgil has *sinīt* before the penthemimeral caesura and a full stop (*Aen.* x. 433):

    tela manusque sinit. hinc Pallas instat et urget.

In a few passages he has a lengthening for which no such

justification is easily discoverable and which must be set down as Homeric or pseudo-Homeric licences : *Aen.* iv. 64 *pectorĭbūs inhians*, ix. 610 *terga fatigamūs hasta.* Roman metricians (e.g. Velius Longus, 52. 9 κ., in the first century of our era) had a theory that *h* might contribute to quantity by position. They were following Greek writers who had before them lines like

ἢ ὀλίγον οἱ παῖδα ἐοικότα γείνατο Τυδεύς.

But to give *h* this force was no part of the metrical practice of classical poets : for them, 'auctŭs hymenᾱeo' or 'languentĭs hyacinthi' did not differ from, or was no more normal than, 'gravidŭs auctumno'. But the discussions of the grammarians seem to have given rise to a belief that *h ought* to contribute to quantity by position. It is the practice of the early Christian poets (so that, e.g. a hexameter may begin with *vir humilis*), while the 'paganus pervicacissimus' Claudian avoids it.

(*c*) Lengthening before a mute and a liquid :

similis volŭcri, mox vera volūcris.

A mute and a liquid are easily pronounced together and both can be put in the following syllable, 'volŭ-cri'. Here a limitation at once comes into view. If one of the letters is in one word and the other in another, this cannot be done. *ĕt ripam* alone is possible, not *ĕ-tripam*. So, too, in compounds : 'ŏbrepo' and ἐκρεῖ are necessary, 'ōbrepo' and ἔκρεῖ are inadmissible.

But, while shortening is excluded in these cases, lengthening freely takes place in Greek even when both consonants are in a following word :

ἀρῑπρεπέᾱ Τρώεσσιν. ὄφρᾱ πρόσθ' ἄλλων.
φίλᾱ φρονέων. μετὰ πρώτοισιν.

There are great differences in this matter between different poets, different dialects, and different periods of poetry. In Homer and Hesiod lengthening is the rule, whether the two consonants are in the same word as the vowel or in the next one: καί τε πρὸ ὃ τοῦ ἐνόησεν: τά τ' ἐσσόμενα πρό τ' ἐόντα. Shortening is infrequent, and usually has some special, though it may be slight, justification (οὐδὲ γὰρ οὐδὲ Δρύαντος υἱὸς ..., Ἀφροδίτη, proper names: τειχεσιπλῆτα, προτραπέσθαι, words otherwise excluded from dactylic verse. Add Il. xi. 69 τὰ δὲ δράγματα: xv. 142 ἵδρυσε θρόνῳ). The reader of Homer would be surprised to meet with ἔτρεμεν or with τείχεᾰ Τρώων. Shortening occurs in Homer only when the liquid is λ or ρ, not with μ or ν.[1]

The opposite extreme is found in Attic comedy. Shortening is invariable, except that βλ and γλ sometimes lengthen the syllable, and γμ, δμ, γν, δν regularly do.[2] Tragedy admitted lengthening, πᾰτρός, νεκρός. This 'correptio Attica' belongs to the history of iambic verse. In Roman comedy also and in spoken Latin shortening was the rule. Lengthening belonged to serious, finished, and formal verse; it came in with Ennius's introduction of the hexameter, but compared with Homer the Latin hexameter admits it very sparingly. *Tenēbrae, latēbrae, pharētra* are found, and a line may end with *patres* (Stat. *Silv.* v. 3. 215), or *libro* (*Georg.* ii. 77). Here the ictus is on the syllable lengthened. But this is not invariably the case ('iuvat íntegrós accedere fontes', Lucr.). In a compound like *navifragus* the *i* is always short, and when the two consonants are in a separate word lengthening is rare, and is usually a direct and deliberate reminiscence of Homer (*spiculaquē clipeique, Aen.* vii. 186). Endings like *mercentur Ātridae, Etruriā crevit, moeniā Troiae* are common. In other metres also,

---

[1] πᾰτρός, according to Ebeling, occurs about 120 times (and the dative πᾰτρί about 60 times). πᾱτρός appears in *Il.* vi. 479 (and nowhere else):
καί ποτέ τις εἴπῃσι· 'πατρός γ' ὅδε πολλὸν ἀμείνων',
but here there is evidence for the reading εἴποι.

[2] Regularly in Latin also: Mr. Housman contends (and he is probably right) that *cycnus* must be the spelling, not *cygnus*, if the first syllable is to be short.

lengthening is very rare when the mute and liquid are in the next word. Catullus has it in his experiments in pure iambi (the *Phaselus* : 'Propontidā trucemve Ponticum sinum, per impotentiā freta', where, according to Christ, he is using weak longs to depict the rapid movement of the vessel: so in his lampoon on Caesar, 'ultimā Britannia', xxix. 4). Latin seems to have had no natural tendency to such effects; they were lessons learned from the metrical practice of certain Greek poets. They were not native to Athens either; rather, Attic tragedy learned them from the Ionian epic and the Ionian iambics of Archilochus.

(*d*) Shortening before consonants other than a mute and a liquid occurs very seldom in either language. Pindar has ἐσλός, and there are a few examples of shortening with μν (Aes. *Agam.* 990, Eur. *Bacch.* 71 ὑμνήσω; see Christ, *Metrik*, p. 14). Apart from these, shortening occurs only with σκ, σπ, στ and στρ, ζ, in Latin also with initial *squ*. In one or two instances shortening can be avoided by giving to *i* the sound of *y* ('Ιστίαιαν, *Il.* ii. 537, τε σκιή, Hes. *Erga* 589), but in a greater number of cases nothing of the kind is possible and it becomes unnecessary to assume it at all. Shortening occurs chiefly with proper names (Ζάκυνθος, Ζέλεια, Σκάμανδρος) or words which otherwise could not find a place in a hexameter (σκέπαρνον, *Od.* v. 237).[1]

---

[1] Shortening with consonants like *sc*, *str* is rare, and therefore presumably difficult or repellent. It may be asked, 'How was it possible at all?' There is the extreme view that even in English, in a word like 'rēstrĭction', the first syllable *is not* short, but is only inconspicuous beside the strong stress accent on the second syllable. The answer is perhaps this: a rule that the syllable *cannot* be short would be true only if pronunciation were always so rapid as just to avoid 'gabbling' or 'mumbling' consonants; but the delivery of ancient verse (and probably the pronunciation of Greek and Latin generally) was not so rapid as that, and hence there was no insuperable difficulty about making a syllable with *sp* or *str relatively* short. Metre is not concerned with

IN EPIC VERSE

Roman poets are less strict. In the early drama—even in anapaests, the metre most akin to dactylic verse—there are numerous shortenings which have no place in the hexameter, or in the stricter prosody of the Augustan age. The Law of Breves Breviantes (*infra*, p. 90) sanctions not only *molĕstórum*, but also *volŭptátem* ; as it sanctioned, too, the shortening of a naturally long vowel in *dŏmĭ mánsit*. But even in hexameters there are things for which there is no analogy in Greek. There is, to begin with, the large exception that down to the time of Lucretius a final *s* is frequently attenuated and has no metrical effect :

> tum laterali(s) dolor, certissimu' nuntiu' mortis,
>
> (Ennius.)

'frequently', but not regularly, for it often causes length by position:

> Corneliu' suaviloquenti
> ore Cethegūs Marcu' Tuditano conlega. (Ennius.)

Lucretius has this neglect of *s* freely, Catullus has it once ('tu dabi' supplicium', in what may have been his earliest poem, though put last in our editions), and Cicero, in 46 B.C., calls it *subrusticum*. If it persisted later, it was in comedy only.

z was not always in Italy distinctly a double consonant ; it was more like English *z* or *s* (cf. *Saguntum* for Ζάκυνθος: *zenatuo*, Faliscan gen. of *senatus*, &c.). Hence it was perhaps rather easier for Virgil to put *Zacynthus* at the end of a line than it had been for Homer (*Aen*. iii. 270). Seneca in iambics has 'tranquillă Zephyri' (*Agam*. 433).

Shortening before *sc, sp*, &c., is found chiefly in Lucretius ('cedere squamigeris: mollia strata', &c., and even 'pendentibu(s) structas') and in the *Satires* of Horace, where it occurs nine times ('praemia scribae, saepe stilụm vertas', &c. In i. 3. 44

ultimate questions of phonetics, but only with the grouping of syllables which can be classified more or less reasonably as long and short.

('non fastidire. strabonem') it is rendered easier by a full stop). Propertius has it five times (or six times if we include iii. 1. 27, Scamandro).[1]

The formal heroic Epos rejected it almost entirely. Virgil, who has *Zacynthus* only once, has this also only once, and with the help of a full stop, *Aen.* xi. 309 'ponite. spes sibi quisque'. Shortening before *sm* in the case of the word *smaragdus* is found in various Roman poets, including Tibullus, Propertius, Ovid, Lucan, and Statius. Silius has *Zacynthus* several times. If it was difficult, though not absolutely interdicted, to shorten the syllable, to lengthen a short vowel in a preceding word was also difficult or repellent. What the Roman poets do is to avoid rather carefully such a collocation of words as would necessitate it. Ennius has *stabilitā scamna solumque*; Catullus, in hexameters, has one such lengthening:

nulla fugae ratio, nullā spes ; (lxiv. 186.)

Tibullus has *pro segetē spicas*,[2] and one other instance. L. Müller (*De Re Metrica*, p. 390) collects six examples in all in epic verse. Besides these there are a few in Seneca and Martial, and Juvenal's *occultā spolia* (viii. 107). The extreme scarcity of the effect seems to make it clear that the avoidance of it was deliberate.

2. Ancient verse, with its syllables carefully placed in contiguity, 'ut tesserulae omnes', naturally abhorred 'hiatus'. If a word ends in a vowel it must be definitely closed or dismissed by running up against the consonantal beginning of the next word. If the next word began with a vowel the two vowels were left facing each other with some sort of unsatisfactory 'rift' or 'gap' between them. It was not only in

---

[1] Catullus had written *unda Scamandri*. With the probable exception of Propertius, later poets 'showed more respect for metre than for the gods', as L. Müller remarks, by calling the river *Xanthus*.

[2] Unless we should read, with some editors, an abl. in *-i*, *segeti*.

verse that this effect was disliked. When prose was elaborated and its rhythm studied, hiatus there, too, was avoided. The Isocratean prose of the fourth century rejects an arrangement of words like ἐπεὶ ἤδη οὐδείς.[1]

The chief device by which hiatus was avoided was elision. When two vowels came together the preceding one was thrust out or forced out of the metrical scheme (*elidere*, ἐκθλίβειν). It disappeared, it had no effect. But, it must be remembered, it is only *for metre* that it disappears. That it disappeared entirely in pronunciation is incredible. Perhaps it did so, or all but did so, in a few cases, when it was an extremely slight sound. The final ĕ of *quĕ*, *vĕ*, *nĕ* may have been almost inaudible; it had a tendency to efface itself in ordinary pronunciation apart from verse (cf. *vin*, *viden*; *nec* beside *neque*; *ac* beside *atque*; and it has been rendered probable that the final ĕ of some words like *inde*, *unde*, *nempe* was similarly attenuated or dropped in dramatic or colloquial verse). But the elided vowel is often by no means a slight one. In Latin it is often long. In *quarē ăge* it is the short *a* of *age* that forms the second syllable of the dactyl. How was the ē pronounced? It is difficult to say. Ancient verse must be thought of as delivered more slowly than our verse or than an English reader tends to deliver it. The metrical scheme consists of spaces or compartments which have some room in them, room it would seem for a rather sudden change. The sound of ē is begun in the second compartment of the dactyl, but instead of going on till a consonant stops it or till it runs up against a consonant, it is supplanted, after occupying some slight and not exactly measurable part of the space—*vocalis ante vocalem correpta*—

[1] Though Latin treated long final vowels very differently from Greek, the Romans also disliked the accumulation of such effects: Rhet. ad Herenn. iv, § 18 'compositio est verborum constructio aequabiliter perpolita. ea conservabitur si fugiemus crebras vocalium concursiones, quae vastam atque hiantem orationem reddunt, ut haec est: "baccae aereae amoenissimae impendebant."'

by the short *a* that follows. In ordinary speech, apart from verse, something similar may have happened; *magnŏ opere* becoming *magnŏ opere* and then *magnŏpere*.[1]

It is chiefly in Latin that this extreme kind of elision is found. There is a great difference in this matter between the two languages. Short syllables are freely elided in both, and especially those short syllables that are of very frequent occurrence in the terminations of nouns or verbs (*a*, *ε*, *o*, *ă* and *ĕ* in Latin), but Greek treats long syllables differently.

In dactylic verse it shortens the long syllable, if the syllable that follows is short, πλάγχθη ἐπεὶ ...; and is careful to avoid placing words so that two long vowels come together (πλάγχθη ἤδη would be strange in Homeric verse, though *quar(ĕ) omnes* presents no difficulty in Latin).

In other forms of verse, and conspicuously and strictly in iambic and trochaic verse, Greek arranges words so that a

---

[1] It has been thought that in the case of a diphthong one of the two component vowels suffered elision. Certainly, with ἔρρεεν ὕδωρ coming at the end of a line, a beginning such as ἔρρει ὕδωρ might be explained as ἔρρε' ὕδωρ—a case perhaps of the atticization of the Homeric text. But a pronunciation which would be represented by ἄνδρα μο' ἔννεπε is not a thing that it would be well to inculcate or practise. If we hold that an elided vowel did not vanish entirely, it seems clearly best to pronounce οι rapidly. In the case of a single vowel such as η or ω, the theory has to assume that it is made up of two χρόνοι or *morae* (∪∪ or ∪∪) and that one of them goes out. The explanation becomes a rather unreal one; it is difficult to feel or to imagine that this is what actually happens. There is perhaps a feeling in some minds that only ε and ο *can* be short, and η and ω cannot be. But this is an illusion. If it were true, Boeotian λιγουράν (=λιγυράν) would be impossible, and Κάτουλος could not stand for *Catŭlus*, as it does.

Certain Attic spellings attested by inscriptions (ποῶ, ποεῖς) do, however, point to the disappearance of an ι, in a case of similar shortening within a word. But it is doubtful whether these should be admitted in literary texts where ποιῶ is an iambus. There is no difficulty about ποιῶ as an iambus, for οἷος and Ἀθηναῖος can be scanned with their first and third syllables short.

long vowel is not followed by another vowel, whether long or short.

Roman poets sometimes wrote verses with few or no elisions in them, aiming at a special effect of smoothness or rapidity, but no such strictness as this was inherent in the language or in the general principles of Latin verse.

What has been said of Greek verse is not universally true. Reservations or exceptions have to be made.

(a) The terminations οι and αι sometimes suffer elision after the Latin fashion: most frequently in comedy, but such elision is not unknown to epic verse (βούλομ' ἐγώ, *Il.* i. 117) or to dramatic and lyric verse (ἀείρομ' οὐδ' ἀπώσομαι κτλ., Soph. *Trach.* 216). Cf. ὁσημέραι (ὅσαι ἡμέραι). The Lesbian poets have elisions of the Latin type (ἄλλα με κωλύ(ει) αἴδως), but not so frequently as Latin.

(b) The converse of elision may take place, *Aphaeresis*. The second or following vowel may be extruded or suppressed (μὴ 'γὼ νόημα—an example has been found in Homer also, *Il.* i. 277 μήτε σύ, Πηλείδη, 'θέλ' ἐριζέμεναι). This happens to ε or ἄ with a long vowel preceding.

(c) The two vowels may be fused into one new vowel sound. This fusion is *Crasis*: κἀγώ, οὑμός, &c. It is found in the text of Homer (*Il.* viii. 360 ἀλλὰ πατὴρ οὑμός (ὁ ἐμός)), though not in places where the metre makes a long syllable necessary. Its existence in the drama is undoubted: οὑφόρει = ὁ ἐφόρει, τἀμά = τὰ ἐμά, &c. Sometimes the vowel of one of the words prevails, but is changed from short to long by the absorption of the other: τἄρα = τοι ἄρα, ἀδανείσατο = ἃ ἐδανείσατο. There are other cases where something of the nature of crasis happens, though it is not represented in writing, e.g. ἢ λάθετ' ἢ οὐκ ἐνόησεν, ἐγὼ οὔτ' ἐμαυτόν. The word συναλοιφή is used for this by Bickel. It is difficult to say whether in such cases something of the nature of crasis takes place, or something more like elision of the Latin type. 'Elision' is a convenient *metrical* term for all cases in which the preceding vowel has no effect, and only the following one takes a place in the metrical scheme.

Besides vowel-endings Latin also elided a final *m* and its preceding vowel. The attenuation of the *m* in ordinary pronunciation seems to be attested by the great frequency with which it is left unwritten in inscriptions (e. g. Taurasia(m) Cisauna(m) in the earliest of the Scipio epitaphs, but the omission is not only early, it is common in inscriptions of all periods). It is indicated also by forms like *animadverto*. Probably the sound was gradually attenuated; it grew fainter as time went on. Ennius could leave it unelided in a heroic hexameter ('milia militum octo'), and this seems to have been rather more frequent in Saturnian verse. Virgil did not follow Ennius's example. Horace has the effect once, in satire ('cocto num adest honor idem?' ii. 2. 28). The text of Tibullus presents one example (i. 5. 33 'et, tantum venerata virum, hunc sedula curet'); there are two in Propertius and one in Manilius. (Attempts have of course been made to remove these by conjecture, but the conjectures are not very convincing; so it is perhaps better to follow L. Müller in retaining them.) It remains to consider the conditions under which *Hiatus* is admitted.

3. The occurrence of hiatus is a large subject, and a complete account of it would involve a vast number of details and small facts. What is important for the ordinary student is to learn in outline how the practice of poets varied at different periods, to understand some of the general principles which regulate it, and to appreciate the poetic or technical effect which particular writers had in mind when they admitted hiatus.

In the Homeric text as it stood 200 years ago hiatus was very frequent, but about that time Bentley made or had made the discovery of the F,—whereby 'ipsam sanavit artem metricam'—with the result that the number of cases was immensely reduced. Most of the harsher examples of it disappeared (εὖ ϝειδώς—Ἀπόλλωνι ϝάνακτι, &c.). Still, in spite of this, hiatus in Homer is fairly frequent, more frequent than in later Greek epic (Σμινθεῦ, | εἴ ποτέ τοι..., τίσειαν Δαναοὶ | ἐμὰ δάκρυα, &c.). Sometimes it is rendered easier by a pause in the sense. Sometimes it occurs between a long and a short syllable, an easier thing than hiatus between syllables of the same quantity, easier between □ ◻ than between □ □.[1] Lyric poetry and Attic drama were far more strict. In the drama, when hiatus does occur, there is usually some sort of interjection or exclamation or repetition (ὦ οὗτος..., ὦ εἶα... ἴτε βάκχαι ἴτε βάκχαι. Christ, *Metrik*, p. 40).

ἄ, ε, and ο, we have seen, are readily elided, especially in common terminations. ι and υ are less accommodating. ἄστυ could not suffer elision at all. ι, when it is a verbal suffix, is frequently elided (εἴμ'(ι), τίθημ'(ι), τίθησ'(ι)): in the indeclinable ἔτι and ἄλλοθι it is elided almost as readily as ε in ἄλλοτε. The ι of the dative is much less frequently elided (χρυσείῃ κερκίδ' ὕφαινεν, *Od.* v. 62). Elision of ὅτι is rare and doubtful. τί is not elided, τε is elided with great frequency. Disyllabic prepositions are readily elided, but πρό refuses to become πρ'.

Besides these and similar cases, there is, in Greek dactylic verse, the hiatus which accompanies the shortening of a long vowel or diphthong. Whether this can be regarded as an obscure case of elision has already been discussed. For the ordinary reader it is not that, nor does he quite feel it to be a case of real hiatus; it is rather a hiatus that is paid for or atoned for, and so cancelled, by loss of quantity.

When Catullus wrote the line (lxvi. 11):

qua rex tempestate novo | auctús hymenaeo

he was deliberately introducing two Greek effects into his

[1] L. Müller remarks that the line 'quid struit aut qua spe | inimica in gente moratur' would be *vitiosus* with 'hostili' for 'inimica'.

verse; and many things that are exceptional in Roman versification are of this type, experiments intended to show learning and taste, though the taste is sometimes a little eccentric. The early drama shows no great abhorrence of hiatus, though many instances of supposed hiatus have been removed by emendation in one way or another, and there are clear cases where Plautus selects an unusual word or arrangement of words to avoid hiatus. Sometimes (though not always or even more frequently than not) it occurs when there is a change of speaker,[1] and it is well established, though not very frequent, at the juncture between two parts of a long line (after the first four feet of a trochaic tetrameter or iambic 'Septenarius'). But Ennius in his epic, both in regard to elision and hiatus, had adopted very strict principles of versification. In this matter he does not follow Homer. He has fewer elisions than Virgil, and hiatus is not certainly found in the extant lines except twice in the case of a final *m* ('milia militŭm octo : dūm quĭdĕm unus homo'; and perhaps 'inimicitiáṃ agitantes'), and, with shortening, in *Scipiŏ invicte*.

Latin verse, as it is known to us in literature from Ennius to Juvenal, and in many writers later than Juvenal, is characterized by great strictness in the observance of metrical rules. In the use which he made of elision, especially in the *Aeneid*, to add dignity and volume to his verse ('omnia praecep(i) atqu(e) animo mec(um) ante peregi'), Virgil stands rather apart from other poets. He is great enough, like Homer, to be a law to himself. Post-Augustan poets, though they owed much to him in many ways, followed rather the norm of Ovid in the mechanism of their verse. Hiatus also is used with some freedom by Virgil, and he has effects in which later poets did not venture to follow him. Perhaps they thought that some of them were due to his having left the *Aeneid* unrevised

[1] This is not wholly unknown in Greek : an example has been found in Menander.

at his death. They knew that incomplete lines were due to that cause, and impressive though the effect of them sometimes is (as in 'numina magna deum', *Aen.* ii. 623) they never tried to repeat it.

Types of hiatus admitted by Virgil can be very definitely classified:

i. After a syllable on which the *ictus* of the verse does not fall.

(a) Two instances of hiatus after a short syllable, where there is a marked pause in the sense:

addam cerea pruna.   honos erit huic quoque pomo.
(*Ecl.* ii. 53.)
et vera incessu patuit dea.   ille ubi matrem.
(*Aen.* i. 405.)

These are very exceptional.

(b) Hiatus of the Greek type, with shortening of a long vowel. Sometimes this brings into dactylic verse a word otherwise inadmissible[1]:

insulae̾ Ionio in magno.   (*Aen.* iii. 211.)

Sometimes the effect is to bring the same syllable into a line with two different quantities, a thing sometimes affected by poets from Homer's Ἄρες, Ἄρες downwards:

valē vălĕ, inquit, Iolla.   (*Ecl.* iii. 79.)
Hylā Hylă, omne sonaret.   (Ib. vi. 44.)[2]

The shortening of *vale* here has nothing to do with the 'Law

---

[1] For elision of *insulae* was not allowed; elision of a word of Cretic form (− ∪ −) was carefully avoided. Ennius had written 'Scipiŏ invicte'; Catullus, 'uno in lectulŏ' (lvii. 7), with less excuse for his hendecasyllabic metre, readily admitted 'lēctŭlō' (Accius in his *Annales* had the harsh hexameter-ending *maxime Athenae*).

[2] The effect aimed at was the presentation of a sound dying away or an echo dying in the distance. This interpretation of the poet's intention does not invalidate the metrical explanation; the metrical graecism is the means by which the effect is achieved.

of Breves Breviantes' (which could shorten *cavĕ* and similar words *before a consonant*. Cf. 'vade valē cavĕ ne titubes', in Horace). The second *vale* is, to start with, exactly like the first; it suffers shortening by what is substantially a Greek principle of versification.[1]

Such shortening, however, does not seem to have been entirely unknown to the Latin language. It appears to belong to Latin most clearly in the case of monosyllables followed by a short syllable. Plautus has *ita me dĭ ament* (*ĭta me dĭ ament* in trochaic verse, as he would have *sed ĭta me dí ament* in iambics, *ita mé di amént* in anapaests (*Persa* 492), as Catullus has *non ita me di ament* in elegiacs, xcvii. 1). This shortening probably answers to actual pronunciation of Latin. If it were merely a piece of Greek metrical practice we should expect it to occur in dactylic or anapaestic verse only. It is found in verse that is more or less informal or conversational: Lucilius, *quid servas quŏ eam?* (*Sat.* xxx. 21); Catullus, *te in circo, tĕ in omnibus* (*libellis*: *tabernis*, L. Müller); Horace, *Sat.* i. 9. 38 *si mĕ amas*. Virgil has it in the *Eclogues* (viii. 108) *an quĭ amant* (also in ii. 65), and even in epic verse, *Aen.* vi. 507 *tĕ, amice, nequivi*. A monosyllable was elided only when the following syllable was long[2]; before a short syllable it was shortened.

(c) In a line of the *Georgics* (i. 437)

Glauco et Panopeae et Inoo Melicertae

Virgil has the effect just described (in *Panopeăe*), along with hiatus after *Glauco*, where *o* is not shortened. He is reproducing a line of Euphorion:

Γλαύκῳ καὶ Νηρῆι καὶ εἰναλίῳ Μελικέρτῃ.

---

[1] In Horace's line 'vade, vale, cavĕ ne titubes' there is no *metrical* question about *cave*. The syllable *was* short, and no metrical principle had to operate upon it to make it so.

[2] The only exception in Virgil appears to be *Aen.* vi. 629 'sed iam age'. *Qui* is elided in Lucilius 505 (1029), if the text can be trusted:

sicuti te, qui ea quae speciem vitae esse putamus.

Γλαύκῳ in Greek verse might be followed by a vowel without much difficulty. Virgil's *Glauco* is almost as abnormal as Horace's *et Esquilinae alites*; not quite so abnormal, for Horace's line is iambic, and iambic verse is less tolerant of such effects.

ii. After a syllable on which the *ictus* of the verse falls, L. Müller (*De Re Metrica*, p. 375) defines four cases in which hiatus occurs, but perhaps the four cases can be reduced to three.

(a) After one of the two dominant caesurae, the semiquinaria or semiseptenaria:

munera sunt lauri | et suave rubens hyacinthus.[1]

(*Ecl.* iii. 63.)

hanc sine me spem ferre tui, | audentior ibo.

(*Aen.* ix. 291.)

In the second of these lines there is a marked pause in the sense, and it is that pause rather than any merely metrical division that is the real cause of the hiatus. If so, this class (a) would be merged in class (d), *infra*. In the line

ter sunt conati | imponere Pelio Ossam (*Georg.* i. 281.)

the hiatus seems to contribute to the sense of effort and the adaptation of sound to sense; i.e. there is again a cause other than the mere occurrence of the penthemimeral caesura.

(b) With a proper name or a Greek name:

Nereidum matri et Neptuno | Aegaeo, (*Aen.* iii. 74.)

a line which also illustrates (a) by its hiatus after *matri*.

[1] The close of this line would be felt to be a Graecism, and probably the hiatus also—a Graecism or, we might say, an annexation for Latin of an effect of Greek verse. The whole history of Roman poetry, on its formal side and from one point of view, may be thought of as a series of such 'annexations' or conquests of literary provinces; more or less successful annexation, with such modifications or restrictions as make the thing effective in Latin verse.

(c) With two short syllables coming before and after, or at all events before:

> evolat infelix et femineo | ululatu.
> stant et iuniperi et castaneae | hirsutae.

(d) With a rhetorical pause or pause in the sense:

> si pereo, | hominum manibus periisse iuvabit.

(Which also illustrates (c); there may be more than one justification for a metrical effect.)

L. Müller adds, 'It cannot be doubted that Virgil had the authority of Ennius for these exceptions to metrical rule'. But there are doubts. (c) at least, if not (b), suggests much rather the example of the 'cantores Euphorionis' than of Ennius: and 'castaneae hirsutae' is in the *Eclogues*, where Virgil was more influenced by an Alexandrian than in his later works.

(c) and (d), he further states, are avoided by other classical poets, explaining Ovid's 'purpureae Aurorae' as justified by a proper name.

The writer of a complete *Historia Metrorum* would be bound to tabulate the practice of each of the more important classical poets. What is attempted here is only to define and illustrate certain types. For the appreciation by the ordinary reader of metrical effects in a poet like Statius or Valerius, the main thing is to have some clear idea of the effects employed by Virgil. They are not admitted with much frequency even by him, and the general conclusion is obvious that hiatus was kept within very strict and well-defined limits by the classical poets of Rome.

CHAPTER III

THE ELEGIAC COUPLET

THE word ἔλεγος is scarcely distinguishable from θρῆνος; it meant a lament for the dead, Horace's *querimonia* (*Ars Poet.* 75): ἐλεγεῖον was a metrical term for the form of verse, the couplet consisting of hexameter and pentameter. The Romans, however, used the word 'elegi' in the latter sense, or at all events in a wider sense than the Greeks of the classical period.

The elegiac couplet appears in literature early in the seventh century B.C., associated with the names of Callinus and Archilochus. It is a variation upon the heroic hexameter, in the direction of lyric poetry; the couplet is a short stanza or strophe, and elegiac poets can be classed under 'Poetae Lyrici' in the wide sense of that phrase. Though accompanied in early times by the flute, it cannot be reckoned as 'melic'. It is clear that at a quite early date it became a measure that was merely recited, not necessarily sung. It arises in a period of unrest in Greece. The more placid Epos, with its prolonged tale of a heroic past, has now beside it forms of verse which express what is of nearer and more everyday interest. In Callinus the verse is used for a war song (tradition puts Callinus rather before Archilochus), and it has been thought that this was its original purpose, a cry of alarm when an enemy is approaching and a summons to arms. But this is uncertain, as is also the derivation of the word ἔλεγος; it may be foreign, possibly Carian: if it is Greek perhaps the most plausible derivation is from the exclamation ἔ: ἒ λέγε ἒ λέγε ἔ. The verse is used to commemorate the dead by Simonides, and from being the verse of the epitaph (ἐπιγράμματα ἐπιτάφια or ἐπικήδεια) it became the verse of the epigram in general. But it had already taken on various tones: an erotic, though pensive, tone in Mimnermus, and in Mimnermus's contemporary, Solon, a note of vigorous and patriotic exhortation. In all its forms it is, of course, far more personal than the Epos: the personality of the Homeric singer remains in the background—Hesiod is less reticent, as is also the author of the Hymn to Apollo—whereas the main purpose of elegiac verse is to give expression to the feelings or thoughts of the poet.

The 'Pentameter' is constructed on a different principle from the hexameter. It falls into two equal parts, and the division between them is marked by the end of a word. It is $2\frac{1}{2} + 2\frac{1}{2}$ feet. In the second half only dactyls are admitted; it is a fairly common principle of structure that the primary rhythm should become apparent at the close. There is catalexis twice; and it was this that made it appropriate for the expression of grief or other emotions. It did not roll on confidently to its close like the hexameter, but twice sank or waned or 'died away in pain'.[1]

It is called 'Pentameter' as early as the fifth century B.C. It was the πενθημιμερές twice; the actual words or sounds amounted to five dactylic units or μέτρα. The scansion of it as five consecutive feet ($-\smile\smile\ |\ -\smile\smile\ |\ --\ |\ \smile\smile-\ |\ \smile\smile-$) is heard of, but this is the view only of some late metricians. It is two groups of dactyls, each καταληκτικὸν εἰς συλλαβήν:

$$-\smile\smile-\smile\smile-\bar{\Lambda}\ |\ -\smile\smile-\smile\smile\bar{\Lambda}.$$

But this description of it is not altogether free from difficulty.

---

[1] Ὅθεν πεντάμετρον τῷ ἡρωικῷ συνῆπτον, οὐχ ὁμοδραμοῦντα τῇ τοῦ προτέρου δυνάμει, ἀλλ' οἷον συνεκπνέοντα καὶ συναποσβεννύμενον ταῖς τοῦ τελευτήσαντος τύχαις· οἱ δ' ὕστερον πρὸς ἅπαντας ἀδιαφόρως· οὕτω Δίδυμος ἐν τῷ περὶ ποιητῶν (Orion).

THE ELEGIAC COUPLET

If there was a pause as long as a long syllable after the first part (κενὸς δίχρονος or δίσημος), why is not the last syllable of that part a *syllaba anceps*?[1] Why not, say,

$$\mu\nu\rho\acute{\iota}\alpha\ \tau\epsilon\rho\psi\acute{\alpha}\mu\epsilon\nu\bar{o}s\ |\ o\check{\iota}\chi\epsilon\tau\alpha\iota\ \epsilon\acute{\iota}s\ A\acute{\iota}\delta\eta\nu?$$

But that is not a legitimate line. It becomes legitimate if we write νίσσεται for οἴχεται, so that the syllable is long 'by position'. The verse then is continuous. If so, why the end of a word? why not—a line that actually occurs in Euripides—

$$\mathring{\omega}\ \phi\acute{\iota}\lambda os,\ \mathring{\omega}\ \phi\acute{\iota}\lambda\epsilon\ B\alpha\kappa\chi\epsilon\hat{\iota}\epsilon,\ \pi o\hat{\iota}\ o\iota o\pi o\lambda\epsilon\hat{\iota}s?$$

The answer to that question seems to be that the first syllable of Βακχεῖε would have to be prolonged in a way that belongs to song, and is quite unnatural in mere recitation. It would have to be τετράσημος or ⏗. The exceptions quoted—from verse that is not 'melic'—are apparent rather than real: ἡμεῖς δ' εἰς Ἑλλήσ|ποντον ἀπεπλέομεν (Ἕλλης πόντον).

The two groups or phrases or κῶλα are connected in a somewhat peculiar fashion. Neither hiatus nor elision is allowed (elision is at all events extremely rare—practically forbidden). The last syllable of the first half must be either long by nature and followed by a consonant, or long by position.

The hexameter in an elegiac couplet does not differ in any important way from the hexameter of the epic. Two points may be noticed:

(a) The 'bucolic' division of a hexameter was a favourite one when it was the penultimate line of an epigram (see p. 18). It was a division which had the effect of linking the two lines together. A group of connected words began before the end of the first line.

---

[1] Compare e.g. the Archilochian juxtaposition in Horace ('Asynartete'):

reducet in sedem vice. | nunc et Achaemenio.

(b) A σπονδειάζων or line ending in — — | — — is avoided in elegiac verse. A line like

cara deum suboles, magnum Iovis incrementum

is most naturally followed by a marked pause. It is too eminently fitted to be the last of a series to be happily placed as the first of a couplet.

Both of these facts illustrate the close connexion between the two lines. But in spite of this connexion the lines are very rarely 'hypermetric' or metrically continuous. There is Simonides' ingenious introduction of the name Ἀριστογείτων into elegiac verse (*supra*, p. 5). After this nothing, till we come to a couplet of Callimachus:

ἥμισύ μοι ψυχῆς ἔτι τὸ πνέον, ἥμισυ δ' οὐκ οἶδ'
εἴτ' Ἔρος εἴτ' Ἀίδης ἥρπασε, πλὴν ἀφανές.

Callimachus had much influence on Roman poets, and this couplet may have had its effect. But it did not cause Roman poets to make elegiac couplets hypermetric. It may have suggested the effect in hexameters.

The two parts of the pentameter are set down, as it were, in juxtaposition, with a diaeresis between them, not linked together like the two parts of a hexameter. Their internal structure must next be considered. There the principle of 'caesura' comes into play. Coincidence between the end of a foot and the end of a word is subject to restrictions, which are as usual more rigid in Latin than in Greek. Meleager (*Anth. Pal.* v. 165. 2) has agreement of word and foot in the second half of the line (σύμπλανε, πότνια νύξ), and Theognis has a pentameter in which word and foot actually agree throughout (456; quoted by Christ, *Metrik*, p. 208):

οὕτως ὥσπερ νῦν οὐδενὸς ἄξιος εἶ.

The Greek line, with its monosyllabic endings, though unusual, is not repellent; nor are monosyllabic endings in English repellent:

In the Pentameter aye | falling in melody back.

THE ELEGIAC COUPLET

A Latin line, constructed on the plan of the Greek one, e. g. :

illic saltem nunc advena plurimus est

is scarcely endurable. The explanation may be that in Latin, when a word coincided with a spondee or dactyl or trochee, the accent inevitably coincided with the *ictus*, and, being a stress accent, over-emphasized it. In Greek, accent could coincide with *ictus* without attracting special attention; in English, accent takes the place of quantity, and the metre is nowhere without it.

Apart from the rarity of a monosyllabic ending the Greek pentameter is subject to little restriction regarding the incidence of word-endings. In Latin, on the other hand, there is a gradual elimination of the unfit or survival of the fittest. Elegiac verse was introduced by Ennius, and written by him with some smoothness and finish, as far as the few extant examples enable us to judge. A few pentameters of Lucilius survive (*Sat.* xxii) and show no advance in technique. Catullus's elegiacs are by no means on a par with his epyllion in neatness and euphony. Some of them are not 'duriusculi' (as Pliny thought some of his hendecasyllabics), but 'durissimi', e. g. (lxxiii. 6):

quam modo qui me unum atque unicum amicum habuit

(*me* elided: elision in the middle; two elisions in the second half; ending in a word of three syllables),

ei misero eripuisti omnia nostra bona

(two elisions running, one in the middle of the line: three neuters in *ă* in an awkward string). Cornelius Gallus came next, and we may conjecture that he attained a greater degree of smoothness, though Quintilian calls him 'durior' (*sc.* 'Tibullo et Propertio'). In Tibullus—Propertius—Ovid the further progress lies revealed. Tibullus and Propertius still have endings in a word of three syllables (though not frequently):

> haesura in nostro tela gerit latere. (Tib. i. 10. 14.)

Similar to this is an ending in a word of five syllables ('harundinibus'); a quadrisyllabic ending ('Pierides') seems to have been somewhat more euphonious, and maintained itself longer. In Ovid a word of two syllables is the rule: exceptions are extremely few. Ovid is careful also to make the last syllable of the line actually long (unlike Tibullus's 'laterĕ'), not relying on the *syllaba anceps* or the following pause. These are improvements in themselves, though there is a certain monotony in his unvarying correctness. Accent and ictus are separated by the disyllabic ending; but so they are also with 'látere' and 'Piérides'.[1] Christ suggests that the 'feminine' or trochaic division of the dactyl allowed the line to flow more easily to its close, as compared with the 'masculine' caesura in 'gerit| latere'. The arrangement of words is often highly symmetrical and regular, especially in Ovid, but also in the elder poets. One of the commonest effects is that of an adjective at the end of the first half agreeing with a substantive at the end of the second:

> et dare captivas ad fera vincla manus,

or the converse:

> aspicio patriae tecta relicta meae.
>
> (*Ex Ponto* i. 2. 48 and 50.)

But an ending in an adjective is rare, apart from the possessive adjectives *meus, tuus, suus*. The composer of elegiac verse should be careful to make his line end with a substantive or a verb. The rule applies to hexameter also. It is a principle of symmetry and emphasis that a line should not end with an

---

[1] Unless the accentuation *Piérides* still survived or could be felt. Zielinski thinks that Ciceronian rhythm affords evidence for it (*Clauselgesetz*, p. 233).

unimportant or otiose word, and this is even more clearly true of the ending of a couplet.

In what precedes elegiac verse has been considered as it is written in the best periods of Greece and Rome by considerable poets. The pentameter was not always preceded by *one* hexameter. Inscriptions show the practice of substituting for a couplet a group of three lines:

τόνδε ποθ' Ἕλληνες Νίκης κράτει ἔργῳ Ἄρηος
Πέρσας ἐξελάσαντες ἐλευθέρᾳ Ἑλλάδι κοινὸν
ἱδρύσαντο Διὸς βωμὸν Ἐλευθερίου.

This appears in the *Anthology* (vi. 50) with a pentameter interpolated after the first line, εὐτόλμῳ ψυχῆς λήματι πειθόμενοι (see Wilamowitz, *Sappho und Simonides*, p. 197). In later times there were eccentricities both in theory and practice. There were theorists who held that the last syllable of the first half was a *syllaba anceps*:

hoc mihi tam grandĕ munus habere datur.

And a late Greek epigrammatist, Philippos, wrote pentameters, κατὰ στίχον, i. e. without any intervening hexameters (*Anthol.* xiii. 1). If there was any abuse of the metre in earlier writers it lay in using it for purposes other than those for which it was originally intended. Callimachus used it for long narratives in his *Αἴτια* (though shortly before his time it had seemed to Aristotle incredible that anybody should write a narrative poem in a metre other than the heroic hexameter), and he was followed by Ovid in the *Fasti*, and by Propertius in some shorter pieces. Callimachus also set the example of using elegiac verse for a lampoon or personal attack in his *Ibis*, a theme which for long had been claimed by iambic verse. Callimachus's poem may have been short enough to count as an epigram, but Ovid's *Ibis* is not.

CHAPTER IV

ANAPAESTS

An anapaest is the converse of a dactyl, ἀντίστροφος τῷ δακτύλῳ, ⏑⏑−, not −⏑⏑. But the rhythm is the same; it is ἴσος, *par* (2 : 2, ⏑⏑ | ⏑⏑).[1]

It is doubtful, however, whether an anapaest is exactly and in all respects the converse of a dactyl. In a dactyl there is a strong ictus on the first part of the foot, and the first two times always take the form of a long syllable.[2] In an anapaest the second part of the foot is normally, but not always, a long syllable, and the *ictus* may have been less marked. If we represent a dactyl by $\overset{\text{-}}{\text{-}}\cup\cup$, an anapaest may have been $\cup\cup\overset{\text{-}}{\text{-}}$ ($\overset{\cdot}{\cup}\cup$ | $\overset{\cdot}{\cup}\cup$). The first part of the foot is often a long syllable; with this and resolution in the second part an anapaest becomes $\text{-}\overset{\cdot}{\cup}\cup$. The slighter *ictus* perhaps helps to account for a strange fact in Latin verse. In other metres Latin verse shows a great reluctance to put the *ictus* on the second syllable of a dactylic word: *cardíne, vertíte* seem to have been repellent to the Roman ear.[3] But the anapaest that in syllables looks like a dactyl—ἀνάπαιστος δακτυλοειδής—is freely used:

inclúte | parva | prodíte | patria.
saeptum altisono | cardíne templum.

---

[1] Quint. ix. 4. 48: 'rhythmo indifferens est, dactylicusne ille priores habeat breves an sequentes; tempus enim solum metitur, ut a sublatione ad positionem idem spatii sit.'

[2] There are some rare and rather disputable instances of the resolution of the long syllable of a dactyl in lyric verse. And it is possible that Ennius admitted ⏑⏑− or ⏑⏑⏑⏑ for a dactyl even in hexameters.

[3] Zielinski, however, thinks that Ciceronian rhythm points to such an effect (*Clauselgesetz*, p. 230).

ANAPAESTS

The origin of anapaestic verse and its relation to dactylic metres lie beyond the survey of metrical history. There is no evidence. The second part of a common type of hexameter—the hexameter with *caesura semiquinaria*—coincides in syllables with an anapaestic dimeter catalectic, and may have been derived from it:

$$- - \cup\cup - \cup\ \cup \underline{\cup}$$
Πηληιαδέω Ἀχιλῆος
ψυχὰς Ἄιδι προίαψεν.

As a separate verse this was called Paroemiacus, almost certainly—though it has been doubted—because it was the verse in which proverbs or παροιμίαι were expressed (φεύγων μύλον ἄλφιτα φεύγεις—ἀγαθοὶ δ' ἀριδάκρυες ἄνδρες). Such proverbs occur in hexameters, in Homer and Hesiod, sometimes with only one short syllable at the beginning (παθὼν δέ τε νήπιος ἔγνω, beside ῥεχθὲν δέ τε νήπιος ἔγνω). When an anapaestic dimeter, or line of four anapaests, had been developed to accompany the march of troops or of a chorus,[1] the catalectic form of it agreed in appearance with the verse-proverb, but must have had a different rhythm, for, whereas the dactylic half-verse was three feet with a kind of anacrusis (∪, −, or ∪∪), the anapaestic line was one of more than three feet and must have had the time of four.

Associated with the ἐμβατήρια of Tyrtaeus at Sparta, and later used for the entrance and exit of the chorus in the Attic theatre, anapaestic verse was obviously a march-rhythm.[2] The

---

[1] There is evidence for it also as an exhortation or accompaniment for rowers: Serv. on *Aen.* iii. 128 'Cretam proavosque petamus: celeuma dicunt, et bene metro celeumatis usus est, id est anapaestico trimetro hypercatalecto'. If this nautical use is ancient, we can see why Cratinus wrote the verse κατὰ στίχον for a chorus of seamen in his Ὀδυσσῆς (fr. 144):

σίγα νυν, ἅπας ἔχε σιγάν,
καὶ πάντα λόγον τάχα πεύσει·
ἡμῖν Ἰθάκη πατρίς ἐστιν,
πλέομεν δ' ἅμ' Ὀδυσσεῖ θείῳ.

[2] Like the iambic trimeter anapaests could also halt or limp. A

short syllables accompany the raising of the foot (ἄρσις), and with the long syllable it is set down again (θέσις). Two anapaests accompany two steps, together they make a βάσις (the Roman *passus*, five feet as a measure of length). Two anapaests make a μέτρον, four are called a 'Dimeter'; they are scanned κατὰ διποδίαν like iambi or trochees, in spite of their greater length. This being the nature of the anapaest, it seems clear that it is and was distinctly felt to be an 'ascending' rhythm; we must not follow J. H. H. Schmidt in applying to it the methods of modern music and scanning anapaests as dactyls with anacrusis

$$(\cup \cup \vdots - \cup \cup \mid - \cup \cup \mid - \cup \cup \mid - \lambda).$$

The name ἀνάπαιστος implies this, and it is confirmed by the regularity with which a word ends with the end of the second foot:

διθρόνου Διόθεν | καὶ δισκήπτρου
τιμῆς ὀχυρὸν | ζεῦγος Ἀτρειδᾶν.

The same question has been raised about iambic verse, which Schmidt treated as trochaic with anacrusis. About both the testimony of antiquity is that the rising movement gave an effect of greater vigour and energy—the downward dactylic and trochaic movements one of greater fluency and facility—

' cholanapaestic' metre is found, on stone, in lines addressed by a gouty patient to Asclepius :

τάδε σοὶ Διόφαντος ἐπεύχομαι·
σῶσύν με, μάκαρ σθεναρώτατε,
ἰασάμενος ποδάγραν κακήν.

(Kaibel's *Supplementum Epigrammatum Graecorum*, in *Rhein. Mus.* 34. 210.) Wilamowitz pointed out the appropriateness of the movement of the verse, suggestive of a hobbling gait. When Diophantus recovers, he returns thanks in dactylic hexameters.

The verse consists of three anapaests and an iambus, a metre which requires further investigation. It is found (with accent taking the place of quantity) in early Byzantine hymns. But it is also as early as Sappho (γλυκύπικρον ἀμάχανον ὄρπετον).

ANAPAESTS

and in the case of iambi Quintilian expressly says that this effect was felt throughout the line, not merely at the beginning of it. It must have been even more clearly so in anapaests. In a hexameter or iambic trimeter the rhythm may be said to be reversed at the *caesura*; in an anapaestic dimeter the initial effect was definitely repeated or renewed in the middle of the line. Sometimes it is further emphasized by the concurrence of a rhetorical effect, repetition or anaphora (νῦν ἐπάκουσον, νῦν ἐπάρηξον. Aes. *Cho.* 725).

The chief forms of anapaestic verse are the following:

(a) The early ἐμβατήρια of Tyrtaeus, in which the catalectic form of line is repeated:

ἄγετ᾽ ὦ Σπάρτας εὐάνδρου
κοῦροι πατέρων πολιατᾶν,
λαιᾷ μὲν ἴτυν προβαλέσθε,
δόρυ δεξιτερᾷ δ᾽ εὐτόλμως.

That is ‿‿ – | ‿‿ – | ‿‿ – | – or ‿‿ – | ‿‿ – | ‿‿ – | ⌣ or ‿‿ – | ‿‿ – | ‿‿ – | – ⊼ or ‿‿ – ‿‿ – ‿‿ ⌣ –. The third foot may be a spondee (which it rarely is in the drama), and the long syllable of the anapaest is not resolved.

(b) The acatalectic dimeter of tragedy and comedy (with the catalectic line at the close of a group of lines) used mainly for the εἴσοδος of the chorus. This is the most important and most familiar form of anapaestic verse; it will be considered more fully.

(c) In the Greek drama dimeters of a freer and more lyrical cast, in θρῆνοι and other emotional passages, sometimes using frequent spondees to express distress or perplexity (*Ion* 859 f. ὦ ψυχά, πῶς σιγάσω;) and sometimes admitting complete resolution in passages of greater excitement or surprise, either once in the line or twice or even in all three feet save the last:

τίς ὄρεα | βαθύκομα | τάδ᾽ ἐπέσυ|το βροτῶν;[1]

---

[1] A resolved line of this type served the metricians as an example of

Similarly resolved anapaests are found on a larger scale in the ὑπόρχημα of Pratinas, 1-4 (Wilamowitz, *Sappho und Simonides*, p. 132 f.).

(d) A longer line, tetrameter or Ἀριστοφάνειον, composed of an acatalectic and a catalectic dimeter. It is found in ἐμβατήρια:

ἄγετ' ὦ Σπάρτας ἔνοπλοι κοῦροι | ποτὶ τὰν Ἄρεος κίνασιν

(unless this should rather be regarded as two separate lines; the long line as written by later poets does not admit a spondee in the seventh place). Epicharmus is said to have composed whole plays in this metre, and it is used by Aristophanes, especially in the *parabasis*. At Rome Plautine drama uses also very frequently an acatalectic line of 8 or 4+4 anapaests. The catalectic line was one of the many metres written by Varro in his *Saturae*. In Aristophanes there is regular diaeresis after the fourth foot, and the seventh foot is not a spondee, though spondees are very freely admitted elsewhere (*Nub.* 961):

λέξω τοίνυν τὴν ἀρχαίαν | παιδείαν ὡς διέκειτο,
ὅτ' ἐγὼ τὰ δίκαια λέγων ἤνθουν | καὶ σωφροσύνη 'νενόμιστο.

Anapaestic verse, in its current and unmistakable forms, may be called 'dipodic' and 'dimetric'. Groups of two feet are combined with groups of four. A group of three or of six

---

composition in the foot called 'Pyrrhic' (or rather 'Pyrrich', for it is pyrrichius, from the dance πυρρίχη). A pyrrhic (⏑⏑ = —) can hardly have had any real use or existence in metrical practice. Dionysius, *De Comp. Verb.* c. xvii, gives the line:

λέγε δὲ σὺ κατὰ πόδα νεόχυτα μέλεα.

A resolved dactyl, or anapaest (⏑⏑ ⏑̇⏑), would be indistinguishable from a pyrrhic dipody. This particular line calls attention to the metre in which it is composed: κατὰ πόδα = foot by foot. 'Foot by foot rehearse the measure, verse that flows in channel strange.' (It is difficult to believe with Wilamowitz and Prof. Rhys Roberts that the line has also another meaning, and refers to the rent limbs of Pentheus.)

anapaests—a tripody or trimeter—is too rare and disputable to be considered here.

In its collocation of words—the technical matter of bricklaying—anapaestic verse, as we should expect, resembled dactylic in admitting the shortening of a long vowel before a following vowel—'vocalis ante vocalem corripitur':

οἴχεταῖ ἀνδρῶν. (Aes. *Pers.* 60.)
τὼ Θησείδα δ' | ὄζω Ἀ|θηνῶν, (Eur. *Hec.* 123.)

(in the latter of which passages the shortened syllable carries the *ictus* and may be compared with Plautus's *íta me | dí ament*, in trochaic verse). But such shortening is far less frequent in anapaests than in epic verse; it is in fact rare. And of course it is rarer still in Latin, where 'vocalis ante vocalem corripitur' was never a prevalent *metrical* principle; the principle came into play *within a word* — e.g. fieri—more frequently than in Greek, and as we have seen above (p. 46, i. b) a monosyllable was shortened in verse, and in actual speech, when the following syllable was short. There is an example in a tetrameter of Varro's:

non quaerenda est homini, | quĭ habet | virtutem, paenula in imbri.

Anapaestic verse was not so congenial to Latin as iambic or trochaic. Plautus does not employ this shortening to any appreciable extent, but other metrical devices are rather notably frequent in his anapaests: (1) fusion of two vowels into one long one, 'filio͡, nuptii͡s', scanned as spondees; (2) shortening on the principle of 'Breves Breviantes',

forĕs án | cubiti ác | pedĕs plús | valeánt.

It is possible, and it has been maintained by some, that, instead of synizesis, we should see in the former of these cases also the operation of the same law, resulting in two short syllables ('filĭŏ, nuptĭĭs').

It remains to consider the systems of anapaestic dimeters which are so conspicuous in the drama. Their special purpose was to accompany the entrance, πάροδος or εἴσοδος, of the chorus,[1] but occasional passages of similar anapaests are found elsewhere, and the πάροδος usually does not consist of anapaests alone, but of anapaests *plus* μέλος.

In the Greek drama anapaestic systems are made up of groups of lines (three, four, or five or more lines, as the poet chose to arrange them) which end with a paroemiacus or catalectic line, and which are continuous in their metrical structure. There is no hiatus or *syllaba anceps* at the end of a line; the composition is hypermetric, hypermetron, or what was sometimes called πνῖγος, as giving the reciter no rest or breathing-space.

A monometer or line of two anapaests is occasionally admitted. It may be the penultimate line:

τῆσδ' ἀπὸ χώρας
ἦραν, στρατιῶτιν ἀρωγάν,

or may mark some kind of pause in the thought.

---

[1] In Ar. *Poet.* c. xii the πάροδος is defined as πρώτη λέξις ὅλου χοροῦ. It is not a μέλος. Westphal argued that it must have been recited, for if it were sung the movement of the choreutae would be ludicrously slow.

The other choric passages are στάσιμα, and a στάσιμον is defined as τὸ ἄνευ ἀναπαίστου καὶ τροχαίου, i.e. without anapaestic systems and trochaic tetrameters. Trochaic tetrameters are not found in the πάροδος of an extant play, but the schol. on Ar. *Ach.* 204 says that tragic and comic poets employed them, ἐπειδὰν δρομαίως εἰσάγωσι τοὺς χορούς, ἵνα ὁ λόγος συντρέχῃ τῷ δράματι (leg. δραμήματι). The close of the *Oed. Tyr.* is a surviving relic of a trochaic ἔξοδος (ὦ πάτρας Θήβης ἔνοικοι κτλ.).

In a normal tragedy the entrance of the chorus is a formal and stately affair, occupying some time. The choreutae enter in their ordered ranks or groups, to assume a rectangular formation (τετράγωνον σχῆμα). At the close of the play the situation was very different. The audience are stirred or overwhelmed by the fear and pity which the catastrophe has excited. Elaborate and prolonged evolutions would be out of place. Hence the anapaests are often only a few lines (πολλαὶ μορφαὶ τῶν δαιμονίων κτλ.).

Diaeresis is regular after the first μέτρον or dipody, except that the division is in a few instances later by one short time:

πτερύγων ἐρετμοῖσιν | ἐρεσσόμενοι.
μαλακαῖς ἀδόλοισι | παρηγορίαις.

Coincidence of word and foot is freely admitted in anapaestic verse, both in Greek and Latin. It may extend throughout a line or more than one line:

ὡς καὶ τῆς νῦν φθιμένης νυκτὸς
μεγάλοι θόρυβοι κατέχουσ' ἡμᾶς.

The form ◡ ◡ ◡ ◡ (proceleusmaticus) is not admitted. Only one example is quoted, and that is in comedy:

διὰ σὲ δὲ | φοιτᾶν. (Ar. *Clouds* 916.)

The inverted anapaest (– ◡́ ◡) is subject to considerable restrictions. A line made up of four such feet is inadmissible, and a line like

ζυγὸν ἀμφιβαλεῖν δούλιον Ἑλλάδι (Aes. *Persae* 50.)

is infrequent. It may not precede an anapaest; this would result in bringing four short syllables together (–◡◡ ◡◡–). Most commonly it is followed by a spondee, as in τῆσδ' ἀπὸ χώρας, a group of syllables that make an 'Adonius', which closed a sapphic stanza.

To the Romans the composition of Anapaestic verse presented special difficulties, and their practice is consequently different from that of the Greeks. In early Roman drama the proceleusmaticus (◡ ◡ ◡́ ◡) is freely admitted, not only in comedy, but also in tragedy; and the diaeresis in the middle of the dimeter is less strictly observed. Greek anapaests not only had diaeresis in the middle of the line, but quite frequently ended each anapaest with the end of a word; in Latin such an arrangement meant divergence throughout of ictus and accent:

inclúte parvá prodíte patriá.[1]

---

[1] Compare lines of Anaxandrides (quoted by Lindsay, *Captivi*, p. 77):
φυσκῶν, ζωμοῦ, τευτλῶν, θριῶν,
θυννίδες ὀπταί, φυκίδες ἐφθαί.

Pacuvius is credited with a deliberate attempt to write anapaests on a new principle, exemplified in the lines:

> agite, íte, evól|vite, rápite, coma
> tractáte per ás|pera sáxa et humum.

Here there is more agreement between accent and ictus, facilitated by the abolition of the diaeresis. Marius Victorinus, who mentions the experiment, of course gives no hint that agreement with accent was arrived at ('Pacuvius novare propositum volens noluit intra binos pedes finire sensum'), nor do we know whether Pacuvius persisted in his experiment or tried it on a large scale. It could not succeed or establish itself. The result was too unlike the Greek norm; and to compose in this vein must have been extremely difficult. To write verse that observes two different principles is a *tour de force* which may be difficult in the extreme, e.g. to write hexameters in English that observe *both* accent and quantity. In Latin anapaests complete success was impossible. Pacuvius has to end his lines with 'comá, humúm'. To achieve coincidence of accent and ictus the line must either end with a word of one syllable, which no doubt it might occasionally do, as in Accius's

> delubra tenes, mysteria qùae,

or with one of a very limited number of quite exceptional words such as 'nostrás', 'tantón', 'abít' (where the abnormal accent is due to loss of a syllable). It is notable that Terence never uses anapaests in his few cantica, although they are the favourite metre in the cantica of Plautus.

With a catalectic ending the conditions are reversed. Here the agreement of ictus and accent was a thing not difficult to

(The exact coincidence of accent and ictus here is of course quite accidental. Accent diverged from *ictus* just as readily:

διθρόνου Διόθεν καὶ δισκήπτρόν.

Accent has no place in Greek metre till Babrius, and in Babrius it is regarded only in one syllable of the line.)

ANAPAESTS

attain, but difficult to avoid. So it is not surprising to find Plautus writing catalectic dimeters continuously (κατὰ στίχον or *iugiter*):

> deféssus súm pultándo.
> hoc póstremúmst. vae vóbis, &c.   (*Stichus* 313 f.)

Plautus also uses the catalectic line as a concluding line or *clausula* after a group of acatalectic dimeters, as do the tragic poets: Accius, *Philocteta*:

> unde ígni' cluét mortálibu' clám
> divísus: eúm dictú' Prometheús
> clepsísse doló poenásque Ioví
>   fato éxpendísse suprémo.[1]

This ending is found also in the *Saturae* of Varro (Κοσμοτορύνη):

> dum nos ventus flamine sudo
> suavem ad patriam perducat.

But it is not consistently and invariably used by the early poets, and it was entirely abandoned by Seneca. Plautus, besides writing catalectic dimeters, frequently makes his longer lines (tetrameters) catalectic. One or two lines are catalectic in a passage otherwise acatalectic: *Persa* 783-4:

qui illúm Persam átque omnés Persás atque étiam omnés persónas

male di ómnes pérdant, íta miseró Toxílus haec míhi concívit.

It is difficult to see why Plautus did not make all his long lines of this type. Aristophanes had done so, without any inducement in the shape of coincident accent and ictus. And the same question arises about iambic verse. The catalectic form ('septenarius') makes coincidence in the penultimate

---

[1] In the second line 'dĭctŭs Prōmetheus' shows that the incidence of the *ictus* did not enforce length by position. It was when the ictus fell on a vowel originally long *by nature* that the long quantity was revived or protected ('mánĕ manē' begins a trochaic line).

syllable extremely easy of attainment and all but invariable. Yet Plautus often writes the complete 'octonarius', without having much precedent for it in Greek comedy as far as we know (though the Ἰχνευταί of Sophocles has revealed a passage of considerable length in satyric drama).

In the Roman drama anapaests are not associated with marching or with the εἴσοδος or ἔξοδος of a chorus. They may happen to be used when a personage is entering, as in *Trin.* 840 f., but that does not make them 'march-anapaests' (Lindsay, *Captivi*, p. 80). There was no regular chorus, and the 'orchestra' was occupied by the seats of senators. The fishermen in the *Rudens* enter with iambic septenarii. Anapaestic verse could be used as a lyric anywhere in the play. Many of the more complex forms of Greek lyric were unworkable in Latin, and anapaests were one of the simpler metres that took their place.

Seneca's practice would have seemed very strange to the Greeks of earlier times. His treatment of anapaests is in keeping with what he does in the case of other metres. He sometimes writes a long passage in Sapphics, without an Adonius anywhere; sometimes a long passage in Asclepiadeans without a shorter closing line (Glyconeus). So in anapaests his last line is often a dimeter like the rest. He does, however, show some tendency to use a monometer as a closing line, often in the form $- \cup \cup - -$:

> quid plura canam? vincit saevas
> cura novercas. (*Phaedra* 357.)

Or the second dipody of the last line takes that shape:

> nec sit terris ūltĭmă Thūlē. (*Med.* 379.)

In the *Agamemnon* (310 f.) he has dimeter and monometer alternating, a form unknown to Greek tragedy. In linking his lines together Seneca is less careful than the Greek dramatists. Hiatus and *syllaba anceps* occur sometimes, without being justified by the close of a period or by a marked

ANAPAESTS

pause in the sense. But the instances are few, and some of them have been removed by emendation. They are notably more frequent in the *Octavia* than in the other plays, and this difference in metrical practice is one of the fairly numerous and considerable reasons for assigning that play to a different author. The author has also a tendency to make a monometer end in a short syllable ('pulsata fretă', 316, 'fletibus oră', 330), and he has an unusual lengthening before a mute and a liquid in 'plura referrē prohibet praesens' (890).

CHAPTER V

IAMBIC VERSE

I. The Iambic Trimeter and Senarius

'Trimeter' and 'Senarius' are not merely different words for the same thing or words of precisely the same meaning. The former designates a handling of the metre that was distinctively Greek, though practised also by later Roman poets: 'senarius' is the more appropriate word for the heavier and more amorphous type of line which prevailed at Rome before the Augustan age.

In both languages there were several distinct veins of iambic writing and types of iambic verse, each with principles and restrictions of its own. Quintilian (*Inst. Or.* ix. 4. 139 f.), speaking of the variation of rhythm in oratory to answer to various emotions, illustrates this by iambic verses: sometimes we aim at the 'tumor tragoediae', which depends mainly on iambi and spondees; the iambus with its rising movement, he would say, gives an effect of imperious energy, and the spondee of course lends solemnity to the utterance:

ēn īmpero Argīs, scēptra mihi līquīt Pelops

(words of Atreus, perhaps from a play of Accius); the verse of comedy, he proceeds, gains 'celeritas' at the expense of 'gravitas', it admits 'trochees' (by which he means what we are accustomed to call 'tribrachs') and pyrrhics:

quid ĭgĭtur făcĭam? non eam ne nunc quidem:

further, 'aspera et maledica', when expressed in verse, take the shape of iambi:

> quis hoc potest videre, quis potest pati,
> nisi impudicus et vorax et aleo?'

Quintilian is here quoting, from Catullus (xxix), lines which admit no spondee and consist of pure iambi throughout. This was a refinement on the abusive verse of Archilochus. The effect was one of measured and dexterous 'celeritas', like the flashing of a rapier in a skilful hand or the flight of a well-aimed missile.[1]

Iambic verse has no early history. It comes into view suddenly in the middle of the seventh century B. C., written in a finished and exact form by Archilochus of Paros, to whom notable advances and innovations are attributed in several different kinds of metre. It existed before, no doubt, probably in a ruder and more popular form, with the licences which are later seen in comedy. It belongs clearly to the Ionians, and it had some place in the popular festivals of Demeter and Iakchos, which flourished among the Ionians and their kindred of Attica—festivals connected with the rise of the Attic drama.

The study of iambic verse begins most conveniently with the most regular form of it that had a wide vogue—Catullus's absolutely pure iambi we may postpone, as an exceptional and rather artificial or fanciful thing—the trimeter of Archilochus and the tragedians. The practice of Archilochus differs so slightly from that of tragedy that he need not be separately treated. It was his verse that tragedy adopted, λεκτικώτατον τῶν μέτρων—'alternis aptum sermonibus' (Hor. *A. P.* 81)—as

---

[1] Quintilian's phrase about Archilochus, 'breves *vibrantesque* sententiae' (x. 1. 60), compares his thoughts or meanings to the hurtling of a spear through the air, or perhaps to a thunderbolt (compare the saying of Cicero, which Quintilian quotes [ix. 4. 55]: 'Demosthenis non tantopere vibrarent illa fulmina,' &c.).

nearer to real life or actual debate than the elaborate and stately hexameter. There are various indications that the natural texture or tendency both of Greek and Latin was iambo-trochaic (alternation of short and long) rather than dactylic or anapaestic, though both languages lent themselves readily enough to the latter forms of verse also.[1]

The iambus is a foot of three times ($\cup\cup\cup$), its rhythm duplex or διπλάσιος (the ratio of the parts 2 : 1, or in actual order 1 + 2). The second and third times go together, taking normally the shape of a long syllable ($\cup -$); when they do not do so the ictus is on the second syllable of the foot ($\cup \mid \overset{\cdot}{\cup} \cup$). It is a rising foot; the slighter or weaker part precedes the stronger. But though the ancients recognized and often discuss the single iambus, Greek composition in iambics dealt not with single iambi, but with pairs or dipodies (whence the name trimeter[2] for a line containing six feet): $\cup - \cup -$. Of the four syllables in such a group there was one that might be heavier without detriment to the general effect—the first. To make the third long would efface the structure of the group: $\cup - - -$ is amorphous. The iambic line consisted of three

---

[1] Cicero (*Orator* 189): 'versus saepe in oratione per imprudentiam dicimus . . . senarios vero et Hipponacteos effugere vix possumus; magnam enim partem ex iambis nostra constat oratio' (where Cicero would have ended with the fault he is describing if he had written, 'partem éx iámbis cónstat nóstra orátió'. He shuns that, and gives us instead, as in the previous clause, the favourite prose ending of a double Cretic $\cup\cup \cup -$): ib. § 191, he speaks of the view that iambic rhythm belongs specially to oratory, 'quod sit orationi simillimus'; it therefore belongs to the drama too: 'qua de causa fieri ut is potissimum propter similitudinem veritatis (= reality, real life) adhibeatur in fabulis, quod ille dactylicus numerus hexametrorum magniloquentiae sit accommodatior.'

[2] Terentianus:

sed ter feritur; hinc trimetrus dicitur,
scandendo binos quod pedes coniungimus.

('feritur', is beaten: each of three groups of syllables has its dominant *ictus*.)

such dipodies, and it followed that the first, fifth, and ninth syllables might be long:

$$\underset{\smile}{-} - \smile - \mid \underset{\smile}{-} - \smile - \mid \underset{\smile}{-} - \smile -.$$

For feet of three times, the longest possible κῶλον, according to Aristoxenus, was one of six feet or eighteen times. The trimeter then may be one κῶλον; but in fact and in practice the trimeter insisted on being divided, in very much the same way as the hexameter. It resented equal division; like a hexameter it refused to be $2 + 2 + 2$ or $3 + 3$ when it was embodied in words: a line like

ἀμηχάνων | ἀλγηδόνων | ἐπιστροφαί

is not admitted in tragedy, and Aeschylus's line (if he wrote it in this shape)

Θρῄκην περάσαντες | μόγις πολλῷ πόνῳ

may be a case of sound deliberately made to answer to sense:

The line too labours and the words move slow.

When elision occurred the division was tolerated:

ὦ πᾶσα Κάδμου γαῖ', ἀπόλλυμαι δόλῳ,

and of course the end of a monosyllabic word might occur in the middle of the line if the word was proclitic and not enclitic:

οὔ μοι τὰ Γύγεω τοῦ πολυχρύσου μέλει

is a perfectly euphonious line. Exceptionally, also, a break in the middle of the line might emphasize a contrast:

ἀτιμίας μὲν οὔ, προμηθίας δὲ σοῦ. (*El.* 1036.)

The trimeter then, like the hexameter, prefers to be $2\frac{1}{2} + 3\frac{1}{2}$ or $3\frac{1}{2} + 2\frac{1}{2}$. Often, of course, as in a hexameter like

Peliaco quondam prognatae vertice pinus

or

caerula verrentes abiegnis aequora palmis,

the division is very slight, and exists rather for metre than for the sense or for rhetoric. It was possible for a comic poet to make a trimeter consist of one long compound word (*Wasps* 220):

ἀρχαιομελισιδωνοφρυνιχήρατα,

though we may perhaps suppose a very slight division after σιδωνο.

The analogy between these divisions and those of the hexameter is so close that it seems necessary to call them *caesurae*. If they are *caesurae*, the fact is of some importance for recent metrical methods and discussions.

The syllables of an iambic trimeter admit of being construed as trochees with *anacrusis*:

$\overset{\smile}{} \vdots -\cup -\overset{\smile}{} \mid -\cup -\overset{\smile}{} \mid -\cup - \wedge .$

(In a trochaic dipody, which is the converse of an iambic one, it is the *fourth* syllable that is *anceps* or permitted to be long.) This method of scansion, which is in agreement with modern musical notation, was adopted by J. H. H. Schmidt and others in the nineteenth century, and—for lyrics at all events—the principle has had considerable currency in this country, since it was set forth by Jebb in the introductions to his editions of plays of Sophocles. It has advantages. It may be contended that it gives a better and clearer account of certain forms of verse than does iambic scansion. As regards the trimeter of the drama—verse that is spoken or recited rather than sung—this matter of the *caesura* is perhaps the most tangible objection that can be brought against it. With trochaic scansion it is difficult to see that there is any cumbrousness or heaviness or rupture into two parts in the line of Aeschylus quoted above:

Θρή|κην περάσαν|τες μόγις πολ|λῷ πόνῳ.

The normal divisions of the Trimeter would have to be called *diaereses* and not *caesurae*, on the trochaic theory. Further, the difference in ἦθος, in feeling or effect, between trochaic and iambic verse is discussed so often and so conspicuously by the ancients that it is difficult to believe that the difference consisted only in the presence or absence of one syllable at the beginning.[1] We have seen above that the structure of anapaests is far from suggesting obviously that they should be scanned as dactyls with anacrusis; and it may be added that the anacrusis is no more plausible in the case of dochmii (∪ − − ∪ −), φρενῶν δυσφρόνων ἁμαρτήματα is not readily thought of as φρε|νῶν δυσφρόνων ἁ|μαρτήματα.

The essential structure of the tragic trimeter has now been explained. If we speak of it in terms of feet, we may say that only the first, third, and fifth may be heavy or spondaic. There must be a caesura in the third foot or in the fourth. Subordinate, but still quite important principles of structure remain. A clear understanding of the nature of the verse was one of the contributions made by English scholars to classical research. It was made in the beginning of last century. One of the rules is still known by the name of Porson (*Lex Porsoni*).

(i) Resolution. Unlike the long syllable of the dactyl in a hexameter, resolution of which is found only in two or three dubious lines of Ennius (*supra*, p. 56), the long syllable of an iambus could be replaced by two short syllables. This was done very sparingly by Archilochus, not more than once in a line:

$$\stackrel{\cup\ \ \ \cup\cup}{κλαίω\ |\ τὰ\ Θασί|ων\ οὐ\ τὰ\ Μαγνήτων\ κακά.}$$

---

[1] There is a passage in Quintilian (ix. 4. 136) which seems to show that when a series of syllables occurred which could be analysed as iambi (∪ − ∪ − ∪ − ....), the 'rising' effect was not felt only at the outset ('iambi ... *omnibus pedibus* insurgunt et a brevibus in longas nituntur et crescunt'). The believer in trochaic scansion should read the iambic tetrameters in the Ἰχνευταί of Sophocles (291 f.) with an open mind, or a mind as unprejudiced as he can make it. He will not feel them to be merely trochaic tetrameters with a syllable prefixed.

Tragedy at first was similarly strict, but gradually assumed greater freedom. When Euripides brought it down from heroic heights to a level nearer that of everyday life, its vocabulary and metre underwent a corresponding change. In metre resolution became more frequent. Euripides has resolution as often as four times in a line:

πενία δὲ σοφίαν ἔλαχε διὰ τὸ δυστυχές.

Comedy admitted resolution with great freedom, leaving untouched only the last foot of the line. In all forms of the verse, at all periods, the last foot is a regular disyllabic iambus, ∪ ≐ .[1]

When the long syllable of the first, third, or fifth foot was resolved, the result might be − ∪́ ∪, a group of syllables of dactylic form, but differing from a real dactyl in the incidence of the *ictus*. Tragedy admitted − ∪́ ∪ only in the first and third foot, not in the fifth.

When resolution took place, and the three syllables were not within the same word but divided between two words, the strict rule, observed by Archilochus and the tragedians, was that the two short syllables which stood for the long should be in the same word (∪ | ∪ ∪, not ∪ ∪ | ∪), as in τὰ Θασί(ων), or in Aeschylus:

Σκύθην ἐς οἶμ|ον, ἄβα|τον εἰς ἐρημίαν.

---

[1] A line in the *Frogs* appears to be an exception :

καὶ κωδάριον καὶ ληκύθιον καὶ θυλάκιον

(l. 1203). The line would be normal if the first syllable of θυλάκιον could be supposed to be short. But all the earlier evidence makes it long, and the only instance of its shortness given by L. and S. is in a late epigram in the Anthology (*Anth. Pal.* viii. 166), which has no metrical authority. Further, the context demands a word exactly equivalent in its syllables to κωδάριον and ληκύθιον. The deviation from rule is similar to that which is sometimes necessitated by a proper name.

In comedy the rule is not observed, though it is not broken with great frequency:

ἐμὲ μὲν σὺ πολλοὺς τὸν | πατέρ' ἐ|λαύνεις δρόμους.
(Arist. *Clouds* 29.)

(ii) An anapaest was admitted by tragedy only in the first foot (ποταμῶν τε πηγαί . . .), and that under the condition that the three syllables must be in the same word. An exception was made in the case of proper names:

ἐμοὶ μὲν οὐδεὶς μῦθος, Ἀντιγόνη, φίλων.

Comedy admitted an anapaest in all places but the last:

κατάβα, κατάβα, κατάβα, κατάβα.—καταβήσομαι.

(iii) The rule of the 'final cretic' (*Lex Porsoni*) when a line ends in a word of 'cretic' form ($-\smile -$), the preceding syllable must be either short, or a word of one syllable connecting itself with the word that follows; it may not be long and the last syllable of a word of more than one syllable. Thus

ὡς τοῖσιν ἐμπείροισι καὶ | τὰς συμφορὰς

is a quite legitimate line, but

Ἄτλας ὁ χαλκέοισι νώτοις οὐρανόν

is so exceptional—in tragedy—that doubts arise about the text. Comedy did not observe the rule, and it was entirely disregarded by Roman poets, even when they wrote iambic verse with the greatest strictness and finish, in the Augustan age and later.

The Porsonian canon has hitherto been a mere 'empirical fact'. The practice of the Greek tragic poets commends itself to the ear as euphonious, but no definite *cause* for it was suggested by Porson himself, or for long after him. Recently a promising attempt to assign a cause has been made by K. Witte (*Hermes*, 1914, p. 229 f.). His theory may be summarized as follows:—The iambic trimeter, like the heroic hexameter, fell naturally into two parts, and the favourite and most frequent division of it was the penthemimeral :

$$\underset{}{\smile} - \mid \cup - \mid \overset{a}{\underset{}{\smile}} \parallel - \cup \mid - \overset{b}{\underset{}{\smile}} \mid - \cup \mid - \, .$$

Further, the effect of this division was heightened, with extreme frequency, by making the syllable before it long. If a precisely similar effect followed at *b*, four syllables later, the division at *a* would no longer be dominant. Hence if a line begins

ψυχήν τ' ἄριστοι,

it may be completed by the words

κεὐγένειᾰν ἐκπρεπεῖς,

where the -αν is short, but a quadrisyllabic word, or group of words, with the last syllable long may not follow the caesura. Similarly (though here the argument becomes somewhat less convincing) with a hephthemimeral division :

Ἕλληνες οὐ μενοῖεν, ἀλλὰ σέλμασιν,

the hephthemimeral division (which *must* be preceded by a short syllable) may not be followed by a similar division which would obscure or eclipse it, i.e. not by a similar division with the added emphasis of a long syllable before it.

That is a brief statement of Witte's principle, and it appears to be sound, at all events as regards the dominant penthemimeral caesura, and the rule once evolved may have been extended to lines with the less frequent hephthemimeral. In a line like

$$\mid - \quad \cup - - \mid - \cup - \quad - \mid$$
non ut superni villa candens Tusculi

there are two conspicuous groups of syllables arranged in a way that rather distorts or destroys a trimeter, a metrical effect belonging to lyrics and to a wholly different type of verse,

$$- \cup \quad - - \mid \quad - \cup \quad - \quad -$$
Πυθῶνί τ' αὔξῃς οὖρον ὕμνων.   (Pind. *Pyth.* iv.)

Witte points out that, in the rare violations in Greek tragedy of Porson's Law, the last five syllables of the line sometimes go very closely together in sense, or the words are bound together by elision[1]:

ἅ μοι προσελθὼν σῖγα σήμαιν' εἶτ' ἔχει.
(Soph. *Phil.* 22.)

Now elision at this point—before the final cretic—is distinctly preferred by Seneca. The effect of 'villa candens Tusculi' did not repel Horace, but it did repel him. In the great majority of the lines in Seneca that end in a word of three syllables, there is elision before that word. If we next come back to Horace we find that in Epode xvii, a poem of a dramatic cast rather than Archilochian iambi, the only violation of Porson's rule is 'homicidam Hectorem'.

Tragedy, as it had an exalted, Ionic and poetic, diction of its own, was also stately and regular in metre. The comic poet can make an effective use of the difference. Thus in the *Peace* Hermes, being a god, naturally speaks the language of tragedy. When Trygaeus knocks at the gate of Olympus, he begins:

πόθεν βροτοῦ με προσέβαλ'—

(βροτοῦ, for θνητοῦ, is tragic, and we may suppose that the sentence was to end with words like ἐξαίφνης φάτις). But he is startled by the apparition of the gigantic beetle, and he goes on:

ὦναξ Ἡράκλεις,
τουτὶ τί ἐστι τὸ κακόν; TP. ἱπποκάνθαρος.

'ὦναξ Ἡράκλεις' and the form τουτί belong to everyday colloquial Attic. The former is also metrically untragic. The

---

[1] Witte proposes to deal with the first line of the *Ion* by writing it:

Ατλας ὁ χαλκέοισι νώτοισ' οὐρανόν,

with elision before the cretic. But this seems doubtful in Attic tragedy: it would be more plausible in Archilochus, in verse written in actual Ionic.

resolution in τί ἐστ|ι τὸ κα|κόν; is not irregular or not glaringly irregular, for the article τό goes closely with κακόν.

The trimeter of Attic comedy enjoyed a large measure of freedom. Some of its features have already been mentioned. But it remains a very different thing from the 'senarius' of the early Roman drama. Most notably, it never admits a spondee in the second or fourth foot.

It might be supposed that the admission of an anapaest would carry with it the admission of a spondee, but this is not the case. Further, the anapaest is not admitted indiscriminately and in any shape. It is admitted most readily—with great readiness—when all three syllables are in one word (κατάβα, κατάβα κτλ.). A long word has a longer pause after it than a short word, and if a long word ended with one of the short syllables the foot was broken or strained asunder becoming less suitable to take a place among iambi. The effect is therefore infrequent, and it has been observed that in Greek it occurs within a dipody, not between two dipodies:

ἐπίσ|κŏπŏς ἥ̆||κω.
δεῦρ|ŏ πᾰλῑν || βαδιστέον.

The Latin senarius is stricter in this respect, and it has been suggested that it was so because it ignored dipodic structure; it had no quadrisyllabic group within which a wrongly divided anapaest could find shelter. Hence the line (*Asinaria*, Prol. 11)

Demophilu' scripsit, Maccu' vortit barbare

may be regarded as proof that, though Plautus's full and formal name, at all events in his later life, was T. Maccius Plautus, he was also known as Maccus. 'Maccŭ̄' | vōrtit' divides an anapaest wrongly.

The comic trimeter could divide itself in ways that were

excluded from tragedy, even emphasizing a strange division by change of speaker (*Birds* 175):

Π. βλέψον κάτω. ΕΠ. καὶ δὴ βλέπω. Π. βλέπε νῦν ἄνω.

The 'proceleusmaticus' (∪ ∪ ∪ ∪), arrived at by resolution of an anapaest, is very rare in Greek comedy, much rarer than in Latin, but there are undoubted instances of it. A good example is a line of the comic poet Plato:

οὗτος, τίς εἶ; | λέγε ταχύ· | τί σιγᾷς; οὐκ ἐρεῖς.

The trimeter of the satyric drama calls for very brief notice. It may be said to be intermediate between the tragic and the comic trimeter, but not in the sense that it is half-way between them. It is nearer the tragic form of verse—notably so in the recently recovered Ἰχνευταί of Sophocles—and differs from it chiefly in admitting the anapaest more freely, in places other than the first. Anapaests are fairly frequent in the *Cyclops*. A fragment of the 'Προμηθεὺς Πυρκαεύς' of Aeschylus:

λινᾶ δὲ πίσσα κωμολίνου μακροὶ τόνοι

shows, by its anapaest in the fourth place—an ordinary word, not a proper name—that the play must have been a satyric drama and not a tragedy.

The history of iambic verse at Rome is in many points obscure and complicated, much more difficult than the history of the trimeter in Greek. It falls into two sharply distinguished periods, or rather phases, which overlap in time. (1) The 'senarius' of the early drama, which ignored dipodic structure and admitted spondees in all places but the last—not only in the first, third, and fifth—was used in tragedy from Livius to Accius, and by Cicero in his versions from the Greek; it is found later in the fables of Phaedrus, and probably continued to be used in comedy in imperial times[1]; (2) a stricter form of

---

[1] M. Pomponius Bassulus, who wrote comedies under Trajan or Hadrian, composed his own epitaph, which is extant on stone. Presum-

verse or 'trimeter', conforming to Greek rule substantially, though not in all details, was introduced first by 'iambographi' in Cicero's time, Catullus and his friends; and in the Augustan age tragedy in the hands of Varius and Ovid all but certainly adopted a similar type of verse, not materially different from the trimeter of Seneca. Horace would not have condemned as loose or inartistic the spondaic lines of Ennius:

in scaenam missos cum magno pondere versus,

if his friends Pollio and Varius had still been writing lines of the same type.[1]

The verse of the early drama is a vast subject of investigation, on which much has been written. It cannot be dealt with here, but a gap would be left in the history of the metre if its nature were not briefly indicated. It is somewhat cumbrous or ponderous, especially in tragedy, less agile in movement than Greek iambic verse. The effect is due to very frequent spondees (or their equivalents, dactyl and anapaests) and also often to frequent elision:

quianám tam advérso augúrio et ínimico óminé
Thebis radiatum lumen ostentum tuum?   (Accius.)

ably the verse is that which he was accustomed to write:

ne more pecoris otio transfungerer,
Menandri paucas vorti scitas fabulas
et ipsus etiam sedulo finxi novas, &c.

The second line has spondees in the second and fourth place, as have some of the lines that follow. Compare also the iambics of Apuleius on a toothpowder (*Apologia*, c. vi).

[1] It has been supposed that when Horace described Pollio's tragedies in the phrase

Pollio regum
facta canit *pede ter percusso*,

he meant to imply that the lines were of the strict Hellenic type. But this seems doubtful. He may have been thinking vaguely of 'trimeter' as the name for the verse of tragic dialogue, however constructed. In the passage of the *A. P.* quoted above (l. 258) he speaks of the 'trimeters' *of Accius* ('hic et in Acci | nobilibus trimetris').

(In these two lines, as it happens, the fourth foot *does* conform to Greek rule, *ĕt ĭnī* and *ĕn ōst.*) Cicero could write in the old tragic vein with such exactness that his lines sometimes sound almost like a parody of Pacuvius or Accius:

haec interemit tortu multiplicabili
dracónem, auríferam obtútu adsérvantem árborém.

Yet Cicero, in an often-quoted passage, speaks of the verses of comedy as shapeless and inharmonious: 'comicorum senarii propter similitudinem sermonis sic saepe sunt abiecti, ut nonnumquam vix in eis numerus et versus intellegi possit' (*Orator* 184). In the Ciceronian and Augustan ages literary Latin was being rapidly polished, hellenized, stereotyped in Hellenic moulds. Feeling and appreciation for its older and more spontaneous forms was dying out or was impaired. The older verse was not really formless. It observed rules of its own, ultimately prescribed by the nature of the Latin language, many of which have been made clear by modern research. But it was a defect in the old Roman drama that the verse of tragedy and the verse of comedy were so much alike—not that they were exactly alike, but there was no such difference as in Greek. While the metrical difference was less consistent and less obvious, the old Roman poet differentiated tragedy by a tumid vein of style, an often turgid and bombastic type of diction, derived partly perhaps from Aeschylus, but partly no doubt from the contemporary 'Asiatic' or at best decadent rhetoric of Greece. The differentiation was clear enough, and could be utilized by the comic poet after the fashion of the scene from the *Peace* quoted above: Plautus in the *Rudens* makes the aged priestess address her suppliants in tragic language, and in very regular cretic verse:

nempe equo ligneo per vias caerulas
esti' vectae?

How the early Latin poets came to handle the metre as they

did is obscure. Were there forms of Greek verse, current in popular entertainments of the time, that were looser than the trimeters of Aristophanes or Menander?[1] Did the native Saturnian verse set an example of indifference to the quantity of the syllable on which the *ictus* did not fall? Did the incidence of the Latin accent—always on the penultimate syllable if that syllable is long—accidentally or κατὰ συμβεβηκός aid and enforce the iambic rhythm, so that less attention to quantity was necessary? In a line like

labórans, quaérens, párcens, ílli sérviens

the coincidence is obvious. Apart from the first and last feet of the line—where there is divergence, if these feet are formed by disyllabic words—there is a great deal of coincidence in the verse of the early drama. A syllable which is both long and accented usually carries the ictus. A line like

et vos a vostris abdúxi negotiis

is comparatively rare. When it does occur the abnormal effect is generally atoned for by the line's ending in a quadrisyllabic word (like *negotiis* here) of obviously iambic cadence.

---

[1] A Greek trimeter with a spondee in the wrong place is not a wholly unknown thing, though foreign to the Attic drama. Kaibel, *Epigrammata Graeca* 502 (Thebes, third or fourth century) κεῖται γὰρ νηδὺν εἰς ἐμὴν ὁ Νήδυμος. Herondas's admission of a spondee in the fifth foot of his scazons is a similar irregularity; the recently recovered iambi of Callimachus are as strict in this respect as those of Catullus. The old Roman poet of course found anapaests with great frequency in the second and fourth places in Greek comedy. He may have said to himself, 'If an anapaest, why not a spondee?' But the Greeks discriminated, admitting the one and excluding the other. Priscian (Keil, *G. L.* iii. 426) has a discussion of the question whether the Roman type of iambic verse was ever written by the Greeks. He seems to quote one or two Greek lines (now unrecognizable owing to the state of the text), but arrives at the answer 'No'. Probably the line quoted above should be regarded as simply incorrect.

The early dramatic verse handed on to the verse of later tragedy—the Latin trimeter—a marked liking for spondees and anapaests. The liking for anapaests is not shared by the iambographi. Catullus shuns them, and instances in the *Epodes* of Horace are few and dubious (*infra*, Part II, Chap. III, § 2).

It became an all but rigid rule that the fifth foot must be a spondee, and it is put as a rule by Diomedes: 'iambicus tragicus, ut gravior iuxta materiae pondus esset, semper quinto loco spondeum recipit (he means 'habet'). aliter enim esse non potest tragicus.' The Latin iambic line was at all times reluctant to end in two pure iambi. In Plautus it does so chiefly with a word of three or four or more syllables ('cīvĭtătĕ cāelĭtŭm, testĭmōnĭīs'). It specially abhorred an ending in two separate words, each a pure iambus. The few exceptions there are have to be justified by the proclisis of a preposition, 'in-malam crucem'. Horace has such an ending only twice in the first ten epodes (v. 7 and ix. 33):

per hoc inane purpurae decus precor,

and nowhere in the seventeenth, though Horace is far from having a spondee always in the fifth place (*infra*, pp. 231 f.). In Seneca, according to L. Müller, there are only six instances of an ending in ∪−∪−, all of them cases of a word of four syllables (*Med.* 512):

Phoebi nepotes Sisyphi nepotibus.

As many as six examples cannot reasonably be removed by emendation, when the text is otherwise flawless. One other instance would have to be added—with a word of three syllables — if *Herc.* 20 is rightly read as 'sparsa nurĭbŭs implĭs'.

The admission of the anapaest is carried further by Seneca than by the Greek tragic poets.

(a) An anapaest in the first foot need not be one word or within one word:

> nec ad omne clarum ...
> vide ut atra nubes ...

and it may take the shape of a proceleusmaticus (*Med.* 670):

> păvĕt ănĭ|mus, horret.

(b) There is at least one instance of an anapaest in the third foot (*Oed.* 796):

> inter senem iuvenemque, sed propior seni.

But by far the greatest exception or extension is the ready admission of an anapaest in the fifth foot.

(c) In the first 500 trimeters of the *Hercules* and the first 500 of the *Medea*, 1,000 lines in all, an anapaest in the fifth place occurs 217 times or rather oftener than once in every five lines. This anapaest in Seneca is subject to considerable restriction. The two short syllables are very seldom in a separate word: a line like

> alte illa cecidit quae viro *caret Her*cule

is extremely rare. There is only one instance in the 1,000 lines of the *Hercules* and *Medea*, and that instance is rather apparent than real; it is *satis est*, where *est* is an enclitic. In the vast majority of cases, there is a word of three syllables, either complete or elided. Statistics are as follows:

	Herc.	*Med.*
Type, *Argolicas agit, propior seni*	103	89
Type, *deserui aetheris*	13	12
	116	101 [1]

It is a further and rather curious fact that before a cretic word, like *aetheris*, Seneca shows a strong preference for

---

[1] The *Octavia* shows no divergence in this respect from the other plays. For the first 500 trimeters the numbers are 102 and 11.

elision. He has no liking for the ending which is so frequent in Horace,

>   villa candēns Tūscŭlī, Silvane tutōr fīnĭum.

In the 1,000 lines under review this ending occurs only three times (*Herc.* 255 'regni vindices', 397 'voces amove', 495 'penates Labdaci'— nowhere in the first 500 trimeters of the *Medea*). This is an indication that ἰαμβοποιΐα in the Archilochian sense should be thought of as a distinct vein of metrical composition, similar no doubt, but differing in certain definite ways from the iambics of tragedy. The divergence might be illustrated also by pointing out—what it seems safe to say— that the pure iambics of Catullus ('phaselus ille', &c.) would never be used by any good poet in the drama, or at all events in the *diverbium* of a drama. Seneca, as it happens, writes in a *canticum* the iambic dimeter, which is the second verse in the couplet of Horace's *Epodes*. In the incantation scene in the *Medea*, 771-86, he writes a piece of sixteen lines in the metre of the *Epodes*, trimeter followed by dimeter. Probably he chose the metre because Horace had used it for a scene of witchcraft (Epode v), but what we may call the Horatian ending occurs only once (though once in as few as sixteen lines), 784:

>   Lernaea passae spicula.

In the *Agam.* 795 f. he has another piece of sixteen lines in dimeters throughout. In these the Horatian ending occurs as often as six times. Seneca's lyrics are throughout largely Horatian.

These may seem small points; but they inculcate what is an important principle for the study of the highly elaborated verse of the ancients. It is necessary to study metrical forms κατ' εἶδος ἕκαστον. An epic hexameter is different from a lyric hexameter, and both are different from the hexameter of satire. So it is, too, with iambic verse.

EXCURSUS

On Four Further Questions

(a) *Choriambic substitution.*—Recent writers on metre have made much of the supposition that $-\cup\cup-$ could readily take the place of a diiambus or $\cup-\cup-$. This idea is applied to the explanation of various metres, and the occurrence of $-\cup\cup-$ in the trimeter is appealed to in support of it. 'By anaclasis the two short syllables of the iambic dipody' ('Viersilbler') 'may come together in the interior of the foot.' But the instances producible are extremely few. In three of the passages of tragedy there is a proper name:

Ἱππομέδοντος σχῆμα καὶ μέγας τύπος.   (*S. c. Th.* 488.)

Παρθενοπαῖος Ἀρκάς· ὁ δὲ τοιόσδ' ἀνήρ.   (Ib. 547.)

Ἀλφεσίβοιαν, ἥν ὁ γεννήσας πατήρ.   (Soph. *Fr.* 785.)

An example in Herondas's scazons is also a proper name:

τῆς Ὑγιίης.

Apart from these there seem to be only:

φαιοχίτωνες καὶ πεπλεκτανημέναι,   (*Cho.* 1049.)

and in comedy:

εἶεν· ἀκούω,   (Ar. *Pax* 663.)

and two instances found by Wilamowitz in Simonides, one with the choriambus in the middle of the line:

ἃ δὴ βοτὰ | ζώομεν οὐ|δὲν εἰδότες

(l. 4 in the passage beginning ὦ παῖ, τέλος μὲν Ζεύς: *Sappho und Simonides*, p. 271 and p. 153).

These passages form a rather slender basis for the view that choriambic substitution was an important and characteristic feature of the metrical art of the Ionians. Milton may have had the passages of Aeschylus in view when he freely admitted a choriambic effect in English:

> Purples the East—
>
> Better to reign in Hell—

It is fairly common in English verse:

> Dángerous sécrets, for he tempts our powers. (Shelley.)
>
> Reády to spríng; waíting a chánce; for this. (Tennyson.)

Is it that in a language in which accent comes into play it matters less which of two syllables has the *ictus* or stress, so that a trochee can take the place of an iambus? Such a possibility would perhaps account for some of the perplexing varieties of the Saturnian measure in Italy, when, for example, 'Hércŏli' takes the place of 'Mĕtélli' ('donum danunt Herculi—dabunt malum Metelli').

(*b*) *The Roman disregard for 'Porson's canon'.*—No certain explanation has been given of the divergence between Greek and Roman verse in this respect. We may perhaps suppose that the facts are something like these:—The observation of the rule by the Greek tragic poets was instinctive, unconscious or half-conscious, the result of an innate sense for euphony and propriety of rhythm. It was not formulated as a rule of composition, and did not come to the Romans as a precept. Their own early verse differed widely from Greek verse in many ways, so that a subtlety like this was not thought of, and when they began to write iambic verse on more strictly Greek lines, they were still influenced by the heavy and spondaic character of their early verse, and they did not study Greek metrical practice with the minute scrutiny bestowed upon it in a later age by Elmsley and Porson. Further, there was perhaps in Latin a special reason for liking an ending in a word of three syllables; accent and *ictus* agreed, there was notable coincidence in the fifth *ictus* of the line, and also in earlier places ('vílla cándens Túsculi'). The Porsonian rule would have fettered the composer, so the conditions regarding a trisyllabic word undergo some modification; they are relaxed to facilitate such endings.

When Livius Andronicus set himself to produce Greek plays at Rome in the metres of the Greeks, he might conceivably have laid upon himself the rule that no line may begin or end with a word of two syllables. But it would not occur to him to do that. It would have been a highly artificial restriction, and in words like *probant, domos* the quantity was sufficiently conspicuous to make them workable as iambi. They had to be admitted, but lines ending in words of three or more syllables were preferred. Of the extant senarii of Ennius about 34 per cent. end in words of two syllables, of those of Accius about 38 per cent.[1] Of the first 100 lines of the *Oed. Tyr.* of Sophocles 62 end in words of two syllables; of the first 100 lines of the *Philoctetes*, 58. If we now turn to Seneca a remarkable result presents itself: of the first 100 lines of the *Hercules* 84 end in disyllables; of the first 100 lines of the *Thyestes*, 87. The dislike of a disyllabic ending has been replaced by a preference for it! But, of course, no Porsonic rule is enacted. There is, on the contrary, a preference for its violation. The Romans had always liked spondaic effects in tragedy, and the liking now takes what a Greek would call a comparatively legitimate shape. It is an all but rigid rule that the fifth foot must be a spondee, and this precluded the observation of the Porsonian canon.

(c) *The nature and history of the old spondaic senarius at Rome.* — It is in general extremely difficult to compose verse that is regulated by two different principles, such as quantity and accent, at the same time. But when Andronicus and Naevius saw their way to beginning and ending a line with a word of two syllables—when they found that the effect was not repellent to the ear—they had surmounted the chief difficulties.[2] In the middle of the line it was not very difficult to keep quantity and accent in agreement. Given the regular incidence of the Latin accent and the normal caesura of an iambic line, agreement resulted almost mechanically:

ibis Libúrnis | ínter alta navium.

The Latin accent was not a strong enough stress to enable a short syllable to take the place of a long, but when two or three longs

---

[1] I count those lines in Ribbeck's text which are fairly certain, neither formed by conjecture, nor possibly parts of trochaic tetrameters: 108 lines of Ennius, 284 of Accius.

[2] Some words of two syllables had perhaps, in certain positions, no appreciable accent at all. They were of the nature of enclitics in phrases like 'operám dabit' or 'voluptás mea'. These belong to colloquial Latin, and it may be due to their frequency in comedy that Plautus more often ends a line with a word of two syllables than the tragic poets do.

came together it differentiated them. Thus an iambic effect could be obtained without the quantitative strictness of the Greek trimeter. In shaping the verse as they did Andronicus and Naevius undoubtedly created something which suited the genius of the Latin language. Barbaric looseness and irregularity is the impression which this verse gives when we first turn to it from the verse of the Greeks. But the impression is largely a mistaken one. The verse is an artistic thing, and has its own laws (compare what is said above, p. 82, regarding 'abdúxi negotiis'—the compensation provided).[1] The proof that it suited the Latin language lies in the fact that the admission of spondees in the second and fourth places was a thing which gained ground. It did not gradually die out. This can be roughly tested by counting in the three great tragedians the number of lines which satisfy Greek rule—which have a pure iambus both in the second and in the fourth place. We may call these 'trimeters' and the other lines 'senarii'.

In Ennius the proportion is about 1 : 3 (i.e. one line in four is a 'trimeter'). I have surveyed 96 lines, practically all that can usefully be taken into account: 70 are senarii, 26 trimeters; but if we allow final *s* to make quantity by position, only 22 are trimeters. In Pacuvius the proportion is about 1 : $4\frac{1}{2}$. In Accius it is about 1 : $6\frac{1}{2}$ (273 lines surveyed: 37 trimeters, or 33 if *-s* is allowed to lengthen a syllable). Accius survived into the first century B.C., and in that century a revolt or new movement took place. Catullus writes not only 'trimeters', but also the extremely strict and artificial form of iambic verse which admits no spondees at all. What, then, is Cicero's position? Cicero had a great admiration for the old poets, and could imitate their style admirably, as we have seen. But he was not unaffected by the new movements, and he knew the Greek poets very well. His

---

[1] Terentianus says that comic poets aimed at a resemblance to real speech:

ut quae loquuntur sumpta de vita putes,

they were deliberate artists in their handling of verse:

in metra peccant arte, non inscitia,

and he adds that Roman poets went further in this direction than Greek:

magis ista nostri.

imitations of Pacuvius and Accius are akin to Horace's line (see *infra*, p. 233, footnote):

alitibus atque canibus homicidam Hectorem.

The effect is frequently obtained *without* spondees in the second or fourth places. Of 111 extant iambic lines of Cicero 35 are trimeters, i.e. the ratio in his case approaches 1 : 3. Whether Pollio wrote 'trimeters' only is perhaps doubtful, but it is highly probable that Varius and Ovid did.

It was not only in this matter of the admission of spondees that the verse of the early drama was in agreement with the genius of the Latin language and the nature of Latin accentuation and pronunciation. In its prosody, as well as in metre, it differed widely from the verse of the Augustan age. It shortened many syllables which were long by nature or position, and which were *always* long for the hellenizing metricians. For them *voluptas* and *domi* are always a bacchius and an iambus, ∪ – – and ∪ –. But the reader of Plautus and Terence will again and again find such syllables shortened—treated as short for the metre, that is, though whether the second syllable of *voluptas* was ever in fact exactly as short as the first is another question. Most of these shortenings come under a rule or principle known as the 'Law of Breves Breviantes'. There is not precise agreement about its formulation, but the essence of it is that before an accented syllable the second syllable of an iambus is shortened: as in *vŏlŭptátem inesse tantum, domĭ mánsit*.[1] These shortenings, it should be

---

[1] For a full statement of facts and details the reader should consult Professor Lindsay's account of Plautine verse in the Introduction to his larger edition of the *Captivi*. 'Brevis brevians' was a name given to the first syllable of an iambus, which was supposed to shorten the syllable that followed. Its shortness was clearly a contributory cause: 'frīgefacio' does not shorten its *e*, but 'călefacio' does; 'molĕstórum' is admissible in Plautine verse, but the second syllable of *fūnestus* cannot be shortened. The accent that was the other contributory cause was the accent on the third syllable of the group, or the accent on the first, or both. The result is found without an accent on the third syllable, as in Terence's line:

ex Graecis bónĭs Latinas fecit non bonas.

added, do not belong only to iambic verse, but are found in the verse of the drama generally, e.g. in anapaests:

nōbís dătŭr bŏ̆nă | paūsă̆ lŏquēndí.　　(Accius.)

It cannot be doubted that these phenomena in prosody answer to the actual pronunciation of Latin in the living speech of the time. They were not 'licences', or things done *metri gratia*—an explanation which is seldom really tenable, for all but the most incompetent poets could easily have written a line or a passage quite differently if they had chosen. The old poets were neither metrical blunderers nor deliberate and laborious metricians. They wrote fluent verse by the ear, verse which was to be delivered in a theatre, and have its rhythm for the audience (whether that audience knew anything of metre or not). The feeling for this old verse was perhaps beginning to be impaired when Cicero wrote that some of the senarii of the comic poets are so *abiecti* or debased that no *numerus* can be found in them. But what seems to prove conclusively that the shortenings answered to real pronunciation is the fact that the principle operates upon the form of Latin words. Only something that existed in current speech could do that. In some words of iambic form the last syllable has become ambiguous, short, but capable of resuming its length when the ictus of verse fell upon it ('mihi, tibi, sibi: ibi, ubi: vide, cave'—so that 'căvĕ' can find admission to the hexameter of Horatian satire); in others the second syllable definitely ceased to be long ('bene, male: modo' when it is an adverb). In compounds 'patĕfacio, calĕfacio' supplant 'patēfacio, calēfacio'.

(*d*) *The length of the first syllable in an impure or heavy iambus.*—The iambic dipody $--\cup-$ can hardly have consisted of two parts in the ratio of 4 : 3, making a total of seven times ($\cup\cup\ \cup\cup\ |\ \cup\ \cup\cup$). Aristoxenus speaks of a syllable that is ἄλογος, and a heavy trochee seems to have been called χορεῖος ἄλογος. The syllable was not a simple multiple of the short syllable or of the χρόνος πρῶτος, and the ratio of the two parts of the foot was μεταξὺ δυοῖν λόγοιν γνωρίμοιν (2 : 2 and 2 : 1 being γνώριμοι λόγοι). What it was has been a subject of much discussion. The various views are collected and summarized by Mr. White (*Verse of Greek Comedy*, p. 5, § 16). Voss and Lehrs did give the

syllable the time of a normal long. Westphal, taking Aristoxenus's
μεταξύ to mean 'midway between', made the syllables 1½ : 2 (ratio
3 : 4, not γνώριμος). It has also been supposed that metrically—
perhaps it would have been safer to say 'for music or singing'—
the syllable counted as short (Schmidt-Jebb: Mr. White does not
mention this view). Böckh gave the foot only the time of three
shorts, but made the ratio between the two syllables 3 : 4 (i. e.
$\frac{9}{7} + \frac{12}{7}$, instead of $\frac{7}{7} + \frac{14}{7}$). Schmidt, followed by Jebb and others,
uses a special symbol for an 'irrational' long (>). The symbol has
some advantages, but it has not been generally adopted. The
question is not one of very great importance for the ordinary
reader of iambic and trochaic verse.

II. THE IAMBIC TETRAMETER CATALECTIC OR 'SEPTENARIUS'

The iambic tetrameter shortened by a syllable was a favourite
verse of comedy:

$$\underline{\smile} - \smile - | \underline{\smile} - \smile - \| \underline{\smile} - \smile - | \smile - | \underline{\smile} ;$$

it was written by Hipponax and Simonides, and so far as we
know it had no place in tragedy. It was vivacious or frivolous,
abusive or argumentative. Terentianus Maurus says of it:

sonum ministrat congruentem motibus iocosis.

The lyric use of it, with the 'scoptic' tone and the manner
of a music-hall song, is well illustrated by Arist. *Plutus*,
290–321 :

καὶ μὴν ἐγὼ βουλήσομαι θρεττανελὸ τὸν Κύκλωπα κτλ.

(a system of five parts: strophe, antistrophe, strophe[b], anti-
strophe[b], epode). Terentianus's line departs from the normal
structure of the verse, the line just quoted from Aristophanes
illustrates it ; there is usually *diaeresis* after the eighth syllable,
at the end of the fourth iambus. The line or στίχος is made
up of two κῶλα, which are dimeters, each of these consisting
of two dipodies.

The closing cadence has been described by some metricians as:

$$\ldots - \cup - \cup \mathrel{\llap{\raise1pt\hbox{$\smile$}}{-}} - \wedge$$

and this modern or trochaic method of scansion perhaps represents the effect of the verse. At all events it brings it into line with the ending of a trochaic tetrameter scazon. Taken as strictly iambic it would end with $\cup - \mid \mathrel{-\!\!\!\cdot}$. Neither of these effects would be given exactly when the verse was not sung but read, and for reading it is not very important to decide between them. The penultimate syllable is never resolved by the Greek poets. Plautus not unfrequently allows it to be represented by two shorts, from which it may be inferred that he did not think of the syllable as τρίχρονος. Roman poets sometimes misunderstood, or at all events treated in a new way, the metres which they adopted. The practice of the Greeks in this instance, though it does not amount to proof, at least affords a presumption that the syllable was felt as a notably long one.

The structure of the verse is affected by its place and purpose. It may be 'melic' outright, a lyric that is sung to music. In other parts it was given in recitative (still with some musical accompaniment). Or it might be merely spoken (ψιλὴ λέξις). Mr. White (*Verse of Greek Comedy*, § 59) distinguishes four grades or types: (1) melic; (2) recitative; (3) melodramatic; (4) spoken. By 'melodramatic' he means the method attributed to Archilochus, παρακαταλογή, in which ordinary speech was supported by some musical notes. But it is not quite clear that in παρακαταλογή the delivery was quite ordinary speech; and, if it was not, παρακαταλογή must be identified with (2) and there is only one grade below it, not two. This doubt, however, does not affect Mr. White's statistics, for he deals with only three grades of iambic 'septenarius', calling the third 'melodramatic'. Whether the ordinary speaking voice in these verses was or was not supported by notes of a musical instrument is not a very important question.

In trochaic verse an 'anapaest' is admitted with some freedom, for it is only a heavy trochee with the first syllable resolved ($\smile \smile -$); a dactyl is very rare. Conversely, in iambic verse a 'dactyl' finds free admission, being a heavy iambus with its second syllable resolved ($- \smile \smile$), but the parallel does not hold further: in comic iambic verse an anapaest is *not* rare, but extremely frequent. These general considerations must be kept in view in considering Mr. White's statistics, which show some curious facts. His 'melodramatic' (spoken) tetrameters closely resemble the trimeter of comedy; there are many dactyls, many anapaests, and of course very many tribrachs (*Verse of Greek Comedy*, p. 64, §§ 175-7). Diaeresis is neglected (i.e. the fourth foot does not end with the end of a word) more frequently than in the 'recitative' tetrameter (once in 4·8 lines as compared with 1 in 7·8). The 'recitative' tetrameter is characterized by extreme severity as regards tribrach and dactyl, and it rejects the anapaest entirely (there is only one doubtful example in 155 lines). In these respects it is far more strict than the 'melic' tetrameter, which, however, is considerably stricter than the 'melodramatic' as regards anapaest and dactyl. The 'melic' tetrameter is otherwise very like the 'melodramatic'. All three have irrational feet very frequently (i.e. the first syllable of a dipody is long): the percentage of irrational dipodies is 70 in the recitative tetrameter, and very nearly as large in the other two (melic 69, 'melodramatic' 67). This is a larger percentage than that of the trochaic tetrameter (65). The trochaic tetrameter rejects the dactyl as persistently as the iambic tetrameter rejects the anapaest. Mr. White's figures for the dactyl in trochaic tetrameters are 6 in 776, but if we disallow two of these (p. 105) the proportion is about 1 in 200.

In the early Roman drama the iambic 'septenarius' was of

course written with un-Greek variations which are found in other metres. Apart from these Plautus's treatment of it is marked by great regularity in the observance of diaeresis. There is almost always the end of a word at the end of the fourth foot. The two parts of the verse are separated more than they are in Greek. It is in keeping with this that *syllaba anceps* and *hiatus* are readily admitted at this point:

hinc med amantem ex aedibŭs | eiecit huiu' mater.
argenti viginti minae | ad mortem me adpulerunt.

If the first part of the line is to be thought of as a separate verse, its last foot should be a pure iambus. This also is the rule in Roman comedy. The exceptions are so few as to raise a suspicion about the soundness of the text where they occur.

The metre has practically no further history in 'classical' times, for no comedy of the imperial age is extant. But it had great vogue in Byzantine times, invaded by accent, and becoming in the end almost wholly accentual:

*Κλαυδίου δὲ φαρμαχθέντος Νέρων ὁ μητροκτόνος
παρεισεφθάρη κάκιστα τοῖς τῶν Ῥωμαίων σκήπτροις.*

(In φαρμάχθέντὸς and in Νέρὼν accent and ictus diverge, but otherwise there is coincidence; κάκιστα has a slight secondary accent on the last syllable, which carries the iambic *ictus*). In later European literature a verse that closely resembles it has wide currency, a line of *six* iambi *plus* a syllable. It is a verse that has hardly any place in ancient poetry. Christ quotes for it only Aes. *Choeph.* 323:

τέκνον, φρόνημα τοῦ θανόντος οὐ δαμάζει.

The words, he adds, are written in the *Codex Laurentianus* as two lyric κῶλα:

τέκνον φρόνημα τοῦ
θανόντος οὐ δαμάζει.

No doubt they are rightly written so. The effect is almost the same as would be given by:

τέκνον, φρόνημα κατ-
θανόντος οὐ δαμάζει.

The words τοῦ θανόντος go closely together, and there is no diaeresis such as is characteristic of iambic tetrameters. There is such a diaeresis, after the third foot, in the 'hypercatalectic hexapody', known as one of the two forms of the Alexandrine of classical French poetry.[1] Christ gives as French and German examples:

Jĕ nē mĕ suīs cŏnnū | qu'aŭ boūt dĕ mā cărriērĕ̄.[2]

(Voltaire.)

Alt wár ich únd der Nácht klagt' ích's durch Tráuerliéder.

(Rückert.)

This line is the modern counterpart of the ancient 'septenarius'. It is shorter by two syllables, but its effect, for the ear of the ordinary reader, is not very different. The ancient line is not felt to be a longer one. The cause of this equality in effect is probably that in a modern language, and especially in English, words are on the average shorter and more numerous. Similarly Milton's decasyllabic line has very much the same effect for the ear as the ancient dodecasyllabic trimeter. There is a very slight pause after a word, and the cumulative effect of these more frequent interstices makes the time of the one line not greatly different from the time of the other. Further, shorter words mean that more thought, more turns or articulations of thought, will be contained in the same number of syllables; the length of the line for the apprehending mind will thus be greater, and it is this mental *tempo* that is important. It is

[1] It is only in quite recent times—in the nineteenth century—that French poets have written the Alexandrine line without diaeresis.

[2] The quantitative symbols ⌣ —, here used by Christ, may be conveniently used for modern verse with the reservation that it is not necessarily quantity in the ancient sense, or always quantity at all, that is meant.

quite possible that if we could hear a trimeter delivered exactly as it was delivered on the stage in the time of Sophocles, the physical or actual time in seconds that it occupied would exceed the time occupied by an English blank verse as it is commonly read.

CHAPTER VI

THE SCAZON OR CHOLIAMBUS

(Τρίμετρος σκάζων, χωλίαμβος, senarius claudus.)

The 'celeritas' of Archilochus's verse was the dexterity and rapidity of movement that belongs to a skilled fencer or swordsman. The measure was a weapon of offence. Hipponax at a later date gave it a slower and more prosaic movement by making the penultimate syllable a long one. As a weapon this was rather a club or cudgel than a rapier. As a line moving on 'feet' it was said to halt or limp, to drag its last foot. Ovid combines the two metaphors in his couplet:

> liber in adversos hostes stringatur iambus,
>   seu celer, extremum seu trahit ille pedem.

The 'scazon' ended in a cadence which was a favoured and familiar one in prose:

> Suffenus iste, Vare, quēm prŏbē nōstī
> homo est venustus et dicāx ĕt ūrbānŭs.

The ending may be described as cretic + trochee (or spondee, the last syllable being *anceps*), and it is of course found also in cretic verse when that is catalectic. A cretic verse catalectic, with the antepenultimate long resolved, coincides with the famous or notorious prose-ending *esse videatur*:

$$- \cup \ \cup \cup | - \cup$$
ἔχετε λειμῶνα τ' ἐρόεντα Μαραθῶνος.

But this resolution never occurs in scazons. There, we may infer, the syllable was too long to be resolvable into two shorts. It was longer than an ordinary long, though perhaps in ordinary reading it was not strictly τρίσημος or exactly equal to three short syllables. One iambus may follow another without perceptible pause, but it is not easy to pass in a moment from a rising to a falling rhythm, $\cup \perp | \perp \cup$. There must be a slight pause $\cup - \wedge - \cup$, or if there is no end of a word, a protraction of a syllable. The 'scazon' is a form of verse for which the trochaic method of scansion provides a natural and intelligible interpretation: 'quem probe nosti' $= - \cup | \perp | \perp \perp$. That any ancient metrician would so describe it is doubtful. But something like this must have been the effect in ordinary recitation. The iambic scazon nearly always has a very marked penthemimeral or hephthemimeral caesura, and the part of a line that follows such a caesura of course begins with a conspicuously trochaic effect.

In analysing the verse in this way we have assumed that the last ictus was on the penultimate syllable, not on the last. But there is a tradition to the contrary, which some modern writers have accepted (Plotius Sacerd., p. 519 K.: 'Hipponacteum trimetrum clodum percutitur sicut iambicum trimetrum archilochium comicum vel tragicum, sed paenultimam longam habet'). The history of the verse is against this. It had considerable vogue at Rome. Introduced by Laevius, Matius, and Varro, it was written frequently by Catullus and later by Martial. The line hardly ever ends in a word of one syllable (except it be the enclitic *sum, est,* &c.); and, monosyllables excluded, the Latin accent inevitably falls on the penultimate syllable ('nósti, urbánus'). The incidence of the verse-ictus on the last syllable would certainly not be attractive to the Roman ear. Would they tolerate the effect 'ností, urbanús' at the end of every line? It is more likely that accent and ictus coincided. Further, it has been thought, and it is probable, that the Latin scazon suggested to Babrius what is the earliest appearance of accent in Greek versification. In Babrius the penultimate syllable has an accent, usually the acute accent, as in:

ἀνὴρ Ἀθηναῖός τις ἀνδρὶ Θηβαίῳ
κοινῶς ὁδεύων, ὥσπερ εἰκός, ὡμίλει.

(Usually too, as here, the vowel is naturally long.) It is reasonable to suppose that in both languages accent aided and reinforced ictus.

It is obvious, theoretically, that if the last foot of an iambic line is to be a spondee, the effect of the ending will be obscured if the preceding foot is also a spondee. We should expect that the scazon, unlike the ordinary trimeter, would have a pure iambus regularly in the fifth place; and this rule is in fact laid down by Roman metricians, Caesius Bassus and Terentianus Maurus. The fifth foot must be a pure iambus; otherwise four long syllables coming together will give the line an obscure and uneuphonious close:

ne deprehensae quattuor simul longae
parum sonoro fine destruant versum.

But the inventor of the verse, Hipponax, lays down no such rule for himself; he admits a spondee in the fifth place:

πάλαι γὰρ αὐτοὺς προσδέχονταῑ χἄσκοντες.

So, too, Herondas in a later age (*Mimiambi* i. 21):

ἀλλ', ὦ τέκνον, κόσον τιν' ἤδη χηραίνεις
χρόνον;

Both writers, however, have the spondee so infrequently as to show that the effect repelled them, and the recently recovered portions of the Ἴαμβοι of Callimachus present no example of it. Had the rule been formulated at Alexandria? Varro, in his *Saturae*, does not observe it (his *Saturae* were a work of his earlier life); his younger contemporary Catullus does, as do all Roman writers of scazons after him.

It is only in the fifth and sixth feet that the scazon differs from the Archilochian trimeter. The first four feet are written in the same way (the second and fourth always pure iambi). The fifth and sixth seem to exchange places. Was it in this way that Hipponax arrived at the verse, by transposing these two feet? The most recent theory of its origin is not unlike that supposition. It is suggested that just as the diiambus could become a choriambus ($-\cup\cup-$), in which the two iambi as it were face each other, so it could also become an antispast ($\cup--\cup$), in which they are set back to back: the scazon was arrived at by making the third of the three dipodies take this shape. But, it may well be argued, variations like the choriambus or antispast must be exact and strict in form, if they are to be recognized—the choriambus always is. Would not Hipponax have made the fifth foot invariably a pure iambus if he had thought of the verse in this way? His practice rather suggests that he made a deliberate change in *one* foot of the Archilochian line, but unconsciously or half-consciously shrank from the group of five long syllables which resulted from making the fifth foot a spondee.

Like almost all forms of verse invented by the Greeks the scazon illustrates adaptation of form to theme or substance. It was used for homely and personal topics, things belonging to everyday life. It is the verse of lampoons, and of epigrams (not necessarily abusive) in Martial. It is used for $Mιμίαμβοι$, in which the mime takes a literary shape—the dialect that of Hipponax, Ionic. And it is used for the popular, familiar, moralizing fable by Callimachus and Babrius. Phaedrus does not use it; but he gets a somewhat similar literary effect by using the old, largely spondaic, senarius, in an age when, as we have seen, tragedy at least, though perhaps not comedy, had adopted the strict canons of the Greek trimeter. Though used for a form of mime, it does not seem to have found any place in regular comedy. It has no place in the Roman drama, and in Greek only two scazons of Eupolis are known, these being a parody or echo of the old iambic poet Ananius (ναὶ μὰ τὰς κράμβας—Ananius had written ναὶ μὰ τὴν κράμβην). The influence of the ἰαμβοποιοί on the old comedy of Athens is undoubted. Cratinus wrote a play entitled Ἀρχίλοχοι, and Hermippus was both an ἰαμβοποιός and a κωμῳδοποιός. Aristotle calls the old type of comedy the ἰαμβικὴ ἰδέα (abusive, personal, critical). But there is no fusion or confusion of style and versification. The trimeter of Aristophanes is *not* the trimeter of Archilochus, but widely different from it, and the verse of Hipponax hardly found admission at all, as far as our evidence goes.

CHAPTER VII

THE TROCHAIC TETRAMETER AND 'SEPTENARIUS'

I. In Normal Form

THE trochaic tetrameter is simple in structure, and presents no difficult or dubious problems. It is in fact the form of verse to which the learner should be first introduced, knowing its English analogue as he does in Tennyson's *Locksley Hall*:

Many a night I saw the Pleiads | rising through the mellow shade.

Every moment lightly shaken | ran itself in golden sands.[1]

It readily appeals to the ordinary ear, and it was a highly popular verse in antiquity, whether in the old festivals of Dionysus or at a triumph in the streets of Rome:

Gallos Caesar in triumphum duxit, idem in curiam.[2]

We have seen that in dactylic verse the close of a group of six feet was marked by making the last disyllabic or spondaic. Similarly, a group of trochees had its close marked by a variation in the foot. The last syllable might be a long one,[3] the

---

[1] These two lines begin with a tribrach, ĕvĕrў, mănў ă.

[2] Some of the verses scribbled on the walls of Pompeii are septenarii:
Bupa (= puella) quae bella es, tibí me misit qui tuus est : vale.
(Conceivably a line from a popular mime.)

[3] (For the quantity of this syllable see p. 106, note.)

foot a spondee or heavier trochee. The shortest possible group is a group of two; and this is the element out of which the trochaic 'tetrameter' is constructed: $-\cup-\overset{\smile}{-}$ is repeated four times, and the last dipody is catalectic. Further, the dipodies are arranged in pairs:

$$-\cup-\overset{\smile}{-} \mid -\cup-\overset{\smile}{-} \parallel -\cup-\overset{\smile}{-} \mid -\cup-\wedge.$$

The learner should first, of course, become familiar with the verse as it is written in Greek tragedy, with very few and very slight variations, before he passes on to comedy, and to the still more varied forms which the verse takes in Roman drama:

καὶ πόρον μετερρύθμιζε καὶ πέδαις σφυρηλάτοις
περιβαλὼν πολλὴν κέλευθον ἤνυσεν πολλῷ στρατῷ.

A tribrach is a very slight variation, and it is very readily admitted. Next to it comes the form of foot arrived at by resolving the first syllable of a heavy trochee, $\overset{\smile}{\cup}\cup-$ (corresponding to an anapaest in syllables, but differing from it in *ictus*). This is readily admitted in the second, fourth, and sixth places. Beyond these two types of resolution there is very little variation, even in comedy. A line of comedy may of course be very different in effect from a 'tragic line, but it is only through the frequency of one or both of these two perfectly legitimate resolutions, as e.g. in Epicharmus's line about shell-fish:

ἃ διελεῖν μέν ἐστι χαλεπὰ καταφαγεῖν δ' εὐμαρέα

(first, fourth, fifth, and seventh feet resolved).

It is misleading to say, as Bickel does,[1] that 'the technique of the verse is in every respect the same as that of the senarius'; and to suggest or imply in particular, as the same writer proceeds to do, that the two forms of verse are similar in their admission of $\cup\cup$ for $\cup$ in the 'Senkung'. The admis-

---

[1] *Einleitung in die Alterthumswissenschaft*, ed. Gercke and Norden, vol. i, p. 260. What he says is true of Seneca.

sion of this in iambics means the admission of an anapaest. What answers to that in trochaic verse is the admission of a dactyl. The anapaest in comic iambics is extremely frequent: a dactyl in trochaic tetrameters is extremely rare.

In tragic tetrameters it occurs only in the case of a proper name. One or two instances in the tragic text, apart from this, have long ago been removed—quite convincingly—by conjectural emendation. In comedy it is so infrequent that attempts have been made to explain it away. Christ proposed to do this by suppressing a short syllable in *Ach.* 318:

ὑπὲρ ἐπιξήνου θελήσω τὴν κεφ'λὴν ἔχων λέγειν,

and by synizesis in *Eccl.* 1156:

τοῖς γελῶσι δ' ἡδέως διὰ τὸν γέλων κρίνειν ἐμέ.

But this solution has not recently found favour, and it certainly seems untenable. There are more instances than Christ supposed. There are two more in Aristophanes, νὴ Δία κἀμὲ ταῦτ' ἔδρασε, *Eq.* 319, and ταῖς ἀφύαις ἥδυσμά τι, *Vesp.* 496. There are several in Epicharmus, and one at least in Menander (Περικειρομένη, l. 150). The safer conclusion seems to be that a dactyl is admissible, but is very rare.[1]

This is precisely in harmony with the history of the verse. According to Aristotle (*Poet.*, c. iv) it was the predecessor of

---

[1] Examples were collected by v. Wilamowitz-Moellendorff in his *Isyllos* (pp. 7, 8). He finds four in Epicharmus, to which should be added Ὀδυσσεὺς αὐτόμολος fr. 2 δαιμονίως ἀπώλεσα, and perhaps B 40 (ed. Lorenz), if Cobet's ἀπ' οὕτινος is right. Of his Aristophanic examples *Av.* 396 and *Thesm.* 436 are open to question; the verse is not strictly the trochaic tetrameter, but trochaic lyrics resembling it. Mr. White (*Verse of Greek Comedy*, p. 100) gives six instances of dactyls in Aristophanes, but two of them are doubtful. In *Av.* 373, the reading χρήσιμον ἤ is not admitted by the editors of the Oxford Text, who excise the ἤ; χρήσιμον ἤ gives a very harsh and conspicuous dactyl. In *Av.* 1113, πρηγορεῶνας ὑμῖν πέμψομεν, synizesis has to be reckoned with, so that πρηγορεῶνας is – ∪ – ∪. Synizesis is much more probable with ε than with ι, and it accounts for some apparent dactyls in Archilochus.

the iambic trimeter in tragedy. Strict and regular in Aeschylus, it attains to some degree of freedom in Euripides, who uses it for a lively altercation in the *Phoenissae* (592 f.). Attic comedy, so far as we know it, did not use it with great freedom or frequency for a casual conversation. Epicharmus, before Aristophanes, had given it greater looseness and flexibility, and this conversational use of it is found, after him, in Menander, from whom it passed to the Roman drama. But in the text of the Roman comic drama, trochaic tetrameters are usually designated 'C' (= *canticum*). It is not quite ordinary speech, as senarii are. In Aristophanes there are passages where it is certainly *canticum* and not *sermo*; e.g. *Ach.* 204–40, where it is combined in antistrophic form with cretics. Where it is not 'melic' outright, it was probably delivered in some sort of *recitative*. Its most conspicuous use in Attic comedy is for the continuous utterance of the poet (through the chorus) in the parabasis.[1]

In the early Roman drama the trochaic tetrameter, like the iambic trimeter and other metres, took shapes which were

---

[1] Statistics are given by Mr. White (*Verse of Greek Comedy*, p. 99 f.) for (*a*) 'melic' tetrameters (of which he recognizes only 116) and 'recitative' tetrameters, either (*b*) in the parabasis (epirrhemata and antepirrhemata), or (*c*) in other places. The differences prove to be inconsiderable. 'The melic tetrameter is somewhat severer than the recitative in excluding the dactyl and in some minor particulars.' The dactyl is so rare that its non-occurrence in 116 lines is of no significance. The anapaest occurs once in 21 lines—in (*b*) it is 1 in 16, in (*c*) 1 in 20. The occurrence of an anapaest once in 21 or 20 lines as compared with once in 16 can hardly have been deliberate on the part of the poet, or readily perceptible to the hearer. The poet unconsciously wrote with slightly greater strictness in lyrics and in the parabasis. Conversation would sometimes make a non-trochaic word almost unavoidable (e. g. πότερον, ἐτεόν). In regard to the admission of a long syllable in the place where it is allowed ($- \cup - \underline{\cup}$), the difference is, again, not very great. In (*b*) and (*c*) together 'sixty-five per cent. of the complete metres' (= dipodies) 'are irrational'. In melic tetrameters the percentage is 56.

unknown to the Greeks. It became a 'septenarius'—seven complete feet *plus* a syllable—instead of being scanned by dipodies (κατὰ διποδίαν). Its Plautine form is described by Professor Lindsay in his Metrical Introduction to the *Captivi* (large edition), pp. 72–5.

The early tragic poets gave it a somewhat graver and more stately movement than it has in comedy, but there is no very marked difference—in this metre there was no very great difference in Greece either between the two forms of the drama.

> ádest, adést fax óbvolúta sánguine átque incéndió;[1]
> múltos ánnos látuit. cíves, férte opem ét restínguité.
>
> (Ennius, *Alexander*.)

With a spondee or its equivalent admissible in every place the line labours and moves slowly:

> Fórtunam ínsanam ésse et caécam et brútam pérhibent phílo-
>   sophí. (Pacuvius.)

In this and other lines there is no pure trochee except at the end (here there is a tribrach, 'phĭlŏsŏphi'). This heaviness must have suited the Latin language and the taste of the Romans; for, as in the case of the senarius, it continues to increase, and the end is a revolt, not a gradual diminution. Accius's septenarii are heavier than those of Ennius.[2]

---

[1] The line probably begins ádĕst adést fax (⏑⏑⏑ – –), though it is not quite impossible that Ennius meant it for an iambic octonarius (ădĕst ădĕst). There are passages in which octonarii and septenarii are mingled.

[2] For the senarius see pp. 79, 88. Out of 128 trochaic lines of Ennius only 16 are 'Greek' or 'tetrameters', i.e. have no spondee (or its equivalent) in an uneven place; out of 124 lines of Accius only 7. Of Ennius's lines 52 are Roman throughout (i.e. have spondees in the uneven places in both halves), of Accius's 70. Of Ennius's lines 20 are strict or Hellenic in the first half, 40 in the second half (a curiously exact result—for the first half presents two opportunities for a misplaced spondee, the second only one). Of Accius's lines 13 are strict in the first

THE TROCHAIC TETRAMETER

It remains to consider the shape it takes in Seneca and some later writers.

Seneca has three passages in trochaic tetrameters (*Med.* 740 f., *Oed.* 223 f., and *Phaedra* 1201 f.). His verses are of course of the Greek type, tetrameters and not septenarii. If Varius or Ovid wrote the verse in tragedy, they also probably wrote it with Greek strictness. Seneca, however, deviates from the Greek norm in one way: he admits a dactyl in the sixth foot (*Med.* 746):

gravior uni poena sedeat coniugīs sŏcĕro mei.[1]

Besides this he *once* in the thirty-four lines has a dactyl in another place (*Med.* 743):

supplicīs (= suppliciis) ănĭmae remissis currite ad thalamos novos.

His treatment of this verse, the reader will have observed, is very similar to his treatment of the iambic trimeter. There he has very seldom an anapaest in a place other than the fifth ('inter senem iuvenemque sed propior seni'; see p. 84). And his dactyl in the sixth foot makes the end of the line exactly like the end of a trimeter.[2] Seneca must have known, and

half, 34 in the second. (In counting these cases I have assumed that final *s* followed by one consonant does *not* make the syllable long. If this is disallowed, the numbers for the more or less strict types would be reduced by 2, 3, or 4—not more than 4 or less than 2—a difference which does not affect the general result.)

[1] As this line has been misunderstood by editors, I may be allowed to call attention in passing to its real meaning. The *socer* is not Creon, but simply Sisyphus: the next line is:

lubricus per saxa retro Sisyphum volvat lapis.

Sisyphus was not strictly the *socer* of Jason, but he was thought of by Seneca as Creusa's grandfather or great-grandfather, and so he was the giver of the bride.

[2] There is the further similarity that Seneca's lines never end in ∪ – ∪ – (*supra*, p. 83). The sixth foot is either a spondee or (less frequently) a dactyl, so that the last three syllables are always preceded by – or ∪∪. And, again, Seneca here also disregards the Porsonian canon (*Phaedra* 1206 'rapite in altōs gūrgĭtēs').

perhaps accepted, the view that a trochaic tetrameter is made up of cretic and iambic trimeter:

$$-\ \smile\ -\ \|\ -\ -\ |\ \smile\ -\ |\ -\quad -\ |\ \smile\ -\ |\ -\ -\quad \smile\ -$$
comprecor ‖ vulgus silentum vosque ferales deos.

In the verse on Caesar quoted above it will be observed that there is much coincidence of accent and ictus:

Gállos Cáesar ín triúmphum dúxit, ídem in cúriam.

The Latin language lent itself to such coincidence in trochaic verse.[1] Conversely, when trochaic verse is written accentually we find a considerable number of lines which can be scanned by quantity:

iúdex érgo cúm sedébit.
cúm vix iústus sít secúrus.

In trochaic tetrameters after Seneca's time the coincidence seems to become more marked. Seneca himself has a few lines in which there is hardly any divergence:

Tántalus secúrus úndas háuriat Pirénidas.
méque ovántem scélere tánto rápite in áltos gúrgites.

In Tiberianus coincidence has become the rule:

ámnis íbat ínter árva válle fúsus frígida,
luce ridens calculorum, flore pictus herbido.

The versification of the *Pervigilium Veneris*—perhaps also by Tiberianus—is not materially different from this.

ruris hic erunt puellae vel puellae fontium
quaeque silvas quaeque lucos quaeque montes incolunt.

In his admission of the dactyl the author of the *Pervigilium* closely resembles Seneca. There is the occasional dactyl in an earlier place:

en micānt lăcrĭmae trementes ... ,

---

[1] So its movement was very obvious: 'aptum est olivam terentibus' (Serv. on *Georg.* ii. 519).

and the penultimate dactyl:

caerulas inter catervas inter ēt bĭpĕdes equos.[1]

Unlike Seneca he is ready to make the sixth foot a pure trochee; the second part of the line sometimes has no spondee ('iūssĭt īrĕ mȳrtĕō').

The first half of the verse usually ends with the end of a word; the composition of the line is marked by *diaeresis*. There is no exception to this rule in Archilochus or Solon, and exceptions in tragedy are extremely few. (Aes. *Pers.* 165):

ταῦτά μοι διπλῆ μέριμν' ἄφραστός ἐστιν ἐν φρεσί

(the conjectural reading μέριμνα φραστός is not attractive) may be compared with Horace's 'arcanique fides prodiga perlucidior vitro' (*infra*, p. 257), or with 'quid enim in-mortalibus atque beatis'. But there is a real deviation from the norm in Soph. *Phil.* 1402:

εἰ δοκεῖ, στείχωμεν. ὦ γεν|ναῖον εἰρηκὼς ἔπος.

In Seneca and in the *Pervigilium* the rule is strictly observed. In comedy it is broken with some frequency—not very frequently, for the lines in which it happens are a small minority. Three occur together in the *Clouds* 607 f., but this is very unusual:

ἡνίχ' ἡμεῖς δεῦρ' ἀφορμᾶσ|θαι παρεσκευάσμεθα,
ἡ σελήνη συντυχοῦσ' ἡ|μῖν ἐπέστειλεν φράσαι,
πρῶτα μὲν χαίρειν Ἀθηναί|οισι καὶ τοῖς συμμάχοις.

Plautus also carries a word over the *iunctura*, but unlike the Greek poets he also has hiatus sometimes at this point, thus disrupting the verse into two separate portions.

---

[1] Mr. Garrod in the *Oxford Book of Latin Verse* has transformed this line into

caerulas inter cavernas inter et virides specus;

'bipedes equos' is Virgilian (*Georg.* iv. 389), and is unquestionably sound, nor is 'catervas' open to any real objection.

The Porsonian canon or *Lex Porsoni* has been incidentally mentioned above as valid for trochaic tetrameters. As in the case of the iambic trimeter it is valid only for Greek tragedy. Comedy and Roman tragedy ignore it. *Clouds* 625:

τὸν στέφανον ἀφῃρέθη· μᾶλλον γὰρ οὕτως εἴσεται.

(For Seneca see p. 108, footnote.) Resolution is regulated by the same principle as in iambi. The two short syllables which stand for a long should be in the same word (e.g. τὸν στέ|φᾰνο̆ν ἀ̆|φῃρέθη). But this is not a hard and fast rule for comedy (Menander, *Samia* 221 τὸ̆ γε̆γο̆νὸς φράσαι σαφῶς).

Trochaeus is a foot that 'runs', and the trochaic tetrameter was described by the ancients as τροχερός or ἀγενής, its movement was ὀρχηστικωτέρα or κορδακικωτέρα. A falling rhythm has not the vigour and energy of a 'climbing' one. Tetrameters were specially used for the πάροδος in comedy, when the chorus enters hurriedly or in excitement: Schol. on *Ach.* 204 (quoted above, p. 62, footnote) γέγραπται δὲ τὸ μέτρον τροχαικὸν πρόσφορον τῇ τῶν διωκόντων γερόντων σπουδῇ. ταῦτα δὲ ποιεῖν εἰώθασιν οἱ τῶν δραμάτων ποιηταὶ κωμικοὶ καὶ τραγικοί, ἐπειδὰν δρομαίως εἰσάγωσι τοὺς χορούς, ἵν᾽ ὁ λόγος συντρέχῃ τῷ δράματι (leg. δραμήματι?).[1] The metre is first used by Archilochus, in very much the same way as iambic verse, for lampoon or invective, personal or 'scoptic' effusions. For this purpose we should expect that celerity would be imparted to it by keeping the foot pure or normal, $-\cup$ rather than $--$. (Compare the 'scoptic' trimeter discussed above, p. 69). This is very clearly the case *in the second half of the line*, if we compare Archilochus with the dramatic poets. There are about sixty tetrameters

---

[1] There is no extant example of tetrameters in the parodos of a tragedy, but *O. Tyr.* 1515 is a survival of its use for the ἔξοδος. The Aristotelian definition of a στάσιμον in tragedy as τὸ ἄνευ ἀναπαίστου καὶ τροχαίου (*Poet.*, c. xii) implies its use in parodos and exodos.

of Archilochus extant (a few more were added by the discovery of the monument to Archilochus in Paros, but these may be left out of account). In the second part of the line there are twelve spondees (and one anapaest). In fifty-six lines of Aeschylus (*Persae* 703-58) there are nineteen spondees, or one in every three lines as compared with one in every five in Archilochus. In Euripides there are rather more spondees: in the *Phoenissae* 588-637 (the altercation of Eteocles and Polynices, fifty lines) there are nineteen (and two anapaests), or one in every two and a half lines. In Aristophanes the occurrence of spondees is much more frequent, as Mr. White's statistics show, one and three-quarters to a line, or two to a line if anapaests are included. Aeschylus, it would seem, retained something of the Archilochian rapidity and precision in the second part of the line, though making it distinctly more spondaic than Archilochus; while in Euripides it is more heavily weighted with spondees, and in Aristophanes— a result which one would hardly have predicted—more heavily still. In the first part of the line there is no difference between the four poets that would be perceptible to a reader. Here, of course, there are two places where a spondee may occur, not only one, and the numbers are greater, and in fact *more* than twice as great; roughly there are five spondees to every four lines or one and a quarter to a line.

In Menander's tetrameters (*Samia* and Περικειρομένη) the Aristophanic proportion of spondees is maintained. Thus the preference of the Roman drama for spondees (which becomes a rigid rule for the fifth foot in Seneca) only carried further a tendency which had shown itself in the drama of Athens.

II. THE TETRAMETER SCAZON

Like the iambic trimeter the tetrameter was converted by the pugnacious Hipponax into a heavy-headed club or cudgel by making the penultimate syllable long.

AND 'SEPTENARIUS'

λάβετέ μου θαἰμάτια, κόψω Βουπάλου τὸν ὀφθαλμόν·
ἀμφιδέξιος γάρ εἰμι κοὐχ ἁμαρτάνω κόπτων.

The second part of the line was no doubt $-\cup \mid -\underline{\cup} \mid \underline{} \mid -\underline{\cup}$.
The history of this verse precisely resembles that of the choliambus. Hipponax and Ananius do *not* make the sixth foot invariably a pure trochee (as Martial would have done if he had written tetrameters):

$$- - \mid \underline{} \mid - -$$
ἀλλὰ πᾶσιν ἰχθύεσσιν ἐμπρεπὴς ἐν μυττωτῷ.

The verse was written by Varro at Rome in his *Saturae*. He has a line of the strictest type:

hunc Ceres cibi ministra frugibus suis porcet,

but other lines show that he did not bind himself by the restrictions seen in this one:

hunc vocasse ex liquida vita in curiāē vōstrae faecem!
sic canis fit e catello, sic e tritico spica.

'Liquida' ($\cup \cup -$) in the third place in the first of these lines, and 'sic e' ($- -$) in the fifth place in the second line,[1] show that Varro is not even following Hipponax; he is making a Latin septenarius limp, heavy though its gait already is through the admission of spondees and anapaests in the first, third, and fifth, as well as in the other places.

---

[1] Like *misit* in the Pompeian line quoted above (p. 103, footnote).

CHAPTER VIII

HENDECASYLLABICS OR PHALAECEI

THE lyric art of Pindar or Bacchylides with its varied cadence was forgotten or neglected in the Alexandrian age, and the tendency of poets was to take some one simple form of line and repeat it unchanged throughout the whole piece. To use a metre in this way was to use it κατὰ στίχον ('iugiter uti' is Terentianus's phrase). This Alexandrian tendency is dominant in Catullus, but not in Horace. The poet who so used a verse for the first time, or who used it conspicuously in this manner, sometimes gave his name to it. Thus a form of verse which had been written by Alcaeus—and written by *him* κατὰ στίχον—came to bear the name Asclepiadean. So, too, the verse with which we are now concerned, though it had been written by Sappho and called Σαπφικόν, came to bear the name of an obscure and presumably Alexandrian poet, Phalaecus. The Romans, however, commonly designated it by the number of syllables it contained, 'hendecasyllabi' (sc. 'versus'). There were other forms of line that contained eleven syllables, but this was the only one to be frequently employed κατὰ στίχον. Mainly lyric in origin, and used occasionally in the lyric parts of tragedy (e. g. Eur. *Orestes* 833), it became with the Romans only semi-lyric in character. It lent itself in Latin to light and casual composition on familiar topics. Like most metres when they passed to Latin, it underwent, after Catullus's time, very strict regulation, and the old freedom of the first two syllables was entirely discarded.

It is this 'stichic' and highly regulated use of it at Rome that brings it into the company of familiar and standard metres like the senarius and hexameter. Its earlier history associates it with lyrics, and problems about its structure arise which can hardly be discussed apart from various forms of lyric verse. The scheme of it in Greek is:

$$\left.\begin{array}{c} \smile\smile \\ -\smile \\ \smile- \\ -- \end{array}\right| -\smile\smile\ -\smile\ -\smile\ -\underset{\smile}{-}$$

i.e. it begins with the 'Aeolic basis', two syllables which are not yet stereotyped in one unvarying shape. Perhaps the most famous Greek example of it is to be found in the first two lines of the stanza in the scolion on the liberators of Athens, or supposed liberators, from the tyranny of Pisistratus:

φίλταθ' Ἁρμόδι', οὔ τί που τέθνηκας,
νήσοις δ' ἐν μακάρων σέ φασιν εἶναι,

(where the first line begins with $-\smile$ and the second with $--$). It is obviously akin to Glyconic verse, and a Glyconic line results if we remove the last three syllables:

cui dono lepidum librum?

Catullus's first poem begins:

cui dono lepidum novum libellum
arida modo pumice expolitum?
Corneli, tibi; namque tu solebas
meas esse aliquid putare nugas.

As the second and fourth lines show, Catullus admits both $-\smile$ and $\smile-$ at the beginning. He does not admit $\smile\smile$, though once he seems to have a tribrach (in a proper name: 'Camerĭum mihi, pessimae puellae'—unless we are to take this as 'Cămēryum'). In the same poem, where the tribrach occurs, he makes the curious experiment of admitting $--$ in place of the dactyl which follows the 'basis'.

Like several other metres the hendecasyllabic admitted of being interpreted as Ionic, and this view of it was taken at least as early as Varro.¹ An 'Ionicus a minori' could take several forms: ∪∪⏤⏑ or ⏤⏑⏤ or ∪∪⏤∪ or ⏤∪⏤∪. Catullus's first line read in this way becomes:

cui dóno | lepidúm no|vum libéllum.

That the verse was commonly so read in classical times is not to be believed; the rapid and turbulent or unhinged movement of Ionics is quite out of harmony with the tone and theme of most hendecasyllabics. But at a later time hymns were written in it with variations which show that the writer thought of it as Ionic. Besides the Ionic theory of its nature there was the view that the line consisted of part of a hexameter and part of a senarius, two-and-a-half feet of each ($\pi\epsilon\nu\theta\eta\mu\iota\mu\epsilon\rho\grave{\epsilon}\varsigma\ \delta\alpha\kappa\tau\nu\lambda\iota\kappa\grave{o}\nu + \pi\epsilon\nu\theta\eta\mu\iota\mu\epsilon\rho\grave{\epsilon}\varsigma\ \iota\alpha\mu\beta\iota\kappa\grave{o}\nu$):

⏤ ⏤|⏤ ∪∪|⏤   ∪⏤ | ∪ ⏤|⏑
cui dono lepidum || novum libellum.

Both these views of it would lead to the belief that the first syllable *ought* to be long, and after Catullus's time it became the regular practice of Roman poets (so far as we know it) to make it so. Horace no doubt would have begun his lines with a spondee, if he had written any hendecasyllabics, and Martial invariably does so. Sidonius calls the verse

triplicis metrum trochaei
spondeo comitante dactyloque
dulces hendecasyllabos.

---

¹ Terentianus Maurus, 2833–48: 'Idcirco' (because, if an anapaest be inserted after the first two syllables of a hendecasyllabic line, a Sotadean results, ⏤⏤ [∪∪⏤] ⏤∪∪⏤∪⏤∪⏤⏑):

genus hoc Phalaeciorum
vir doctissimus undecumque Varro
ad legem redigens Ionicorum
hinc natos ait esse, sed minores.

Atilius Fortunatianus says: 'Varro in Cynodidascalico Phalaecion metrum ionicum trimetrum appellat, quidam ionicum minorem.'

Terentianus Maurus analyses the verse in various ways, beginning with the division suggested by what was probably the prevalent theory of its origin:

        cui dono lepidum | novum libellum,

and taking next the division

$$--\;|\;-\cup\cup\;\|\;-\cup-\cup-\breve{\cup}.$$

In Statius's poems on the 'Via Domitiana' (*Silv.* iv. 3) and on the 'Birthday of Lucan' (*Silv.* ii. 7), the longest and most elaborate pieces of hendecasyllabics that we have from the first century of our era, the great majority of the lines are of one or other of these two types:

        Lucani proprium | diem frequentet
        quisquis collibus | Isthmiae Diones
        pendentis bibit | ungulae liquorem.

It is noticeable further in the practice of Statius and Martial that elisions are very few and very slight. There is a careful avoidance of elision which is foreign to Catullus. Coincidence between word and foot is not avoided. There are many lines in which only one foot does not end with the end of a word:

        Baetin, Mantua, provo|care noli.

Coincidence throughout, however, is quite rare (*Via Dom.* 91):

        Poenos Bagrada serpit inter agros

(where spondee, dactyl, and the three trochees are all separate words).

PART II

CHAPTER I

GREEK LYRIC VERSE

I. ARCHILOCHUS, ALCMAN, AND SAPPHO

WHATEVER forms of lyric verse existed prior to the Homeric poems or contemporary with them—and it seems probable that shorter lines, more or less Aeolian, existed, out of which a hexameter could be formed—the first 'lyric' verse that presents itself in literature or to the view of the historian is the elegiac couplet. The ancients would not classify it as 'lyric', but it is clearly a change in the direction of lyric poetry. Tradition made Callinus or Tyrtaeus its founder, along with Archilochus, but for our present purpose we may ignore the dubious question of priority and contemplate it as one of the various advances in metrical art made by the poet of Paros. Archilochus was looked upon by ancient critics as a poet of the same quality as Homer, though he attempted nothing on the scale of the epos,[1] and in particular as an originator of new metrical and musical forms. Marius Victorinus called him 'parentem artis musicae, iuxta multiformem metrorum seriem diversamque progeniem'. Slight as the surviving fragments of Archilochus's poetry are, it is possible

[1] *Quint.* x. 1. 60: 'Summa in hoc vis elocutionis, cum validae tum breves vibrantesque sententiae, plurimum sanguinis atque nervorum, adeo ut videatur quibusdam, quod quoquam minor est, materiae esse non ingenii vitium.'

to discover in them at least three important lines of advance in metrical art.

(i) There is first the vein of composition which we may associate with the word 'epode' as that term is applied to verses of Horace. A well-known and established line or στίχος has a different appendage attached to it to make a couplet. An elegiac couplet is an epode in this sense (the second line a sequel or following verse, ἐπῳδός). It was a further step, and a very important one, to make this appendage consist of feet of a different type, e.g. to make the alternating line an iambic dimeter:

> δύστηνος ἔγκειμαι πόθῳ,
> ἄψυχος, χαλεπῇσι θεῶν ὀδύνῃσιν ἕκητι
> πεπαρμένος δι' ὀστέων,

or, conversely, a normal iambic line might be followed by something shorter that was dactylic:

> ἐρέω τιν' ὑμῖν αἶνον, ὦ Κηρυκάδη·
> ἀχνυμένη σκυτάλη·
> πίθηκος ᾔει θηρίων ἀποκριθεὶς
> μοῦνος ἀν' ἐσχατιήν·

Besides these there was the combination of the longer and shorter iambic line, trimeter and dimeter, which Horace adopted in most of his epodes.

The 'epodic' vein is known to us chiefly in Horace. The recurrent couplet or short stanza has little place in the lyrics of the drama or in Pindar. Pindar or Sophocles set up every time a new fabric of 'manifold music', a fresh piece of metrical and musical architecture; the elements combined were more or less familiar, but the combination of them was devised for the occasion. The simpler 'epodic' vein is seldom seen in tragedy. The elegiac couplet is found only once, for a θρῆνος, in the *Andromache* of Euripides, a μονῳδία ('Ἰλίῳ αἰπεινᾷ Πάρις οὐ γάμον κτλ., l. 103 f.), and in the same play he has a dactylic hexameter followed by a trochaic κῶλον (l. 117):

ὦ γύναι, ἃ Θέτιδος δάπεδον καὶ ἀνάκτορα θάσσεις
δαρὸν οὐδὲ λείπεις.

Many lyric systems have an ἐπῳδὸς στίχος in the sense of a following or closing verse that is different from what precedes. But it seems expedient to speak of this rather as a 'clausula', and to reserve the term 'epode' for something of the nature of a recurrent couplet, of which a normal στίχος forms part. Though written in two 'lines' the group may of course contain more than two κῶλα; there are four in Horace's combination:

horrida tempestas | caelum contraxit et imbres |
nivesque deducunt Iovem; | nunc mare, nunc siluae.

(ii) One of the extant fragments of Archilochus is a line which runs thus:

ἀλλά μ' ὁ λυσιμελής, ὦ 'ταῖρε, δάμναται πόθος.

This also may have been part of an 'epodic' couplet, perhaps with an iambic trimeter before it, as in Horace:

Petti, nihil me sicut antea iuvat
scribere versiculos amore percussum graui.

Horace probably thought of the second part of the longer line as iambic, and divided the whole thus:

$$-\cup\cup\ -\cup\cup\ -\ |\ \underline{\cup}-\ \cup-\ -\underline{\cup}\ \cup-.$$

But Archilochus's syllables can be taken in another way and, whether he meant it or not, the line will serve as an introductory example of a large class of lyrics:

$$-\cup\cup\ -\cup\cup\ --\ |\ -\cup\ -\cup\ -\cup\ -\wedge.$$

Here we have a dactylic and a trochaic group; and the dactylic group comes to a marked close, like a hexameter. It ends in a spondee (though we may expect to find occasionally a *syllaba anceps*, the last foot appearing for prosody as a trochee). Verse of this type (with the trochaic part usually shortened and weighted at the close, $-\cup--$) was written very extensively by Pindar, Bacchylides, and others, and various names have been devised for it, of which 'dactylo-epitrite' was perhaps the most useful and the least ambiguous.

(iii) Another extant fragment of Archilochus runs:

τοῖος γὰρ φιλότητος ἔρως ὑπὸ καρδίην ἐλυσθεὶς
πολλὴν κατ' ἀχλὺν ὀμμάτων ἔχευεν.

$-\underset{\smile}{\cup\cup} - \underset{\smile}{\cup\cup} - \underset{\smile}{\cup\cup} - \cup\cup \mid -\cup-\cup-\underset{\smile}{\,}$
$\underset{\smile}{\,} - \cup - \underset{\smile}{\,} -\cup-\cup-\underset{\smile}{\,}$

(Hor. *Odes* i. 4 'solvitur acris hiems', &c.). The first line consists of a group of four dactyls and a trochaic phrase, the second is iambic (catalectic)). Here the dactylic group ends with a dactyl; it is not brought to a close by a spondee, and the rhetorical pause or pause in sense between ὑπὸ and καρδίην is very slight. Whether Archilochus, like Horace, always made the fourth foot a dactyl is uncertain; Cratinus wrote:

χαίρετε πάντες ὅσοι πολύβωτον ποντίαν Σέριφον
$-\cup\cup \; -\cup\cup \; - \; \cup\cup \; -- \mid -\cup-\cup \; -\underset{\smile}{\,},$

and in this shape the line does not differ in principle from the preceding type (ii). But taking it as it stands in the extant fragment and as Horace wrote it, it is an example of a somewhat different arrangement. The dactylic portion is not completed or secluded or relegated to a separate compartment by a variation in the form of its last foot. The whole cannot be a single κῶλον; according to Aristoxenus the longest dactylic κῶλον is one of four feet, and even if we think of the dactyls as more rapid than ordinary dactyls and equivalent in time to trochees, the feet are still too numerous—for trochees Aristoxenus's limit was six. But if, while preserving the structure, we reduce the number of dactyls, or of trochees, or of both, we shall arrive at lines which are short enough to be single κῶλα, and these will form a new type of metre—

dactyl and trochee not in separate compartments, but in the same κῶλον. Clearly there will be several species:

(a) *With dactyls preponderating and trochees few:*

ὃς μετὰ Μαινάσι Βάκχιος ὄμμασι δαίεται

(Ar. *Lys.* 1285.)

(four dactyls, and trochaic dipody catalectic $-\cup-\wedge$).

ὦ διὰ τῶν θυρίδων καλὸν ἐμβλέποισα

(three dactyls, and trochaic dipody or possibly $-\cup\llcorner-\wedge$).

The same with $\cup\cup$ or $-$ or $\cup$ prefixed:

ἀτελέστατα γὰρ καὶ ἀμάχανα τοὺς θανόντας κλαίειν.   (Stesichorus.)

δαρὸν δ᾽ ἄνεω χρόνον ἧστο τάφει πεπαγώς.
                                                                (Ibycus.)

Ἄναυρον ὕπερ πολυβότρυος ἐξ Ἰωλκοῦ.
                                                              (Simonides.)

(b) *With dactyls reduced in number—reduced to one:*

καὶ μέλι καὶ τὰ τέρπν᾽ ἄνθε᾽ ἀφροδίσια

(this is still two κῶλα, $-\cup\cup-\cup\llcorner\ |\ -\cup-\cup-\cup\stackrel{\smile}{=}\wedge$).

Πάν, Πελασγικὸν Ἄργος ἐμβατεύων

(Phalaecean,

$-\cup-\cup\cup-\cup-\cup-\stackrel{\smile}{=}$ or $-\cup-\cup\cup-\cup-\cup\llcorner-\wedge$).

ποικιλόθρον᾽ ἀθάνατ᾽ Ἀφροδίτα

(Sapphic, $-\cup-\cup-\cup\cup-\cup-\stackrel{\smile}{=}$).

(c) *With both dactyls and trochees fewer in number:*

νᾶι φορήμεθα σὺν μελαίνᾳ

($-\cup\cup-\cup\cup-\cup-\stackrel{\smile}{=}$, Alcaic decasyllable).

ἢ πόλιν ἡμετέραν ἔχει   (Ar. *Thesm.* 1140.)

(the same, catalectic).

The latter is seen also in Ibycus, fr. 1:

GREEK LYRIC VERSE

ἦρι μὲν αἵ τε Κυδώνιαι
μηλίδες ἀρδόμεναι ῥοᾶν
ἐκ ποταμῶν, ἵνα παρθένων

(the next three lines here are complete dactylic tetrapodies, each ending in a dactyl and 'hypermetric' in scansion:

κῆπος ἀκήρατος αἵ τ' οἰνανθίδες
αὐξόμεναι κτλ.).

The survey of these metres has led us into regions which it is not known that Archilochus trod. The shortest κῶλον of the type which has now come into view is $- \cup \cup - \cup - \wedge$ (ὄμμασιν ἐνδίκοις, 'vulgus et arceo') or $- \cup \cup - \cup - \asymp$ (δύσμαχα δ' ἐστὶ κρῖναι, 'Lydia, dic per omnes'). Verse like this is not 'Parian'. It has been called 'Logaoedic' or 'Lesbian' or 'Aeolian'. 'Logaoedic' is a word that was invented by metricians of Roman imperial times. It was applied to lines of the type ὦ διὰ τῶν θυρίδων καλὸν ἐμβλέποισα (five or six feet, six if the ending is $\smile - \wedge$; the maximum number of feet that can form a single κῶλον in trochaic time).

We have now met with two *principles* on which composite metres can be constructed; the principle of separate groups or compartments, dactyls in one group, trochees in another, and the principle of mixture, groups internally heterogeneous, dactyl and trochee in the same κῶλον. The words which come nearest to expressing this difference of principle are the Greek adjectives ἐπισύνθετον and μικτόν (ἐπισύνθετον, 'outwardly compounded', compounded by juxtaposition of groups). But before tracing these two veins of composition further—both of them are extensively illustrated in Pindar and the drama—we must revert to early history, and it will also be desirable to survey first those lyrics in which there is no heterogeneity at all, metres composed of one type of foot only (μέτρα μονοειδῆ or ὁμοειδῆ).

In the time of Archilochus or not long after it, in the

seventh and sixth centuries B.C., there were other developments of music and metre in Greece: Dorian, represented by Alcman at Sparta and Stesichorus in Sicily, and Aeolian or Lesbian, represented by Sappho and Alcaeus. The Dorian poetry is mainly choric, composed for a public occasion and expressing the feelings of a people or of a large company. The Aeolian poetry expresses the feelings of the poet or poetess, and it is often addressed to a particular person.

Stesichorus (or Tisias) of Himera was a poet of considerable versatility and importance.[1] Quintilian describes him as 'epici carminis onera lyra sustinentem'. He related heroic stories in new shapes, for example making Clytaemnestra take the lead in the murder of Agamemnon (as she does not do in Homer); and for these heroic lays he seems to have used metres akin to that of the epos, numerous groups of dactyls, if we may judge by a few extant passages, with only few and short groups of trochees interwoven with them:

οὕνεκα Τυνδάρεος
ῥέζων ποτὲ πᾶσι θεοῖς μούνας λάθετ' ἠπιοδώρου
Κύπριδος· κείνα δὲ Τυνδαρέου κόραις
χολωσαμένη διγάμους τε καὶ τριγάμους τίθησιν
καὶ λιπεσάνορας ...

$-\cup\cup\ -\cup\cup\ -\wedge$
$-\ -\cup\cup\ -\cup\cup\ -\ -\ -\cup\cup\ -\cup\cup\ -\ -$
$-\cup\ -\ -\ \ -\cup\ -\cup\ \ -\cup-$
$\cup-\cup\cup\ -\cup\cup\ -\cup\ -\cup\cup\ -\cup-\ \underset{\smile}{-}$
$-\cup\cup\ -\cup\cup\ ...$ (or $-\cup\cup\ -\cup\ -\wedge$).

(Τυνδαρέου is trisyllabic, by synizesis Τυνδαρεου͡. Two of the lines are preceded by − and ∪, a syllable for which

---

[1] The versatility which we attribute to Stesichorus may perhaps be illusory, things written by various poets having attached themselves to the name 'Stesichorus'. His personality is obscure. But the most sceptical view of him does not impugn the existence of an early vein of lyric poetry in Sicily in the metre here described.

GREEK LYRIC VERSE

modern metricians have used the useful term 'anacrusis'. Here the syllables can be accounted for as belonging to the preceding κῶλον : οὕνεκα Τυνδάρεος ῥέ|ζων ποτὲ πᾶσι θεοῖς κτλ., but this is not always the case. The last κῶλον in the fourth line is one that we have met with as the shortest 'logaoedic' group, – ∪ ∪ – ∪ – ≍.) The longest extant passage is dactylic almost throughout :

Ἀέλιος δ' Ὑπεριονίδας δέπας ἐσκατέβαινεν
χρύσεον, ὄφρα δι' Ὠκεανοῖο περάσας
ἀφίκοιθ' ἱερᾶς ποτὶ βένθεα νυκτὸς ἐρεμνᾶς
ποτὶ ματέρα κουριδίαν τ' ἄλοχον παῖδάς τε φίλους·
ὁ δ' ἐς ἄλσος ἔβα
δάφναισι κατάσκιον ποσσὶ πάϊς Διός.

– ∪ ∪ – ∪ ∪ – ∪ ∪ – ∪ ∪ – ∪ ∪ – ≍
– ∪ ∪ – ∪ ∪ – ∪ ∪ – ∪ ∪ – –
∪ ∪ – ∪ ∪ – ∪ ∪ – ∪ ∪ – ∪ ∪ – –
∪ ∪ – ∪ ∪ – ∪ ∪ – ∪ ∪ – – – ∪ ∪ – ⚲
∪ ∪ – ∪ ∪ –
≍ – ∪ ∪ – ∪ – | – ∪ ∪ – ∪ ≍.

(Heracles landing at Gades from the Sungod's boat, to encounter Geryones. In the third line an 'anacrusis' which cannot be attached to the preceding line. Ancient metricians had to make this line anapaestic, ∪ ∪ – | ∪ ∪ –, &c.; or they made the whole anapaestic and called the dactylic lines 'acephalous'). Tradition ascribes to Stesichorus the invention of the triple or triadic arrangement by which a strophe was repeated and followed by an 'epode'—ἐπῳδός here meaning a strophe that follows another duplicated one, not a line that follows other lines.

Of Alcman's poetry many short fragments survive which show great finish and variety of metrical form, and we have also a considerable part of a παρθένιον, which was monostrophic—the same strophe recurs, without an epode. In this system trochees predominate, a few lines are 'logaoedic', and the penultimate line is one of four dactyls and the last is the Alcaic decasyllable (= 'virginibus puerisque canto'):

ἦ οὐχ ὁρῆς; ὁ μὲν κέλης
Ἐνετικός, ἁ δὲ χαίτα
τᾶς ἐμᾶς ἀνεψιᾶς
Ἁγησιχόρας ἐπανθεῖ
χρυσὸς ὡς ἀκήρατος
τό τ' ἀργύριον πρόσωπον
διαφάδαν—τί τοι λέγω;—
Ἁγησιχόρα μὲν αὕτα.—
ἁ δὲ δευτέρα πεδ' Ἀγιδὼν τὸ Ϝεῖδος
ἵππος εἰβήνῳ Κολαξαῖος δραμεῖται,
ταὶ πελειάδες γὰρ ἁμὶν
Ὀρθίᾳ φάρος φεροίσαις
νύκτα δι' ἀμβροσίαν ἅτε σήριον
ἄστρον ἀϜειρομέναι μάχονται.

The first line is $- \cup - \cup - \cup -$ (= 'non ebur nec aureum'). For the second the preceding strophe has ὁ δ' ὄλβιος ὅστις εὔφρων, $\cup - \cup \cup - \cup --$, so that ὄλβιος answers to (Ἐ)νετικός, $-\cup\cup$ to $\cup\cup\cup$, an indication that in a lyric which is on the whole trochaic we have to reckon with a dactyl which has the time of a trochee. The couplet is repeated four times: lines 1, 2 = 3, 4 = 5, 6 = 7, 8. Then follow two longer trochaic lines, trimeters, the element repeated being $- \cup - \overset{\smile}{-}$. Next come two dimeters of the same type ($- \cup - \overset{\smile}{-} \mid - \cup - \overset{\smile}{-}$), then the dactylic tetrapody (ending in a dactyl, and 'hypermetric' or continuous in scansion with the line that follows), then the Alcaic decasyllable, ἄστρον ἀϜειρομέναι μάχονται (in the next strophe its first foot is a spondee, ἀλλ' Ἁγησιχόρα με τηρεῖ). Aeschylus also, besides Alcman, had a liking for this decasyllable as a *clausula* or concluding cadence, and, like Alcman, he sometimes has a penultimate dactylic κῶλον or κῶλα in a system that is mainly trochaic.

In its general structure Alcman's strophe has something of a 'Parian' character. Several lines are exactly alike, and trochaic throughout, while one is dactylic throughout; so far as it consists of such elements it is 'Parian'. If we call it 'Alcmanian', and take 'Parian' or ἐπισύνθετον as the name for a *genus*, the *genus* will include at least three *species* : (1) the Archilochian and Horatian 'epode' or epodic couplet, (2) Alcmanian, (3) 'dactylo-epitrite' (consisting of the elements $-\cup\cup\ -\cup\cup\ --$ and $-\cup\ --$).[1] A good example of what we are proposing to call by Alcman's name is seen in the lines (Ar. *Av.* 747 f.):

ἔνθεν ὡσπερεὶ μέλιττα
Φρύνιχος ἀμβροσίων ἐπέων ἀπεβόσκετο καρπὸν ἀεὶ
φέρων γλυκεῖαν ᾠδάν.

$-\cup\ -\cup\ -\cup\ -\cup$
$-\cup\cup\ -\cup\cup\ -\cup\cup\ -\cup\cup\ -\cup\cup\ -\cup\cup\ -\overline{\wedge}$
$\cup-\ \cup-\ \cup-\ \stackrel{\cup}{=}$.

It has been proposed to call this 'simplified logaoedic',[2] but the simplification, or separation of groups of similar feet, is carried so far that the term 'logaoedic' ceases to be appropriate. If the word 'logaoedic' is to be retained, it would be most serviceable in the sense that dactyl and trochee occur within the same κῶλον—a κῶλον which includes both is 'logaoedic'; and we may regard ὣ διὰ τῶν θυρίδων καλὸν ἐμβλέποισα— to which the ancients gave the name—as the upper limit or extreme case. Anything longer than that—with the dactyls grouped together, and the trochees in another group—is not 'logaoedic'.

Solvitur acris hiems grata vice | veris et Favoni

[1] A different account of 'dactylo-epitrite' verse, which has found favour with recent metricians, is discussed on p. 177.

[2] By Mr. White, in his *Verse of Greek Comedy*.

will be excluded from the category. Contrast with this the so-called 'Priapean' line:

o colonia quae cupis | ponte ludere longo

‒ ◡ ‒ ◡ ◡ ‒ ◡ ‒ ⋀   ‒ ◡ ‒ ◡ ◡ ‒ ‒ (or ⌣ ‒ ⋀),

which consists of two κῶλα, each palpably 'logaoedic' or μικτόν, a 'Glyconic' and a 'Pherecratean' verse. Glyconic was one of the many measures written by Sappho.

The poetry of Alcaeus and Sappho is known to us very imperfectly, in a few portions of poems, stanzas, or lines that have been more or less accidentally preserved. In quite recent years a few portions of poems of Sappho have been recovered, which are metrically instructive.[1]

The chief forms of verse written by the Lesbian or Aeolian poets are the following:

(1) The Sapphic stanza:

ποικιλόθρον', ἀθάνατ' Ἀφροδίτα.

‒ ◡ ‒ ⌣   ‒ ◡ ◡   ‒ ◡ ‒ ⌣   *ter*
‒ ◡ ◡   ‒ ⌣.

(The fourth syllable may be short or long. Horace made it invariably long, and Horace also preferred the *caesura* seen in

καὶ γὰρ αἰ φεύγει | ταχέως διώξει.

Sappho has no such preference, and very frequently ends a word with the fourth syllable, as in:

*φαίνεταί μοι | κῆνος ἴσος θέοισιν
ἔμμεν ὤνηρ | ὅστις ἐναντίος τοι.*)

(2) The Alcaic stanza:

*ἀσυνέτημι τῶν ἀνέμων στάσιν·
τὸ μὲν γὰρ ἔνθεν κῦμα κυλίνδεται,*

---

[1] They have been made accessible in Diehl's *Supplementum Lyricum*, one of the 'Kleine Texte' published at Bonn (by Marcus and Weber), which contains also parts of two poems of Corinna and Paeans of Pindar.

GREEK LYRIC VERSE

τὸ δ' ἔνθεν· ἄμμες δ' ἂν τὸ μέσσον
νᾶϊ φορήμεθα σὺν μελαίνᾳ

⏓ –∪ –⏓ –∪∪ –∪ –
⏓ –∪ –⏓ –∪∪ –∪ –
∪ –∪ –⏓ –∪ –⏓
–∪∪ –∪∪ –∪ – –

(Horace made the fifth syllable always long, and introduced a diaeresis after it in the first and second lines: see Chap. III.)

(3) Metres of which some were afterwards called 'Asclepiadean', each line beginning with what has been called a 'basis' or 'basis Aeolica', a kind of disyllabic anacrusis, syllables which may be – ∪ or ∪ – or ∪ ∪ or – –. The chief metres of this type are:

Phalaecean:

⏓ ⏓ ⸮ – ∪ ∪ – ∪ – ∪ – ⏓.

Glyconic (with Pherecratean, which is shorter by a syllable, the shortest of the lines of the type):

⏓ ⏓ ⸮ – ∪ ∪ – ∪ –   (Pherecratean, ⏓ ⏓ ⸮ – ∪ ∪ – ⏓).

Metres like the Glyconic, but with more than one dactyl:

(a) μέμναισθ', οἶσθα γὰρ ὥς σε πεδήπομεν. (Sappho.)
– – ⸮ – ∪ ∪ – ∪ ∪ – ∪ –.

(b) ὤνηρ οὗτος ὁ μαιόμενος τὸ μέγα κρέτος
ἀντρέψει τάχα τὰν πόλιν, ἁ δ' ἔχεται ῥόπας.
(Alcaeus.)
– – ⸮ – ∪ ∪ – ∪ ∪ – ∪ ∪ – ∪ –.

Asclepiadean metres:

(α) ἦλθες ἐκ περάτων γᾶς ἐλεφαντίναν
λάβαν τῶ ξίφεος χρυσοδέταν ἔχων
⏓ ⏓ – ∪ ∪ – – ∪ ∪ – ∪ –.

(β) μηδὲν ἄλλο φυτεύσῃς πρότερον δένδριον ἀμπέλω
⏓ ⏓ – ∪ ∪ – – ∪ ∪ – – ∪ ∪ – ∪ –.

The last two metres are obtained from the Glyconic by the introduction of one or of two choriambi (–∪∪–). λάβαν χρυσοδέταν ἔχων is a Glyconic, as is μηδὲν δένδριον ἀμπέλω.

So far we have been describing metres in terms of dactyls and trochees. It is now necessary to explain that a different view of them has recently become current and has been advocated by distinguished scholars. An upholder of it would say to us at this point: 'There are no dactyls in these metres; what you take for a dactyl is really part of a choriambus; primitive Aeolian verse, so far as it divided itself into fixed groups of syllables,' he would probably be cautious enough to make this reservation, 'fell into groups of four syllables. The apparent dactyl in a Glyconic line results simply from an iambus following a trochee: ἄριστον μὲν | ὕδωρ ὁ δέ, ∪ – – ∪ | ∪ – ∪ –.' Postponing the discussion of this theory, which is open to some serious objections, let us first see what can be done with the dactyl and trochee. The 'Aeolist' or 'Indo-European' or 'quadrisyllabist' metricians themselves admit that there *was* verse in which a dactyl and a trochee came together. What metrical elements or phrases are wanted for the construction of the verses of Sappho and Alcaeus?

We want hardly anything beyond the two forms of the shortest κῶλον of the mixed type, which have been mentioned above:

(a) – ∪ ∪ – ∪ –, vulgus et arceo, ὄμμασιν ἐνδίκοις.

(b) – ∪ ∪ – ∪ – – Lydia, dic per omnes, δύσμαχα δ' ἐστὶ κρῖναι.[1]

---

[1] Perhaps discoverable in the Linus-song (Schol. *Il.* xviii. 570). At all events the lines

Φοῖβος δὲ κότῳ σ' ἀναιρεῖ
Μοῦσαι δέ σε θρηνέουσιν

seem to be the least questionable part of the text of it (– – ∪ ∪ – ∪ – ⌴).

GREEK LYRIC VERSE

(b) is written κατὰ στίχον by Aristophanes (*Fr.* 10):

> οὐκ ἐτός, ὦ γυναῖκες,
> πᾶσι κακοῖσιν ἡμᾶς
> φλῶσιν ἑκάστοθ' ἄνδρες κτλ.,

and Eupolis wrote a stanza in it ending with the line (*Fr.* 163):

> μῆλα δὲ χρέμπτεται (= (a)).

(a) coincides in syllables with a very frequent form of the dochmius, which sometimes has (b) attached to it as a *clausula*:

```
 - ∪   ∪ - ∪   -
```
μήτε σε θυμοπληθὴς δορίμαργος ἄ̞τα φερέτω κακοῦ δ'

```
           - ∪   ∪ - ∪   -   -
```
ἔκβαλ' ἔρωτος ἀρχάν.

(a), which has been called, and may conveniently be called, an 'Aeolic tripody', enters into various metres. It is the second part of the first and second lines of an Alcaic stanza (*vulgus et arceo*). It is also the close of an Asclepiadean line (*severis arborem*). With two syllables prefixed it is a Glyconic (*cui flavam religas comam*), and to prefix a 'basis' of two syllables is a regular habit of Aeolian verse. With four syllables prefixed (a kind of double 'basis', in the regular shape of a ditrochaeus, $- \cup - \underset{\smile}{-}$) it is a Sapphic line (*ποικιλόθρον'* | *ἀθάνατ' Ἀφροδίτα*).[1] With the dactyl doubled it is the fourth line of an Alcaic stanza, and the effect of an Alcaic stanza depends on the fact that the third and fourth lines taken together exhibit on a larger scale the movement

---

[1] In one of the recently recovered poems Sappho makes a more curious experiment in construction than this would be, prefixing a cretic to a Glyconic line (*Suppl. Lyr.* 7):

> νῦν δὲ Λύ|δαισιν ἐντρέπεται γυναί-
> κεσσιν, ὥς ποτ' ἀελίω κτλ.

where the line is followed, in a regular three-line stanza, by another Glyconic and a Phalaecean.

seen in the first and second lines separately—the third line is a longer trochaic or iambic phrase than the first part of one of the preceding lines; and dactylic movement, after being as it were longer staved off, comes when it does come in greater volume, two dactyls instead of one. In the first two lines what is prefixed to (a) is an iambic πενθημιμερές, the syllables $\smile - \cup - \smile$.[1] Whether we call this an iambic πενθημιμερές or a ditrochaeus with anacrusis makes no difference to our reading of them; if we adopt the latter description of *odi profanum* it does not mean that we propose to pronounce them 'o—di pro—fanum'. What words Alcaeus would use to describe the syllables we do not know; possibly words that would describe them very imperfectly. Metrical, like grammatical, terminology was probably very scanty and incomplete in early times; so, for example, in the line

ῥίψει χειρὸς ἑλὼν ἀπὸ πύργου, λυγρὸν ὄλεθρον

(ὄλεθρον constructed as ῥῖψιν ὀλεθρίαν would be) Homer writes an exact specimen of the construction now called 'cognate' or 'internal accusative', but it is certain that Homer had no such phrase by which to describe it.

In the third line of an Alcaic stanza the ἰαμβικὸν πενθημιμερές, instead of being prefixed to (a), precedes a ditrochaeus ($\smile - \cup - \smile \mid - \cup - \smile$); or we may say that the line is a trochaic dimeter with anacrusis ($\smile \vdots - \cup - - \mid - \cup - -$), which is in some ways a more convenient description, and if we adopt it we can point to Seneca's use of the line *without* anacrusis:

semper ingentes alumnos.   (*Agam.* 810.)

[1] These syllables are readily prefixed in various forms of composition. They precede an 'enoplius' ($-\cup\cup -\cup\cup --$) again and again in Pindar. They seem even to precede 'anaclastic' Ionics in Aes. *P. V.* 128 μηδὲν φοβηθῇς· ‖ φιλία γὰρ | ἥδε τάξις κτλ. Compare also the line ἀνωλόλυξαν | κισσοφόροις ἐπὶ διθυράμβοις in a poem attributed to Simonides or Bacchylides (*Anth. Pal.* xiii. 28), where it precedes the Alcaic decasyllable.

GREEK LYRIC VERSE

We have now described or constructed the familiar Sapphic and Alcaic stanzas. What can be done with Glyconics? One of the recently recovered poems of Sappho is important for our inquiry. It is written in stanzas of three lines, two Glyconics, and a line which differs from them only in having an additional dactyl:

τὰν δ' ἐγὼ τάδ' ἀμειβόμαν·
χαίροισ' ἔρχεο κἄμεθεν
μέμναισθ', οἶσθα γὰρ ὥς σε πεδήπομεν[1]

– ∪ – ∪ ∪ – ∪ –
– – – ∪ ∪ – ∪ –
– – – ∪ ∪ – ∪ ∪ – ∪ – .

Quadrisyllabic scansion may give a reasonable account of the first two lines:

– ∪ – ∪ | ∪ – ∪ –,

but it does not give an equally good account of the third:

– – – ∪ | ∪ – ∪ ∪ | – ∪ –,

and it becomes still less attractive when a third dactyl is added:

ὤνηρ οὗτος ὁ μαιόμενος τὸ μέγα κρέτος

(Alcaeus—but Sappho also writes the line:

μνάσεσθαί τινά φαμι καὶ ὕστερον ἄμμεων)[2]

– – – ∪ | ∪ – ∪ ∪ | – ∪ ∪ – | ∪ – .

[1] πεδήπομεν = μεθείπομεν.

[2] One of the recent volumes of Oxyrhynchus papyri contains a portion of a poem of Sappho in which this verse was written κατὰ στίχον. The subject was the wedding of Hector and Andromache:

"Εκτωρ καὶ συνέταιροι ἄγοισ' ἐλικώπιδα
Θήβας ἐξ ἱάρας Πλακίας τ' ἀπ' ἀιννάω
ἄβραν 'Ανδρομάχαν ἐνὶ ναῦσιν ἐπ' ἄλμυρον
πόντον κτλ.

Here the shortening συνέταιροῖ is Homeric, and belongs to dactylic verse. The poems in this Oxyrhynchus volume show us both Sappho and Alcaeus (p. 55) interested in Homer, and recalling Homeric events and Homeric phraseology.

GREEK LYRIC VERSE

It is difficult to believe that the longer lines are not dactylic; and if they contain dactyls, is it credible that the syllables – ᴗ ᴗ in the shortest line are something quite different? We have then a series or scale, in which a Glyconic grows by the accretion of dactyls:

(a) τὰν δ' ἐγὼ τάδ' ἀμειβόμαν.

(b) μέμναισθ', οἶσθα γὰρ ὥς σε πεδήπομεν.

(c) ἀντρέψει τάχα τὰν πόλιν· ἁ δ' ἔχεται ῥόπας.

But there is also another series, starting from a Glyconic:

(a) τὰν δ' ἐγὼ τάδ' ἀμειβόμαν—cui flavam religas comam.[1]

(b) λάβαν τῶ ξίφεος χρυσοδέταν ἔχων—Maecenas atavis edite regibus.

(c) μηδὲν ἄλλο φυτεύσῃς πρότερον δένδριον ἀμπέλω—
nullam, Vare, sacra vite prius severis arborem.[2]

The two series are so much alike that it is almost impossible to dissociate them. But if they are parallel and cognate the first two syllables in the second series are a 'basis', and the line does not begin with a quadrisyllabic foot.[3] The scansion

---

[1] Horace made the 'basis' regularly – –.

[2] It was a curious fancy of Prudentius's to make these three lines form a stanza for his preface to the *Cathemerinon* (not altogether unlike what Sappho sometimes does, and not so infelicitous in effect as might be expected):

num quid talia proderunt
carnis post obitum vel bona vel mala,
cum iam quicquid id est quod fueram mors aboleverit.

[3] A similar beginning in a hexameter was recognized as Aeolic, χραισμεῖν, εὖτ' ἂν πολλοὶ κτλ. (*supra*, p. 25). It appears in Sappho's hexameters:

οἴαν τὰν ὑάκινθον ἐν οὔρεσι ποιμένες ἄνδρες,
οἶον τὸ γλυκύμαλον κτλ.

Compare also the wedding song, where a hexameter is disrupted:

ἴψοι δὴ τὸ μέλαθρον
Ὑμήναον
ἀέρρετε τέκτονες ἄνδρες.

μηδὲν ἄλλο | φυτεύσῃς πρό|τερον δένδρι|ον ἀμπέλω

seems to be excluded. That the first two syllables stand apart from the rest is indicated by the fact that they *alone* are variable: they may be – ∪ or ∪ – or – – or ∪ ∪. Every other syllable in an Alcaic or 'Asclepiadean' line of this type is absolutely fixed. If we may assume then dactylic movement or effect in what follows, the simplest description of what happens in our two series will be this: in the former the first *three* syllables of – ∪ ∪ – ∪ – (ὥς σε πεδήπομεν) are duplicated, in the latter it is the first four. The phrase ὥς σε πεδήπομεν begins but is arrested (ὥς σε πεδη- ὥς σε πεδήπομεν), and in the longer line or 'greater Asclepiad' it is so arrested twice.

It is this description or analysis of the verse that will enable a modern reader to find it pleasing. To read 'antispasts' with ease and pleasure (φυτεύσῃς πρό|τερον δένδρι-) is a thing which he might arrive at by assiduous practice, though even that seems doubtful. 'But', it may be said, 'that is an unscientific and unhistorical attitude to assume; if antispasts *were* what the Greeks felt here, the effort must be made.' This may be admitted; but we are entitled to ask that the evidence be strong and conclusive. We must be careful not to make some of the greatest poetry of the Greeks difficult, or even repellent, for the literary student, in obedience to what may be only a dubious and ingenious theory. The discussion of the evidence must find a place in a separate *Note* or *Excursus*.

EXCURSUS

(a) 'Aeolic' Verse.

The 'Indo-European', 'Aeolic', or 'quadrisyllabic' theory which has had much vogue in recent years may be summarized as follows:

Indo-European verse was at first 'syllabic'; syllables were merely counted, they were in no way regulated and might be long or short. Such a group of eight syllables may be represented by the symbols o o o o o o o o. It is a 'carmen' only in the sense of an utterance of fixed length. Two such groups could make a longer line of sixteen syllables (seen in early Indian verse), and there was also a group of twelve syllables. The octasyllabic group began to be regulated at the end, the last four syllables became ∪ − ∪ o (iambic) or − ∪ ∪ − (choriambic), while the first four were still free. When two groups of four syllables come into view the verse may be called a 'dimeter', and the longer verse similarly became a 'trimeter'. From the octasyllabic verse arose the iambic and trochaic dimeters (∪ − ∪ − ∪ − ∪ − and − ∪ − ∪ − ∪ − ∪). Apart from these the chief forms which it assumed were:

(i) o o o o − ∪ ∪ − (the first four syllables unregulated), the 'polyschematist' dimeter.

(ii) o o − ∪ ∪ − ∪ − (two syllables still unregulated), 'Glyconic'. The choriambus has shifted its place and is now in the middle of the line.

(iii) − ∪ ∪ − ∪ − ∪ − (all the syllables now regulated), 'choriambo-iambic'.

The choriambus moves gradually back from the end of the line. On the other theory of the verse it is a dactyl that shifts its place. (ii) is normal 'Glyconic', in (i) the dactyl is nearer the end of the line, in (iii) it is at the beginning of it. Which description is to be preferred?

When stage (ii) is reached a possibility of compromise comes into view. We may say, 'whatever happened before this, in primitiv times, about which we have no direct evidence, it was surely possible that when the "Glyconic proper" was evolved (τὰν δ' ἐγὼ τάδ' ἀμειβόμαν) the syllables $-\cup\cup$ in it could be taken as a dactyl, at a time when a dactylic epos was flourishing; and it was thus that it became possible for Sappho to lengthen the line by introducing another dactyl, and to use this longer line in a three-line stanza with two Glyconics'.

But recent metricians would not admit even as much as this. They regard 'quadrisyllabic' scansion or structure as much more lasting than that, and they find verses in the sixth and fifth centuries which they define as partly 'syllabic' or amorphous. One of them [1] even gives the scheme of a *Sapphic* line as

$$\circ\circ\circ\circ-\cup\cup-\cup--,$$

and the 'polyschematist' dimeter is discovered frequently in the lyrics of the drama.

It must be admitted that there are lyrics in Aristophanes which the Aeolic theory accounts for very neatly. It fits them exactly:

πέτου, πέτου, Νικοδίκη,   ($\cup-\cup-\ |\ -\cup\cup-$, diiambus and
 πρὶν ἐμπεπρῆσθαι Καλύκην   choriambus);

or:

ἐς βαθὺ τῆς ἡλικίας   ($-\cup\cup--\cup\cup-$, two choriambi);

and it is possible that ancient forms of verse would survive in comedy. The theory suits also the second of the recently recovered poems of Corinna, and an ancient vein of verse might also be looked for in σκόλια and *carmina popularia*. But when we turn to the eminently 'Aeolian' poets, the 'Aeolic' theory meets with difficulties. There is no question of four unregulated syllables. In the first four syllables of a Sapphic line, and in the first five of an Alcaic hendecasyllable, the variations are of the most innocent and commonplace description. The ditrochaeus with which a Sapphic line begins is regulated as much as any ditrochaeus ever was in the usual verse of early Greece; and in the Alcaic line the variations are those which are familiar in any iambic πενθημιμερές.

---

[1] Schröder, in *Horazens Versmasse für Anfänger erklärt*. The 'beginner', when he turns to his text of Horace, of course finds the first four syllables absolutely fixed. In Sappho only one of them is variable (the fourth).

Horace regulated the metres still further, making certain syllables invariably long; he fixed all the variable syllables, except the first of an Alcaic line, which he sometimes allows to be short. His lyrics were written to be read, mainly, though the *Carmen Saeculare* was undoubtedly sung. Sappho's verses were things which could easily be sung to the lute, without elaborate musical training and special preparation. They must have been also *read*. They are addressed often to particular persons and they were sometimes of the nature of a poetical epistle, e.g. the now extant poem on her brother's return. So they are regular, like Horace's. The same stanza is repeated with only the slightest variations. The notion that a Sapphic line was in part unregulated or amorphous is the opposite of the truth.

The first two syllables in certain forms of Aeolian verse may be said to be unregulated; but it does not follow quite certainly that this part of the verse was 'syllabic' or amorphous. Several different forms of it, it may be, were definitely recognized and permitted. The same may be the case with the 'polyschematist' dimeter. If the first four syllables of it were entirely unregulated we should expect to find all the sixteen combinations that are arithmetically possible, but it is admitted that only nine of them are actually found.

There are at least three quite definite arguments which we may advance against Aeolic or quadrisyllabic scansion.

(i) The first has been already anticipated. It consists in pointing out that Sappho could extend a Glyconic line by introducing a dactyl—on the dactylic theory, a second dactyl—and use this line in a three-line stanza with two Glyconics; and further (*supra*, p. 134), that rising, as it were, out of the Glyconic, we seem to have *two* parallel scales or series, one obtained by the insertion of dactyls, the other by the insertion of what, on the dactylic theory, are only 'apparent' choriambi ($-\cup\cup-\wedge$), and that the dactylic expansion seems to show that the first two syllables are a disyllabic basis.

But this is not the only form that this argument takes. There is perhaps also expansion or extension by the insertion of a single trochee, notably in the case of scolia. Scansion by means of choriambi, diiambi, and Ionics explains some lines, and then breaks down in others.

A common form of stanza in scolia began with two Phalaeceans, and the Phalaecean, as we have seen, is capable of Ionic or quadrisyllabic analysis.

ὑγιαίνειν μὲν ἄριστον ἀνδρὶ θνητῷ

looks promising for the quadrisyllabist metrician ⋅

∪∪ − − | ∪∪ − ∪ | − ∪ − −,

but the next line is less tractable:

δεύτερον δὲ φυὰν καλὸν γενέσθαι

− ∪ − | ∪∪ − ∪ | − ∪ − −;

the third line:

τὸ τρίτον δὲ πλουτεῖν ἀδόλως

presents to us a five-syllable group,

∪∪ − ∪ − | − ∪∪ −,

but no further difficulty, and the fourth looks like a perfect ' Aeolic ' trimeter:

καὶ τὸ τέταρτον ἡβᾶν μετὰ τῶν φίλων

− ∪∪ − | ∪ − − ∪ | ∪ − ∪ −,

choriamb, antispast, and diiambus. It occurs also in Aristophanes, and is scanned by Mr. White in that way:

ἐστὶ δίκαιον εἰ δημοκρατούμεθα

− ∪∪ − | ∪ − − ∪ | ∪ − ∪ ⏒.

But this line coincides with a double dochmius, and if it is that it is divided in the middle into two equal parts, like

μήτε σε θυμοπλη|θὴς δορίμαργος ἆ|τα κτλ.

Apart from this agreement with a double dochmius, the line also perhaps occurs *with an additional trochee in it*, though the text is not altogether certain:

Τυδείδην τέ φασιν ἐσθλὸν Διομήδεα

and

εὐφροσύναισι, ταῖσδ' ἀοιδαῖς κεχαρημένος,[1]

---

[1] The text of the first line is reported to be φασὶ τὸν ἐσθλόν, and of the other εὐφροσύναις ταῖς δ' ἀοιδαῖς. The lines are brought into agreement with other examples of the closing line (1) by deleting ἐσθλόν, (2) by reading εὔφροσι ταῖσδ' ἀοιδαῖς (there are other conjectures).

that is, by quadrisyllabic division :

$$-\cup\cup-\,|\,-\cup-\cup-\,|\,-\cup\cup-\,|\,\cup\overset{\cup}{\_},$$

where the two syllables at the end, εα, are not at all happily accounted for. On the other theory thé latter part of the line is simply the familiar Aeolian tripody, and what precedes is similar (sometimes called 'first Glyconic' from the place of the dactyl):

$$-\cup\cup\,-\cup\,-\cup\,\llcorner\,|\,-\cup\cup\,-\cup\,\overset{\cup}{\_};$$

and it is impossible to dissociate this line from Sappho's

μελλίχιος δ' ἐπ' ἰμέρ|τῳ κέχυται προσώπῳ,

where quadrisyllabic scansion leaves us with κέχυται προσώπῳ to be accounted for ($\cup\cup-\cup\,|\,--$).

(ii) The second argument is not a new one. Recent material supplied by one of the Aeolists themselves seems to strengthen it a little.

It consists in the fact that a shortening such as is seen in φαίνομαῖ εἶναι belongs conspicuously to dactylic verse, and is also found in Aeolic verse, where the Aeolists deny that there is any dactyl at all.

This shortening of a final vowel before a following vowel is altogether alien to iambic or trochaic verse. It is unimaginable that a trochaic line could begin δέξαῖ ὦ πάντων ἄριστε, or an iambic line with καὶ δέξαῖ ἡμᾶς or πρόκειταῖ οἰκτρός.[1] One of two syllables is assimilated to a short that follows it (as in παῦροῖ ὅμως) or precedes it. Hence it is admitted also in anapaests and in regular Ionics (ἐθελήσεις τί μοι οὖν, ὦ πάτερ, ἥν σου τι δεηθῶ; ∪∪— — ∪∪— —, &c.).

It is seen in Aeolic verse in

        ἀμφί μοῖ αὖτε, Φοῖβ' ἄναξ,   (*Clouds* 595.)
        γῆς τε καῖ ἁλμυρᾶς θαλάσσης,   (*Ibid.* 567.)
        ἐν τῷ τρόπῳ ὡς λέγεις,   (*Knights* 1133.)

and also in the *Persae* of Timotheus:

        ἔνθα κείσομαῖ οἰκτρὸς ὀρ-
        νίθων ἐναλίων βορά,

---

[1] Horace's *Esquilinae alites* is very exceptional. Reasons will be given (Chap. III, § ii) for thinking that the final syllable of *Esquilinae* is not to be thought of as shortened. It is a case of unmitigated *hiatus*. It resembles the *o* of *Glauco*, not the *ae* of *Panopeae*, in Virgil's line:

    Glaucŏ | ęt Panopeăe et Inoo Melicertae.

where quadrisyllabic scansion sunders the two short syllables of
κείσομαι ($-\cup-\cup\mid\cup-\cup-$, μαῖ οἰκτρὸς ὀρ). Mr. White has collected
all such shortenings in Aristophanes, and the result is instructive
in a way that has not occurred to him. The great majority of
course are in anapaestic tetrameters and dactylic hexameters
(*Verse of Greek Comedy*, §§ 798–9). Then he collects those that are
in other metres (§ 800). 'Of these exceptions one is Ionic, four are
trochaic, two paeonic-trochaic, three anapaestic, one enoplic, six
Aeolic, and, as we should expect from the dominating influence of
Homer, twelve dactylic.' Now in the other metres, including the
Aeolic, the text is invariably sound, and there is no doubt whatever
about the shortening. But of the passages classified as trochaic or
paeonic-trochaic there is not one that is free from doubt. In two
of them it is not metrically certain that the syllable *is* shortened
(in *Thesm.* 1150 it is at least as likely that it is elided), and in the
others the text which Mr. White adopts would not be accepted or
allowed to be certain by editors. The passages have been read
otherwise, not solely on metrical grounds, or, if on metrical grounds,
not solely to get rid of the shortening. This is a rather remarkable
fact. It is not a positive proof perhaps. But it certainly strengthens
the belief that when a shortening like κείσομαῖ occurs the foot is
a dactyl.

(iii) Sometimes a familiar Aeolic line, such as the Alcaic deca-
syllable, occurs in a context where the quadrisyllabic scansion
cannot be applied to it.

> τὸ δ' ἔνθεν, ἄμμες δ' ἂν τὸ μέσσον
> νᾶϊ φορήμεθα σὺν μελαίνᾳ

is, according to the Aeolists,

$\overset{\smile}{-}-\cup-\mid--\cup-\mid--\cup\cup\mid-\cup\cup-\mid\cup--$

(-μες δ' ἀϑ τὸ μέσ|σον νᾶϊ φο|ρήμεθα σὺν | μελαίνᾳ). It is difficult,
at the best, to read an Alcaic stanza in this way, and to write Alcaics
with such a scheme in mind would be more difficult still. But
apart from that the last line occurs in contexts where there is no
long syllable before it to make up the Ionic foot. For example, in
Aes. *P. V.* 166–7:

> (πρὶν ἂν) ἢ κορέσῃ κέαρ ἢ παλάμᾳ τινὶ
> τὰν δυσάλωτον ἕλῃ τις ἀρχάν,

where it is plainly preceded by dactyls:

$$-\cup\cup\ -\cup\cup\ -\cup\cup\ -\cup\cup$$
$$-\cup\cup\ -\cup\cup\ -\cup\ --.$$

This we have already found in Alcman, the Alcaic *clausula* at the end of a strophe of some length and immediately preceded by dactyls. In another of Alcman's strophae what answers to it is

ἄλαστα δὲ
ἔργα πάσον (= ἔπαθον) κακὰ μησάμενοι
$-\cup\cup\ -\cup\cup\ -\cup\cup-.$

Here it is difficult to avoid recognizing three dactyls; thus we have a dactylic dipody catalectic ($-\cup\cup\ -\overline{\wedge}$) answering to $-\cup--$. The syllables $-\cup\cup-$ at the end of a line are not necessarily a choriambus.

The Indo-European theory is not the only shape in which quadrisyllabic scansion is imposed upon verse of the Glyconic type. The 'acephalous' form of a Glyconic line can also be taken as Ionic. Thus

ὦ δῆμε, καλήν γ' ἔχεις
ἀρχὴν ὅτι πάντες ἄν-
θρωποι κτλ.

may be either (o) $o-\cup\ |\ \cup-\cup-$ (Aeolic) or it may be $--\cup\cup\ |\ -\cup-\wedge$ (Ionic).[1] One is a survival from primeval times. The other, Ionicization, is a kind of malady that invades verse in later ages. The history of lyric verse is therefore complicated by two quite different possibilities of quadrisyllabic scansion. How long did the former survive (if it ever really existed)? How early did the other begin (that it had some vogue is certain)? For the complete solution of the problems involved in these questions it is probable that much more extensive evidence would be necessary than we now possess. We want some fifth or sixth-century account of metrical composition—a thing not to be hoped for, though it is

---

[1] $-\cup-\underline{\vee}$ is often found among Ionics *a maiori* as an alternative or equivalent. In Sotades it may occur three times running:

σαρκικὸν γὰρ εἶχε χρῶτα καὶ τὸ δέρμ' ὅμοιον
beside   ἂν χρυσοφορῇς, τοῦτο τύχης ἐστὶν ἔπαρμα.
$$-\cup-\cup\ |\ -\cup-\cup\ |\ -\cup-\cup\ |\ -\underline{\vee}\overline{\wedge}$$
and
$$--\cup\cup\ |\ --\cup\cup\ |\ --\cup\cup\ |\ -\underline{\vee}\overline{\wedge}.$$

perhaps just possible that a fifth-century work, such as the Ἐπιδημίαι of Ion might contain very instructive passages bearing on metre. We want also more extensive texts, more of Stesichorus, to name only one early poet, and more of Anacreon, who seems to have been a poet of great skill and versatility. 'Ionicization' will be considered when we have reviewed Ionics themselves and have discussed 'prosodiac-enoplic' verse.

II. SIMPLE OR HOMOGENEOUS METRES (μονοειδῆ)

Doubts and difficulties about lyric verse arise chiefly where feet of different kinds are combined. But there are some lyric systems of a simpler type in which the same foot is used throughout, μέτρα μονοειδῆ, employing only one εἶδος of rhythm. Even here we shall not escape controversy; we may be asked, at the outset: 'Do you mean that for this purpose iambic is one εἶδος and trochaic another? Or do both belong to the same εἶδος, since the ratio between the parts of the foot is the same (2 : 1, λόγος διπλάσιος)?' To this we may provisionally reply: 'Spoken iambic and trochaic verse, trimeters and tetrameters, are certainly very different things, but in strictly lyric compositions iambus and trochee may be regarded as belonging to the same εἶδος. Consider, for example, Aes. *Agam.* 438-48:

> ὁ χρυσαμοιβὸς δ' Ἄρης σωμάτων
> καὶ ταλαντοῦχος ἐν μάχῃ δορὸς κτλ.

Some of the lines almost certainly have an iambic, some a trochaic, beginning. But there is absolutely *no* change in the tone of the passage, the voice of melancholy foreboding is the same throughout. Real iambi have a different ἦθος from trochaics. Is it not safest to suppose that for Aeschylus such a system was not iambic in one place and trochaic in other, but, throughout, either or neither or both?'

We have thus been dragged back into the turbid waters of controversy at the very outset:

> rursus in bellum resorbens
> unda fretis tulit aestuosis.

But let us try to select examples which raise no large questions. Doubts about a detail here and there we can hardly expect to escape in dealing with any ancient verse. Let us first keep to 'descending' rhythms as far as possible, avoiding iambi and anapaests.

Specimens of simple verse, μέτρα μονοειδῆ, of course fall into three classes according to the nature of the foot or rhythm. If we begin with the shortest there are: (1) trochee (– ⌣, ratio 2 : 1, ⌣⌣ | ⌣); (2) dactyl (– ⌣ ⌣, ratio 2 : 2, ἴσος, ⌣ ⌣ | ⌣ ⌣); (3) cretic or paean (– ⌣ –, ratio 3 : 2, ἡμιόλιος, ⌣ ⌣ ⌣ | ⌣ ⌣). The first εἶδος includes iamb (and tribrach), the second anapaest (and 'proceleusmaticus'). The Greeks did not make the iambus a separate εἶδος from the trochee; obviously trochees and iambi are most conveniently regarded as *sub*-species or different *forms* of the same. Another way of putting this is to say that they are different for μετρική, but the same for ῥυθμική. βαίνονται μὲν οἱ ῥυθμοί, τὰ δὲ μέτρα διαιρεῖται—βαίνω is *scando* and does *not* mean what we mean by 'scan'; when an Englishman 'scans' a verse what he usually does is μέτρα διαιρεῖν.

The following are simple specimens of verse in each εἶδος.

(i) *Trochaic* (or more simply, ἐν διπλασίῳ λόγῳ, if we think that both 'trochaic' and 'iambic' are words of doubtful validity for what is strictly lyrical).

Aes. *Eum.* 916 f.:

> δέξομαι Παλλάδος ξυνοικίαν,
> οὐδ' ἀτιμάσω πόλιν,
> τὰν καὶ Ζεὺς ὁ παγκρατὴς Ἄρης τε

GREEK LYRIC VERSE

φρούριον θεῶν νέμει
ῥυσίβωμον Ἑλλάνων ἄγαλμα δαιμόνων.
ᾆτ' ἐγὼ κατεύχομαι
θεσπίσασα πρευμενῶς
ἐπισσύτους βίου τύχας ὀνησίμους
γαίας ἐξαμβρῦσαι
φαιδρὸν ἡλίου σέλας.

This is the whole stanza or strophe. The learner should at first perhaps confine his attention to the first five lines, since there is in them *nothing* at all doubtful. They run:

```
- ∪ - ∧ - ∪ - ∪ - ∪ - ∧
- ∪ - ∪ - ∪ - ∧
⌴ ⌴  - ∪ - ∪ - ∪ - ∪
- ∪ - ∪ - ∪ - ∧
- ∪ - ∪ ⌴  ⌴ | - ∪ - ∪ - ∪ - ∧ .
```

There is nothing really doubtful, for it is incredible that the two contiguous long syllables in the third and fifth lines should be heavy or irrational trochees (sometimes written − >). The irrational trochee is not a thing that may occur anywhere; the country in which it is to be found is quite definitely mapped out. It comes in the group − ∪ − ⌣ (ditrochaeus), and it comes also, for example, at the beginning of a logaoedic line like

δῆμός τοί σε καλεῖ γυναι-.[1]

To assume it here would make the second line one of *five* feet, and the last would be 3+4. δέξομαι may be either − ∪ − ∧ or − ∪ ⌴. In the antistrophe we must assume protraction of a syllable rather than a pause within a word (δενδροπῆμων δὲ μὴ πνέοι βλάβα).

The remaining five lines are not so completely free from

---

[1] Of course when this is taken as 'Aeolic' (− − − ∪ | ∪ − ∪ −) it is not there (cf. *supra*, p. 136).

what is dubious. Is the third iambic? (It is certainly not at all like a trimeter, for it is divided as no trimeter—outside conversation in comedy—could be ; so too in the antistrophe.

τρέφοι χρόνῳ | τεταγμένῳ· | γόνος [δ' ἀεί].)

Or should the lines be written

θεσπίσασα πρευμενῶς ἐ-
πισσύτους βίου τύχας ὀνησίμους ?

Or may we leave them as they stand, *without* thinking of the second as 'iambic'? The last line but one presents a different problem. It consists of six long syllables. What was it? Certainly *not* three irrational or heavy trochees. It is not quite so unlikely—but still improbable—that it was $-\,{>}\,\smile\,-\,{>}\,\smile$. Without Aeschylus's music all we can do is to suppose that it was a line of six syncopated feet, $\smile\,\smile\,\smile\,\smile\,\smile\,\smile$.

Having followed the structure of this lyric the learner should take as an exercise another lyric of the same type, and analyse it for himself, e.g. *Persae* 115 f.

ταῦτά μοι μελαγχίτων
φρὴν ἀμύσσεται φόβῳ,
ὀᾶ, Περσικοῦ στρατεύματος
τοῦδε, μὴ πόλις πύθη-
ται κένανδρον μέγ' ἄστυ Σουσίδος.

Here he may regard ὀᾶ as *extra metrum*. It may not have been that, but without Aeschylus's music we do not know how it was treated. In this example he will find syncopated feet not contiguous as in the passage of the *Eumenides*, but alternating (μὴ πόλις πύθη—ται κέναν—δρον μέγ' ἄστυ Σουσίδος). In the next strophe, 126 f. (πᾶς γὰρ ἱππηλάτας κτλ.), he will be called upon to discover such alternation more frequently, and his knowledge of 'prosody' will be tested by τὸν ἀμφί-ζευκτον ἐξαμείψας (= $\smile\,\smile\,\smile\,-\,\smile\,-\,\smile\,-\,\underset{\smile}{-}$ or more probably, at the end, $-\,\smile\,\smile\,-\,\wedge$). 131 ἀμφοτέρας ἅλιον, a dactylic colon, he will disregard for the present, but he will later come to recognize a liking in Aeschylus for a short dactylic strain just before the close of a trochaic system (e. g. *Agam.* 416 f. = 433 f. and 452 f. = 471 f., where the trochaic rhythm is resumed or reasserted in the clausula). Another simple strophe of the same type is *Agam.* 160–7, Ζεύς, ὅστις ποτ' ἐστίν κτλ. (Here also there is a dactylic phrase before the close, longer than ἀμφοτέρας ἄλιον — πλὴν Διός, εἰ τὸ μάταν ἀπὸ φροντίδος ἄχθος), and the following system, 176 f. τὸν φρονεῖν βροτοὺς ὁδώσαντα κτλ., would furnish a similar exercise.

(ii) *Dactylic* (ἐν ἴσῳ λόγῳ).

Systems that are dactylic from beginning to end are not very common in tragedy. Stesichorus probably wrote purely dactylic lyrics, but the extant passages are not long enough to prove this. Aristophanes has several dactylic systems. Sometimes in tragedy the non-dactylic element is very slight. Thus in the epode in Aes. *Pers.* 897 f. the clausula alone is trochaic (907–8):

(δμαθέντες μεγάλως πλα-)
γαῖσι ποντίαισιν,

while strophae α', β', and γ' alike have two trochaic phrases each, one as a *clausula* and one earlier (866 οὐδ' ἀφ' ἑστίας συθείς, 870 Θρηκίων ἐπαύλων).

Dactylic verse differs from anapaestic in several ways. An anapaest may take dactylic shape ($-\smile\smile$), but a dactyl never takes anapaestic, it is never $\smile\smile-$. Resolution is extremely rare, rarer than in lyric anapaests. The 'dimeter' or tetrapody is very frequent, but not dominant as in anapaests.

A rule of Aristoxenus makes the maximum colon in this type of rhythm (τετράσημον, $\smile\smile\smile\smile$) a group of four feet. Various shorter κῶλα are possible, besides, and some have more vogue than others. A few of the prevalent groups may be enumerated.

(a) Dimeter or tetrapody, ending either in $-\cup\cup$ or $--$:

πολλάκι δ' ἐν κορυφαῖς ὀρέων, ὅκα
θεοῖσιν ἅδῃ πολύφαμος ἑορτά.   (Alcman.)

When the last foot is a dactyl the construction is 'hypermetric'; another dactylic line must follow, without hiatus.[1]

(b) Tripody, complete or catalectic:

ὦ Διὸς ἁδυεπὲς φάτι,
τίς ποτε τᾶς πολυχρύσου.   (*O. T.*)

It may also begin with a spondee:

παμμίκτων τ' ἐπικούρων.   (*Pers.*)

Catalectic:

ἀέναοι νεφέλαι.   (Ar. *Nub.*)
ἀμφοτέρας ἅλιον.   (*Supra*, p. 146.)

(c) Dipody or 'monometer', usually ending in a spondee, and often making with a tetrapody the lyric counterpart of a 'bucolic' hexameter, but found also in the form $-\cup\cup\ -\cup\cup$.

One of the few wholly dactylic systems in tragedy occurs in the *Phoenissae* of Euripides (l. 784 f.):

ὦ πολύμοχθος Ἄρης, τί ποθ' αἵματι
καὶ θανάτῳ κατέχει Βρομίου παράμουσος ἑορταῖς;
οὐκ ἐπὶ καλλιχόροις στεφάνοισι νεάνιδος ὥρας
βόστρυχον ἀμπετάσας λωτοῦ κατὰ πνεύματα μέλπει
5 μοῦσαν, ἐν ᾇ χάριτες χοροποιοί.

ὦ ζαθέων πετάλων πολυθηρότα-   ἀντ.
τον νάπος, Ἀρτέμιδος χιονοτρόφον ὄμμα, Κιθαιρών,
μήποτε τὸν θανάτῳ προτεθέντα, λόχευμ' Ἰοκάστας,
ὤφελες Οἰδιπόδαν κομίσαι, βρέφος ἔκβολον οἴκων,

---

[1] In *Pax* 789-90 Mr. White assumes this dactylic ending before anapaests:

ὄρτυγας οἰκογενεῖς γυλιαύχενας $-\cup\cup-\cup\cup-\cup\cup-\cup\cup$
ὀρχηστὰς ναννοφυεῖς σφυράδων $----\cup\cup-\cup\cup-$.

The effect is at best very rare, and it may be doubted whether the lines are rightly so divided.

GREEK LYRIC VERSE

5 χρυσοδέτοις περόναις ἐπίσαμον·
μηδὲ τὸ παρθένιον πτερόν, οὔρειον τέρας, ἐλθεῖν | πένθεα
γαίας
Σφιγγὸς ἀμουσοτάταισι συν ᾠδαῖς,
ἅ ποτε Καδμογενῆ τετραβάμοσι χαλαῖς
τείχεσι χριμπτομένα φέρεν αἰθέρος εἰς ἄβατον φῶς
10 γένναν, τὰν ὁ κατὰ χθονὸς Ἀΐδας
Καδμείοις ἐπιπέμπει· δυσδαίμων δ' ἔρις ἄλλα.

The only serious doubts arise in regard to the division of κῶλα. The seventh and ninth lines are clearly tetrapodies. Line 4 is likely to be tetrapody + dipody (bucolic division suggested by the words—but we cannot be quite sure that the division was there): line 8 may have the same division. Line 6 may be supposed to be. 3 + 3 + 2. Lines 2 and 3 would perhaps be best taken as 2½ + 3½, divided as hexameters (line 3 contains an effect that is not permitted in the epic hexameter, *supra* p. 21).

The dactylic lyric in the *Clouds* is well known (275 f.):

ἀέναοι νεφέλαι,
ἀρθῶμεν φανεραὶ δροσερὰν φύσιν εὐάγητον
πατρὸς ἀπ' Ὠκεανοῦ βαρυαχέος
ὑψηλῶν ὀρέων κορυφὰς ἐπὶ
280 δενδροκόμους ἵνα
τηλεφανεῖς σκοπιὰς ἀφορώμεθα
καρπούς τ' ἀρδομέναν θ' ἱερὰν χθόνα
καὶ ποταμῶν ζαθέων κελαδήματα
καὶ πόντον κελάδοντα βαρύβρομον·
285 ὄμμα γὰρ αἰθέρος
ἀκάματον σελαγεῖται
μαρμαρέαις ἐν αὐγαῖς.
ἀλλ' ἀποσεισάμεναι νέφος ὄμβριον
ἀθανάτας ἰδέας ἐπιδώμεθα
290 τηλεσκόπῳ ὄμματι γαῖαν.

The first line is catalectic, $-\cup\cup\ -\cup\cup\ -\overline{\wedge}$, with a very natural pause after the vocative. There is of course no reason against hiatus between this line and the next. The next is no doubt 4+2. Then follow two tetrapodies of the type first seen in Alcman, then a similar dipody (δενδροκόμους ἵνα); then four dimeters or tetrapodies of the same hypermetric type; next 2+3, probably (in the antistrophe 'εὐστέφανοί τε θε‖ῶν θυσίαι θαλίαι τε). Line 287 was not certainly dactylic. If we read μαρμαρέαις ἐν αὐγαῖς it is a logaoedic line, but it is easily made dactylic by reading it μαρμαρέαισιν ἐν αὐγαῖς (and in the antistrophe παντοδαπαῖσιν ἐν ὥραις). The presence of a logaoedic line is not incredible, but it would be more likely if it were the last of the whole system. Here the final clausula is a paroemiac or catalectic anapaestic dimeter.

The dactylic verse of lyrics has several marked characteristics as compared with the hexameter. Spondees are rare, occurring chiefly at the end or at the beginning of a colon.[1] Trochaic caesura is avoided: only one melic hexameter in Aristophanes has it, but in recited hexameters, epic or mock-heroic, it is frequent.[2] Shortening of a long vowel before another is not excluded (e.g. παρθένοι ὀμβροφόροι), but it is not frequent.

'Bucolic' division of a group of six feet (4+2) is now and again suggested by the words:

ἔστι τι τῶνδ' ἐτύμως; εἴπ', ὦ πάτερ, | εἴ τι φιλεῖς με.
(*Pax* 118.)

εἰπέ μοι, ὦ χρυσέας τέκνον ἐλπίδος, ἄμβροτε φάμα.
(Soph. *O. T.* 158.)

But that a lyric line of six dactyls was regularly divided in the

---

[1] Θήβας· ἐκτέταμαι φοβερὰν φρένα δείματι πάλλων, *O.T.* In this lyric verse does resemble epic (χραισμεῖν, εὖτ' ἂν πολλοί, *supra*, p. 25).

[2] Forty lines out of 142 have it, according to Mr. White's statistics (*Verse of Greek Com.*, § 363).

ratio 4 : 2 seems to be rather a theory than a thing that can be seen in actual texts. Sappho's divided hexameter:

> ἴψοι δὴ τὸ μέλαθρον
> Ὑμήναον
> ἀέρρετε, τέκτονες ἄνδρες,

is against it. Division between words perhaps does not count for much as evidence of division in a lyric, and some forms of lyric verse even preferred to make a κῶλον end in the middle of a word, but the forms in which this certainly happens are not as a rule purely dactylic. To impose a scheme of 4+2 gives results like these:

> ἡνίκ' ἂν ὀξυλάλον παρίδῃ θή|γοντος ὀδόντα.
> (*Ran.* 815.)
> ἀργαλέων τ' ἐν ὅπλοις ξυνόδων. Κλεο|φῶν δὲ μάχεσθω.
> (*Ib.* 1532.)

In the former passage (where the same strophe is repeated four times) one of the lines consists of five dactyls, and in all four strophae the division suggested by the words is penthemimeral:

> ῥήματα δαιομένη | καταλεπτολογήσει. (828.)[1]

The dactylic system here closes with a trochaic dimeter catalectic as a *clausula*. So also at 883 a short trochaic line closes a system of dactyls. So, too, in *Agam.* 104-21 the penultimate line is trochaic (βλαβέντα λοισθίων δρόμων). This is prepared for by two brief trochaic movements in l. 108 and l. 116; and it prepares the way for trochees in the next strophe, 160 f. So in *Oed. C.* 228-35 there is a trochaic (or iambic) ending.

---

[1] There is an anapaestic pentapody in *Ach.* 285 (= 336): σὲ μὲν οὖν καταλεύσομεν, ὦ μιαρὰ κεφαλή, which has been taken to be a brachycataectic trimeter in logaoedic time. Is it possible that Aristoxenus's limitation was not absolute or universally valid?

(iii) *Paeonic* or *Cretic* (ἐν λόγῳ ἡμιολίῳ).

A 'paeonic' foot, with the ratio 3 : 2, may be – ∪ – ('cretic') or – ∪ ∪ ∪ (first paeon, which is very common), or ∪ ∪ ∪ – (which is less frequent, and quite rare in Aristophanes); the possible forms that intervene, ∪ – ∪ ∪ and ∪ ∪ – ∪, can hardly be said to exist as real elements in metre.

It is now generally agreed that a five-time rhythm is not a fiction of theorists, but was actually in use. Some nineteenth-century metricians explained away paeonics as trochees with syncopation (– ∪ ⌊, ⌊ ∪ ∪ ∪, &c., six times, not five). The discovery of the Delphic hymns helped to establish the reality of cretics. Von Wilamowitz holds that the paeon is *derived from* trochaic verse, the second long in a trochaic dipody having been lightened to answer to a light footfall in the dance (– ∪ ∪́ ∪ taking the place of – ∪ – ∪). But 'derivation' of metres, in which the Greeks expatiated, is a region in which there are very few definite landmarks to guide the traveller.

The simplest extant specimen of purely paeonic verse is in Acs. *Suppl.* 418 f.:

φρόντισον καὶ γενοῦ
πανδίκως εὐσεβὴς
πρόξενος· τὰν φυγάδα μὴ προδῷς
τὰν ἕκαθεν ἐκβολαῖς
δυσθέοις ὁρμέναν.

The next strophe begins with a line of three cretics:

μή τι τλῇς τὰν ἱκέτιν εἰσιδεῖν,

but the rest of it consists of dochmii.

It will be observed that the structure is 'hypermetric'; there is no hiatus or *syllaba anceps*. The number of feet is uneven; either one stood alone, or there is a group of three. The latter alternative is the more probable, as the beginning of the next strophe helps to show. Authorities later than Aristoxenus make a group of three the longest permissible. Aristoxenus laid down the strange rule that as many as five (answering to the number of times in the foot) could form one κῶλον (twenty-five times). It is difficult to believe this, if dactylic κῶλα were limited to sixteen times.

Cretics appear with some frequency in the earlier plays of Aristophanes, and they are common also in Roman comedy. The Ἰχνευταί of Sophocles furnishes several good examples of a cretic lyric in a satyric play. They are frequently associated with trochaics, and sometimes it is not quite certain that we have real cretics. It is not true that all cretics were syncopated trochees, but some apparent cretics may be. The doubt arises in regard to the cretics in the δέσμιος ὕμνος of the Furies in Aes. *Eum.* 328:

ἐπὶ δὲ τῷ τεθυμένῳ
τόδε μέλος, παρακοπά,

(∪∪∪ –, the 'fourth paeon', or ∪∪∪ ⌞, a trochaic dipody). The greatest poem that has come down to us, in cretic verse, is the second Olympian ode of Pindar.[1] There are many difficulties about its metrical construction. They are difficulties of detail which cannot be discussed here. In the following text of the first strophe and epode cretics are marked where they are clear and certain. In two lines bacchii or 'antibacchii' should perhaps be recognized (– – ∪ or ∪ – –), a form of 'paeonic' foot which is rare in the extant Greek drama, but frequent in Plautus.

στρ. α΄.

– ∪ – | – ∪ –
ἀναξιφόρμιγγες ὕμνοι,
   – ∪ – | – ∪ ∪∪ | – ∪ ∪∪ | – ∪ ⌣
τίνα θεόν, τίν᾽ ἥρωα, τίνα δ᾽ ἄνδρα κελαδήσομεν;

---

[1] Another remarkable poem, partly in cretics, but not cretic throughout, is the story of Theseus and Minos in Bacchylides (xvi). The student of cretic verse should read also the two Delphic hymns—of the third century B.C.—in very regular cretics (text in *Musici Scriptores Graeci*, Teubner, p. 435 f.).

GREEK LYRIC VERSE

∪∪ ∪ − | ∪∪∪ −|− ∪ −|− ∪−
ἤτοι Πίσα μὲν Διός· Ὀλυμπιάδα δ' ἔστασεν Ἡρακλέης

− ∪−|∪ ∪∪−
ἀκρόθινα πολέμου·

− ∪ ∪∪| −∪ − | ∪∪∪ −|− ∪ −
5 Θήρωνα δὲ τετραορίας ἕνεκα νικαφόρου

∪ − −|∪∪ ∪ − | ∪ − − | ∪−⏞
γεγωνητέον ὄπιν δίκαιον ξένων

∪ − −| ∪ − ⏑
ἔρεισμ' Ἀκράγαντος

εὐωνύμων τε πατέρων ἄωτον ὀρθόπολιν.

The division of the third line is very doubtful. Between the first and second lines it will be observed that the syllables -οι τίνα θε- do make a paeonic foot. The last line is not certainly cretic throughout. Cretics or bacchii can be found in the first half of it, but it is quite likely that there was a non-cretic clausula, as there plainly is in the epode:

(εὔφρων ἄρουραν ἔτι πατρίαν σφίσιν κόμισον)
ἐπῳδός

− ∪ − | − ∪ −| − ∪ −
λοιπῷ γένει. τῶν δὲ πεπραγμένων

− ∪∪∪|− ∪ −|−∪ −?
ἐν δίκᾳ τε καὶ παρὰ δίκαν ἀποίητον οὐδ' ἂν

∪∪ − − ∪ ∪∪ − | − ∪⏑
χρόνος ὁ πάντων πατὴρ δύναιτο θέμεν ἔργων τέλος·

− ∪ −| − ∪ −|−∪∪ ∪|− ⏑
λάθα δὲ πότμῳ σὺν εὐδαίμονι γένοιτ' ἄν·

− ∪ ∪∪|− ∪ −|−∪ −
5 ἐσλῶν γὰρ ὑπὸ χαρμάτων πῆμα θνάσκει
παλίγκοτον δαμασθέν.

The clausula is clearly trochaic or iambic, and in lines 2 and 3 it is not unlikely that this was foreshadowed by some

trochaic movement, perhaps ἐν δίκᾳ τε καὶ | παρὰ δίκαν ἀποι-,
$-\cup-\cup-\wedge\cup\cup\cup\,|-\cup|\llcorner$. Line 3 can be construed as
paeonic only if we are prepared to bring in a 'second paeon'
and bacchii, thus $\cup\cup\cup-|-\cup-|\cup-\cup\cup|\cup--|\cup-\overline{\wedge}$.
τῶν πατὴρ δύναι- would be a trochaic phrase like those
which can be found in the preceding line. The catalexis
seen in the fourth line is found also in Alcman:

$$-\cup-|--$$
Ἀφροδίτα μὲν οὐκ ἔστι μάργος δ' ἔρως οἷα παῖς παίσδει.

It is found in Plautus, but is rare in Aristophanes' Comedies
It is the cadence which coincides with the end of a scazon
(*supra*, p. 98), and with the familiar 'esse videatur' of Roman
oratory.[1]

In addition to the three great types of verse which we have
now illustrated there are two other kinds of metre which can
be called μονοειδῆ, *dochmiac* and *Ionic*, in which the same
foot (though with considerable variations in both cases) is
used throughout. Regular Ionics are clearly ἐν διπλασίῳ
λόγῳ: $--\cup\cup$ is a duplicated trochee, 4 : 2 for 2 : 1, and
whatever broken or anaclastic Ionics really were, it is not
likely that their rhythm constituted a different γένος or εἶδος.
It is not clear that dochmii did not. They are described as
an ὀκτάσημος ῥυθμός, and there is the authority of Quintilian
and of the Scholiast on *Heph.*, c. 10. 3, for regarding the foot

---

[1] Terentianus speaks of the cretic as a highly effective foot both for
verse and for oratory:

> optimus pes et melodis et pedestri gloriae.
> plurimum orantes decebit, quando paene in ultimo
> obtinet sedem, beatam terminet si clausulam
> δάκτυλος, σπονδεῖος imam, nec τροχαῖον respuo

(i.e. it should be penultimate, followed by dactyl, spondee, or trochee.
With spondee or trochee it is $-\cup-|-\cup$. When a dactyl follows
the ending is really in a double cretic, $-\cup-|-\cup\cup$, the last syllable
being *anceps*. These are the first and second of Zielinski's preferred or
favourite cadences).

as divided in the ratio 5 : 3 or 3 : 5 (τριὰς πρὸς πεντάδα). Dochmii are easy in one way and difficult in another. What they really were and how they were arrived at is a very obscure question. The forms they assume, in syllables, are quite definite, and it is generally easy to recognize and scan and read them. To do this is important for the study of tragedy. It is to tragedy that they belong (though they are of course found in comedy also, where many tragic effects are parodied), and they seem to have been devised to express the intense feelings of distress or suspense or despair which accompany the crisis of a tragic action. (It is a rhythm ἐπιτήδειος πρὸς θρήνους καὶ στεναγμούς, Schol. on Aes. S. c. Th. 98.)

The normal form of a dochmius is ∪ − − ∪ −. Each of the long syllables may be resolved, and both the short syllables may be irrational—actually long, if counting as short (>). An irrational first syllable, with resolution of the second, would give > ∪ ∪ − ∪ −, but whether this form was arrived at in that way is uncertain. Of the many theories which have been advanced about the origin of the dochmius, one, the most recent, Mr. White's, is perhaps the most promising, or the least unpromising. He suggests that it is derived from an iambic tripody, ⏒ − ∪ − ∪ −, by total suppression of the third syllable.[1] The short syllable, he thinks, was not represented by a pause or by protraction of an adjacent syllable (which would leave the rhythm still ἐννεάσημος), but dropped entirely so that the total time is eight χρόνοι and the foot is 'oblique' or 'askew', δόχμιος, twisted or distorted to express mental anxiety or agony.[2] The usual

---

[1] Compare Aes. *Suppl.* 911 :

διωλόμεσθ'· ἄελπτ', ἄναξ, πάσχομεν,

where three iambi precede a dochmius : ∪ − ∪ − ∪ − | ∪ − − ∪ −.

[2] Wilamowitz, in his most recent book (*Sappho und S.*, p. 183), throws out a suggestion which would undermine all such attempts to show that

line consists of two dochmii, and a line of the same form occurs occasionally outside tragedy, e.g. Pindar, *Ol.* i:

ἀκέντητον ἐν δρόμοισι παρέχων,

but this may be an accidental coincidence in syllables. The rhythm of Pindar's line may have been quite different. Dochmii are abundant in the *S. c. Th.*, where they express the alarm and anxiety of the chorus for the fate of their city, besieged by the Argive host; or their agonized appeals to Eteocles (686 f.) to refrain from combat with his brother. Except for a few iambi and cretics[1] the whole of the first utterance of the chorus is dochmiac (78–180), and the opening of it will serve as an example of the metre:

> θρέομαι φοβερὰ μεγάλ' ἄχη·
> μεθεῖται στρατός· στρατόπεδον λιπὼν
> ῥεῖ πολὺς ὅδε λεὼς πρόδρομος ἱππότας·
> αἰθερία κόνις με πείθει φανεῖσ'
> 5 ἄναυδος σαφὴς ἔτυμος ἄγγελος.—
> ἔτι δὲ γᾶς ἐμᾶς πεδί' ὁπλόκτυπ' ὠ-
> τὶ χρίμπτει βοάν· ποτᾶται, βρέμει δ'
> ἀμαχέτου δίκαν ὕδατος ὀροτύπου.

the foot was in itself 'askew'. He thinks that it is a verse that comes in cross-wise, that runs aslant or athwart the structure of the lyric. It does this, he thinks, in the Skolion of Simonides, which he is discussing.

It is perhaps unnecessary to find the emotional effect of dochmii in the nature of the foot itself. — ⏑ ⏑ — ⏑ — is a short and elementary phrase entering into many forms of lyric verse: it is introduced by a 'basis' in the Glyconic (— ⏑ | — ⏑ ⏑ — ⏑ —) and combined with a different group of syllables in the Alcaic (⏓ — ⏑ — ⏓ | — ⏑ ⏑ — ⏑ —). The repetition of the short phrase without such introduction or elaboration gave the effect of despair, agitation, or excited suspense at the crisis of a tragedy.

[1] There are also a few bacchii (104 τί ῥέξεις; προδώσεις, παλαίχθων Ἄρης, τὰν τεάν;), a passage which might be quoted for the view that dochmii are really bacchii with catalexis (but there are serious objections to that theory); and a trochaic or iambic clausula, occurring more than once, akin to lines discussed above (ἄρηξον | δαίων ἄλωσιν).

The only doubtful line here is the first. It seems to begin with a detached anapaest (θρέομαι, ∪∪−); granted that, the rest is dochmiac, with resolution of the first two longs (∪⏜⏜∪−). The rest of the passage is as follows:

```
   ∪ −  − ∪ − | ∪ ∪∪ − ∪ −
  >∪∪ ∪∪ ∪ − | ∪ ∪∪ − ∪ −
  >∪∪ − ∪ − | ∪ − − ∪ −
5  ∪ − − ∪ − | ∪ ∪∪ − ∪ −
   ∪ ∪∪ − ∪ − | ∪ ∪∪ − ∪ −
   ∪ − − ∪ − | ∪ − − ∪ −
   ∪ ∪∪ − ∪ − | ∪ ∪∪ ∪∪ ∪ −.
```

In some passages of this play the form − ∪∪ − ∪ − is very frequent (219–21, 226–8, 692–3, 698–700, 705–7).

Ionic verse is in some of its forms very simple and regular, in others it presents very difficult problems. In its regular shape it is either 'a maiori' ('falling' − − ∪∪ − − ∪∪) or 'a minori' ('rising' ∪∪ − − ∪∪ − −). In its 'broken' shape (Ἰωνικοὶ ἀνακλώμενοι or κεκλασμένοι) it is most frequently ∪∪ − ∪ − ∪ − ⏔ (Anacreontic). The ἦθος of the measure was one of excitement and turbulence, frenzy or ecstasis, of licence and effeminacy.

> euoe, recenti mens trepidat metu
> plenoque Bacchi pectore turbidum
>   laetatur. euoe, parce, Liber,
>   parce gravi metuende thyrso.[1]

It was ἀνειμένον, 'mollissimum rhythmorum genus', asso-

---

[1] Ionic verse would be an appropriate vehicle for this: not so appropriate for the tranquil close of Horace's ode:
> et recedentis trilingui
> ore pedes tetigitque crura.

Horace is giving us here something like a dithyramb on a small scale, in a different metrical medium. Closing in tranquillity the ode successfully depicts what Aristotle would call the κάθαρσις of ἐνθουσιασμός by means of an ὀργιαστικὸν μέλος.

ciated with the 'mollities' or ἀβροσύνη of Ionia and with the orgiastic worship of Dionysus and of Cybele. It could express the abandonment of grief or despair (κεκλασμένος πρὸς τὸ θρηνητικόν). Its intrusion in the realm of metre may be compared with the advent of Dionysus at Thebes, and it sometimes provoked an attitude of protest or resistance like that of Pentheus. Plato would have banished it from his Ideal State, and perhaps had it in mind when he spoke of ὕβρεως ἢ μανίας πρέπουσαι βάσεις. The condemnation would apply most obviously to certain forms of ἀνακλώμενοι, such as Galliambics.

Regular Ionics are quoted from Sappho and Alcaeus: 'a maiori', εὐμορφοτέρα Μνασιδίκα τᾶς ἀπαλᾶς Γυρίννως (– – ∪ ∪ – – ∪ ∪ – – ∪ ∪ – ∪ – –. This is not quite regular throughout, – ∪ – – taking the place of the last Ionic); 'a minori', ἔμε δείλαν, ἐμὲ πασᾶν κακοτάτων πεδέχοισαν (Alcaeus, ∪ ∪ – – ∪ ∪ – – ∪ ∪ – – ∪ ∪ – –, the original of Horace's 'miserarum est neque amori dare ludum neque dulci', &c.).

In its regular form Ionic verse is not necessarily ἀνειμένον or μανιῶδες. It is capable of a certain stateliness and dignity not unlike that of anapaests. In the εἴσοδος of the *Persae* it immediately follows anapaests, and the last anapaestic lines have a certain resemblance to it:

τοκέες τ' ἄλοχοί θ' ἡμερολεγδὸν (∪ ∪ – | ∪ ∪ – – ∪ ∪ – –)
τείνοντα χρόνον τρομέονται (ending in ∪ ∪ – –).

In the first strophe and antistrophe of the Ionics the only variation is occasional syncope (∪ ∪ ⌣), by which the foot in syllables resembles an anapaest:

πεπέρακεν μὲν ὁ περσέπτολις ἤδη ∪ ∪ – – ∪ ∪ – – ∪ ∪ – –
βασίλειος στρατὸς εἰς ἀν-   ∪ ∪ – – ∪ ∪ – –
τίπορον γείτονα χώραν,   ∪ ∪ – – ∪ ∪ – –
λινοδέσμῳ σχεδίᾳ πορ-   ∪ ∪ – – ∪ ∪ – –

θυμὸν ἀμείψας   ∪∪ − −
Ἀθαμαντίδος Ἕλλας,   ∪∪⌣ ∪∪ − −
πολύγομφον ὄδισμα   ∪∪⌣ ∪∪ − −
ζυγὸν ἀμφιβαλὼν αὐχένι πόντου ∪∪⌣ ∪∪ − − ∪∪ − −.

According to a tradition preserved in a scholium on the *Prometheus* (l. 130) Anacreon came to Athens in the time of the Pisistratidae, and thus Aeschylus became acquainted with the secrets of Ionic verse. Certainly he makes very effective use of it, lifting it far above the level of the Anacreontic drinking-song (φέρ' ὕδωρ, φέρ' οἶνον, ὦ παῖ, ∪∪ ∠ ∪ | − ∪ ∠ −). At the close of the *Suppliants* (1018 f.) it expresses gratitude and exultation. In the *Persae* (65 f.) the Persian host is glorified in regular Ionics—unbrokenly regular in the first two strophes, α and α'; in those that follow suffering ἀνάκλασις at the close, until in strophe ε, with a more despondent tone, the metre changes into trochaics outright:[1] ταῦτά μοι μελαγχίτων | φρὴν ἀμύσσεται φόβῳ κτλ. In the *Prometheus* (399 f.) Ionics are the vehicle of grief and commiseration for the sufferings of the Titan. In the *Agamemnon* Ionics are twice used very effectively to present the disastrous results of the beauty of Helen (709 f.):

μεταμανθά|νουσα δ' ὕμνον | Πριάμου πό|λις γεραιὰ κτλ.,

and 744 f.:

παρακλίνασ' | ἐπέκρανεν | δὲ γάμου πι|κρὰς τελευτάς κτλ.,

while in the antistrophe to the latter passage (757 f.) they introduce the poet's protest against old and immoral beliefs:

δίχα δ' ἄλλων | μονόφρων εἰμί· τὸ δυσσε|βὲς γὰρ ἔργον.

[1] In strophes ζ and ζ' there is a further change. Syncopation is frequent: σμῆνος ὣς — ἐκλέλοι — πεν μελισ — σᾶν σὺν ὀρχάμῳ στρατοῦ. The misgivings of the chorus increase, and the flow of the verse is arrested. Ionic verse appears also in the invocation of the ghost of Darius (633-4, 647-50), and it expresses the awe and trepidation of the elders when the ghost appears (694 σέβομαι μὲν προσιδέσθαι κτλ., with an anapaestic *clausula*).

GREEK LYRIC VERSE

Apart from the *Bacchae*, where it is naturally predominant, the extant plays of Sophocles and Euripides show no such extensive and subtle use of the measure. (There is also an Ionic lyric in the *Supplices* of the latter, l. 42 f., where the theme is urgent and despairing entreaty.)

In recent years Ionic verse has been recognized in English. Prof. Gilbert Murray finds the rhythm of ἀνακλώμενοι in Mr. Kipling's ballad of *Mandalay*:

And the súnshine | and the pálm-trees | and the tínkly | temple bélls
On the róad to | Mandaláy.

It is sporadic in other poets, written by them unconsciously, it would seem, without knowledge of the Greek verse and without any thought of Anacreon:

In the mídnight, | in the sílence | of the sléep-time
(Browning.)

(but here it is only in this first line, with its short syllables—'in the', 'in the', 'of the',—that the effect is obvious). It is more continuous in Campbell's *Battle of the Baltic*:

When the sígn of | battle fléw | on the lófty | British líne.

Another form of Ionic can be felt in Lamb's lines:

Áll all are | góne the || óld familiar fáces.
κῆ δ' ἀμβροσίας μὲν κρατὴρ ἐκέκρατο,
Ἑρμᾶς δ' ἔλεν ὄλπιν θεοῖς οἰνοχοῆσαι.

Prof. Gilbert Murray has rendered the Ionic measures of the *Bacchae* in English Ionics. Much of Longfellow's *Hiawatha* reads itself readily as Anacreontic.

If we contemplate the effect in English, it is fairly clear what it is and how it comes about. It comes through stressing heavily the second trochee in a ditrochaeus or trochaic dipody: 'ón the lófty | Brítish líne'. If the third syllable is much stronger than the first the foot can be described as ∪∪−∪, which is an anapaest *plus* a short syllable, a thing which readily becomes catalectic, for an anapaest in English is familiar and frequent. Was it arrived at in the same way in Greek? Possibly; at all events the forms of it can be deduced from such a weighted or ill-balanced ditrochaeus. Ionics were in use long before Anacreon, but if we compare

πῶλε Θρηκίη, τί δή με λοξὸν ὄμμασι(ν) βλέπουσα

with

πολιοὶ μὲν ἡμὶν ἤδη κρόταφοι κάρη τε λευκόν,

we may conjecture that one was derived from the other, when some poet by the help of τύχη or τέχνη happened to try the experiment of giving the second trochee a strengthened *ictus*. The trochaic form of the line re-emerges in some of the later Anacreontea, 36. 16 τὰς δὲ φροντίδας μεθῶμεν, 57. 1 τὸν κελαινόχρωτα βότρυν. If the third syllable is very strong in a group of four, the reduction of the first to a short is only a way of making the same effect a little more obvious. Thus from the ditrochaeus $\stackrel{\_}{\smile}\stackrel{\prime\prime}{\smile}$ we should get both $\smile\smile-\smile$ and $\smile\smile--$. But if $\smile\smile\stackrel{\prime\prime}{\smile}$ has given the reader the clue, he will have no difficulty in reading the next ditrochaeus in an Ionic fashion. The first syllable of *that* need not be reduced. Hence the Anacreontic combination of two Ionic feet $\smile\smile\stackrel{\_}{\smile}\mid-\smile\stackrel{\_}{-}$. The metre which expresses a loose, unhinged, excited state of mind is obtained by disturbing the balance of a trochaic dipody.

Whether this is what actually happened or not, the possibility of such an origin for Anacreontics is of some importance. It is a *trochaic* dipody that has to be disturbed. No similar manipulation, as far as I can see, will elicit any Ionic form from an iambic dipody, $\smile - \smile -$. If trochees and iambi were equally real, an iambic dipody ought to give birth somehow to an *Ionicus a maiori*. The inference would seem to be that, for lyric verse, iambic scansion is illusory. Ancient metricians—

in later times at all events—construed much lyric verse iambically. But the reading of it that really works—like Copernican as compared with Ptolemaic astronomy—is trochaic (involving the assumption of anacrusis in many metres).

The ditrochæus is an element in many forms of verse, and if we set down two 'Anacreontei' other syllabic coincidences are discoverable; we can pick out a 'logaoedic' group of syllables, an 'Ithyphallic' and others:

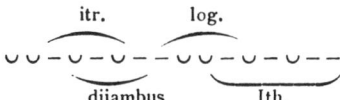

Conversely, some portion of another verse could be taken for Ionic, and the poet might be tempted to construct more of it in such a fashion that Ionic scansion was possible.[1] Owing to the great variety and flexibility of Greek lyric verse, Ionic effects were a thing which the poet could toy with at every turn: Sometimes only the poet's actual hearers would know, from the music, whether the effect was intended or not. Though there has been much discussion of Ionic verse in recent years, Ionic lines still sometimes escape detection and are classed as logaoedic or iambic, e.g.:

τὰ δ' ἄρισθ' ὅσαις προσήκει,

or

προσέχουσ' ἔτυχον ἐμαυτῆς.

[1] Further coincidences besides those here given would appear, if we included resolved forms of Ionic feet, such as ∪∪−∪∪ for ∪∪−−. The two Anacreontei contemplated here make up, with catalexis in the second, the metre of the *Attis* of Catullus (which he got from Callimachus or some other Alexandrian). The theory of ditrochaic origin, which we have provisionally advanced, could be illustrated by reading some of Catullus's lines as *accentual* Latin verse, when a trochaic tetrameter emerges, like that of the *Pervigilium Veneris*, except that that *is* still quantitative and that here resolution of the penultimate foot is the rule :

ádiítque opáca sílvis | rédimita lóca deaé.

Both of these are clearly Ionic, the first an 'Anacreonteus', the second regular Ionics with resolution (∪∪–∪∪ | ∪∪––). They *can* be construed as species of 'logaoedic', no doubt. In what would the difference consist? In the first, taken as Anacreontic, there would be a marked ictus on two syllables:

τὰ δ' ἄρισθ' ὅσαις προσήκει,

the intermediate long syllable would be eclipsed by the other two. If the verse is logaoedic this inequality disappears, or at all events is much less; and there is a possibility of syncopation, προσήκει (or on the Seikelos principle προσήκει), making (probably) the total time of the verse rather longer. In the other verse logaoedic structure presumably would mean *ictus* on a different syllable of ἔτυχον—ἐτύχον, not ἐτυχόν.

How subtle and complicated such effects might be we have no means of determining with certainty. We have seen Aeschylus in the *Persae* prepare the way for trochaics by anaclasis at the end of Ionic strophae. In the lyric of the *Agamemnon*, where μεταμανθάνουσα δ' ὕμνον occurs, the beginning is purely trochaic (*Ag.* 681 f. = 699 f.), but before we come to that line the tendency to Ionics has shown itself:

(πρασ)σομένα τὸ νυμφότιμον
μέλος ἐκφάτως τίοντας.

In the *Prometheus*, 399 f., Ionics (mostly broken or Anacreontic) are followed by trochaics in strophe β', arranged so that they resemble 'Anacreontei' in length and movement:

Κολχίδος τε γᾶς ἔνοικοι
παρθένοι μάχας ἄτρεστοι
καὶ Σκύθης ὅμιλος, οἳ γᾶς ...

(the rest is logaoedic). This lyric system, and the lyrics at l. 128, begins in a way which it is very difficult to explain. There seems to be an anacrusis before Anacreontics:[1]

στέ|νω σε τᾶς οὐ|λομένας τύ|χας, Προμηθεῦ,

[1] Cf. also *Pers.* 652, *S. c. Th.* 720, *Agam.* 686 (and perhaps also 459).

and in 128

> μηδὲν φοβηθῇς· | φιλία γὰρ | ἅδε τάξις
> πτερύγων θο|αῖς ἀμίλλαις.

Do both begin with an ἰαμβικὸν πενθημιμερὲς like 'odi profanum' in Alcaics? There is a similar beginning at 133, within the strophe:

> κτύπου γὰρ ἀχὼ | χάλυβος διῆξεν ἄντρων |
> μυχόν, ἐκ δ' ἔπληξέ μου
> τὰν θεμερῶπιν αἰδῶ·
> σύθην δ' ἀπέδιλος ὄχῳ πτερωτῷ.

It will be seen that the indubitable 'Anacreontei' do not lead to any satisfactory quadrisyllabic scansion of what follows: πληξέ μου τὰν | θεμερῶπιν ‖ αἰδῶ σὺ or αἰδῶ σύθην is not an arrangement that has any merits. The analogy of 418-19 points to the last two lines being logaoedic. The last is the Alcaic decasyllable, with a short syllable prefixed, a clear case of 'anacrusis'.

III. Pindar and the Dramatic Poets

The 'individualistic' or personal lyric of Sappho and Alcaeus as a rule took the shape of a fixed stanza of no great length, repeated, as often as the poet chose, without variation of its structure and indeed with no variation at all except that one or two inconspicuous syllables might be either short or long. The Alcaic and Sapphic stanzas have no place in the drama, or in the processions and choric celebrations for which Pindar composed a paean or an ode of victory. With a chorus and a chorodidascalos, who in early times was the poet himself, much more complex effects could be achieved. Poet and musician were one; the 'structure brave, the manifold music'[1] was 'built' afresh for each occasion. The

---

[1] Browning, *Abt Vogler*, which the late Sir R. Jebb translated into Pindaric verse :

> εἴθε μίμνοι ποικιλόφωνον ἕδος
> δῶμ' ὃ τεύχω δαιδαλόεν . . .

predecessors of Pindar and the dramatists in such composition were not Sappho and Alcaeus, but Alcman and Stesichorus. The Lesbian poets were not without their influence; we have seen, for example, the Alcaic decasyllable (τὰν δυσάλωτον ἕλῃ τις ἀρχάν) still appearing as a *clausula* (especially in Aeschylus). But the prevailing structure is the threefold or triadic one (strophe, antistrophe, epode) which tradition attributed to the choric poet of Sicily.

Aeschylus, so far as extant plays enable us to judge, stands somewhat apart, in his μελοποιΐα, from the other two tragic poets. Stimulated by Anacreon perhaps, if we may believe tradition, he makes a highly effective use of Ionics and Ἰωνικοὶ ἀνακλώμενοι. Further, he has a liking for varying syncopation in a simple metre, getting the effect of tragic gravity or pathos by prolonged syllables:

πολλὰ μὲν γᾶ τρέφει δεινὰ δειμάτων ἄχη
– ⏑ – ⋀ (or ⌣) – ⏑ – ⋀ (or ⌣) – ⏑ – ⏑ – ⏑ – ⋀
– ⏑ – ⋀ (or ⌣) – ⏑ – ⋀
πόντιαί τ' ἀγκάλαι ...
ἀλλ' ὑπέρ—τολμον ἀν—δρὸς φρόνημα τίς λέγοι κτλ.
– ⏑ ⌣ – ⏑ ⌣ ⋮ – ⏑ – ⏑ – ⏑ – ⋀.

Thirdly, he seems to use more often than Sophocles does the type of μέτρον ἐπισύνθετον that has sometimes been called 'dactylo-epitrite'. After Aeschylus measures of the 'logaoedic' type, more or less akin to Glyconics, tend to prevail, and they are indeed frequent in Aeschylus himself. All three poets make an effective use of dochmii at the crisis of a tragic action (*supra*, p. 157).

In Euripides, along with some innovations such as the solo or μονῳδία with its complex music, there are signs of a reversion to the Aeschylean manner. Euripides can make a highly effective use of Ionics when his subject calls for them, as it does in the *Bacchae*. Again, some of his most famous odes (e.g. ’Ερεχθείδαι τὸ παλαιὸν ὄλβιοι κτλ., *Med.* 824) are in 'dactylo-epitrite' verse, and the dactylic *canticum* of the *Phoenissae* (*supra*, p. 148) is perhaps definitely Stesichorean. The heroic lays of Stesichorus perhaps exercised a greater influence upon Aeschylus and Euripides than upon Sophocles. There are indications of it in things other than metre. It was probably from Stesichorus that Aeschylus got his guilty Clytaemnestra and Euripides his innocent *Helen*.[1] The *Ajax*, an early play of Sophocles, has Aeschylean traits, and conspicuously a lyric in 'dactylo-epitrite' verse:

ἦ ῥά σε Ταυροπόλα Διὸς Ἄρτεμις,
ὦ μεγάλα φάτις, ὦ
μᾶτερ αἰσχύνας ἐμᾶς ...

and a somewhat similar Aeschylean vein in the *Rhesus* helps to the conclusion that the play was really an early work of Euripides.[2]

Apart from μέτρα μονοειδῆ, dochmiacs and Ionics, there are two main types of lyric metre in the στάσιμα of tragedy— the εἴσοδος in the early drama being in regular anapaests— namely, 'dactylo-epitrite' and 'logaoedic'.

It is convenient to speak of them in the first instance as 'dactylo-epitrite' and 'logaoedic', words for them which have had considerable currency. But it is by no means clear what would be the best or most exact terms.

The elements of which the former consists are normally $-\cup\cup -\cup\cup --$ and $-\cup -\overset{\smile}{-}$. A dactylic group comes to

---

[1] See Robert, *Bild und Lied*. For Clytaemnestra's dream of the snake that draws blood from her breast, Sophocles substitutes a quite different dream, derived from his friend Herodotus. Stesichorus's παλινῳδία sent Helen to Egypt and only her εἴδωλον to Troy, or at all events gave rise to that version of the story.

[2] 'Dactylo-epitrite', verse 225-41, 527 f. Ionics (ἀνακλώμενοι), 363-4—a touch of Ionic rhythm, as in Aeschylus, where the subject suits it.

a close in a spondee, and the trochaic phrase is the shortest possible, a dipody with the last syllable usually long. Either group may be preceded by a syllable (anacrusis) usually long (or, resolved, ⏑⏑), but sometimes short.

Various names have been in use for this type of metre: 'Dorian' (partly from a hint given by Pindar himself: Δωρίῳ φωνὰν ἐναρμόξαι πεδίλῳ, *Ol.* iii. 6); 'dactylo-epitrite' (from ἐπίτριτος, the Greek adjective for the ratio 4 to 3, the trochaic element being in syllables[1] ⏑⏑⏑ | ⏑⏑⏑⏑, 3+4); 'dactylo-trochaic' (which is too wide in meaning); and most recently 'prosodiac-enoplic'. Various notations or modes of analysis have also been in use for it.

(a) When a syllable precedes the groups −⏑⏑−⏑⏑−− and −⏑−− they can be described as anapaestic and iambic respectively. This was a method adopted by ancient metricians. For the trochaic group it presents little difficulty. Anapaestic scansion becomes questionable when the first syllable is short, as in ἄνω ποταμῶν ἱερῶν; and in a famous opening of Pindar's, reproduced by Aristophanes in *Eq.* 1264, τί κάλλιον ἀρχομένοισιν ἢ καταπαυομένοισιν. Iambo-anapaestic scansion becomes highly questionable when the second group is *not* catalectic, for the whole then becomes *hypercatalectic*, a term which has no clear or satisfactory meaning (−− ⏑ − | −− ⏑⏑ − ⏑⏑ − | −). See *infra*, Excursus, p. 177.

(b) The syllable that precedes is regarded as an anacrusis, a method belonging to modern music which has many advantages.

(c) 'Prosodiac-enoplic' scansion, for which there is some ancient evidence, divides the dactylic group into two equal

[1] Or, 'for mere prosody'. That the second syllable in the apparent spondee is not a real long is shown by the fact that it is not resolved. The first syllable *is* a μακρὰ δίσημος.

GREEK LYRIC VERSE 169

parts, a choriambus and an 'Ionicus a minori' ($-\cup\cup-$ |
$\cup\cup--$), each of six times, ἐξάσημα, and each therefore
equal to a ditrochaeus (which the epitritus is assumed to be).
It has the advantage of avoiding the assumption of a group
of *three* feet, which is difficult for anything that may accompany
a march or procession—a march-rhythm is naturally in
multiples of two, dipodies and dimeters (as in anapaests);
but the poems actually written in this type of metre seldom
belong to a procession (πρόσοδος) and seldom are 'enoplic'
in the sense of accompanying a march or war-dance. It is
not clear that the choriambo-ionic division is more than
a special musical setting or musical arrangement adopted
sometimes and for some purposes and not certainly very
ancient.

For the ordinary reader (b) is by far the most convenient
method, for (besides anacrusis) he has to recognize only *two*
recurring elements, $-\cup\cup\ -\cup\cup\ --$ and $-\cup\ --$. The
reader of Pindar would do well to begin with the fourth
Pythian ode:

$-\cup-\ -$ | $-\ \cup\ \cup\ -\ \cup\ \cup-\overline{\wedge}$
σάμερον μὲν χρή σε παρ' ἀνδρὶ φίλῳ

$-\cup--$ |$-\ \ \cup\cup-\cup\ \cup--$
στᾶμεν εὐίππου βασιλῆι Κυράνας

$-\ \cup\ -\ -$|$-\ \cup\ \cup\ -\ \cup\cup-\overline{\wedge}$
ὄφρα κωμάζοντι σὺν Ἀρκεσίλᾳ.

Clearly, if we adopt simple symbols for the two elements, the
metrical structure of this can be exhibited with great brevity:
for example, ε and E (the initial of ἐπίτριτος and the initial
of ἐνόπλιος—ἐνόπλιος *was* an ancient name for the dactylic
group, whether it was always thought of as dactylic or not).
ε— might stand for the catalectic form of the group, +ε for
the group with anacrusis. On this notation the preceding
lines are ε $E-$ ε E ε $E-$.

170   GREEK LYRIC VERSE

Μοῖσα Λατοί δαισιν ὀφειλόμενον Πυ θῶνί τ' αὔξῃς
οὖρον ὕμνων.

That is ϵ E ϵ ϵ.

ἔνθα ποτὲ χρυσέων Διὸς αἰητῶν πάρεδρος
οὐκ ἀποδάμου Ἀπόλλωνος τυχόντος ἱρέα
χρῆσεν οἰκιστῆρα Βάττον καρποφόρου Λιβύας, ἱερὰν
νᾶσον ὡς ἤδη λιπὼν κτίσσειεν εὐάρματον
πόλιν ἐν ἀργινόεντι μαστῷ.

–⏑⏑ –⏑⏑ –⏑⏑ – – | – ⏑ –⏑̱
–⏑⏑ –⏑⏑ – – | –⏑ –⏑ | –⏑ –
–⏑ – – | –⏑ – – | –⏑⏑ –⏑⏑ –⏑⏑ –⋏
–⏑ – – | –⏑ – – | –⏑⌴ –⏑ –
⏑⏑⏑ – – | –⏑ – –.

In these lines there are variations which would render our brief notation more complicated. There are two groups of *four* dactyls (**E⁴ ?**), in the fourth line of the ode and the sixth, the second of them catalectic (**E⁴ – ?**).[1] In line 7 there is syncopation of a foot or protraction of a syllable in -σειεν εὐ-άρματον (whether the syllable εὐ should be thought of as exactly τρίσημος is a difficult question which hardly concerns the ordinary reader ; on any method of scansion it must be prolonged, it is μακρᾶς μείζων). In the last line there is resolution of a trochee (πόλιν ἐν, ⏑⏑⏑). The devices or variations presented by this strophe provide the reader with the means of scanning about half of the odes of Pindar. Of the recently recovered poems the paean written for an Athenian

[1] On the dactylic theory, a group of four dactyls raises no difficulty, except this slight question of brief notation. The 'prosodiac-enoplic' or quadrisyllabic scansion has more trouble with it. According to Blass (Introduction to *Bacchylides*, p. xxxiv) there are two groups, one catalectic, which together 'tetrapodiae speciem falsam praebent' (ἔνθα ποτὲ χρυσέων, –⏑⏑ –⏑⏑ –⋏, Διὸς αἰητῶν πάρεδρος, ⏑⏑ – – –⏑–⏑̱). Bacch. ix, strophe l. 6, ἄνθεσι ξανθὰν ἀναδησάμενος κεφαλάν is –⏑ – –, –⏑⏑–, ⏑⏑ ⌴, ⏑ ⏑ ⌴. This is not plausible.

GREEK LYRIC VERSE

θεωρία to Delos (*Suppl. Lyr.* v) is a simple example of 'enoplotrochaic' metre (if we may add one more to the many attempts to find a name for this mode of composition). Each strophe began with the words ἰήϊε Δάλι' Ἄπολλον (a 'prosodiacus'; or we may say that the first κῶλον—here it is 'the first κῶλον alone—has an anacrusis):

$$\cup-\cup\cup\ -\cup\cup\ \ -\ \ \overset{\smile}{}$$
ἰήϊε Δάλι' Ἄπολλον·

$$-\ \ \cup\cup-\ \ \cup\cup\ -\ -$$
καὶ σποράδας φερεμήλους

$$-\ \cup\ -\ -|-\ \cup\cup-\cup\cup\ \ -\ \ \overset{\smile}{}$$
ἔκτισαν νάσους ἐρικυδέα τ' ἔσχον

$$-\ \cup\ \cup\ -\ \ \cup\ \cup\ -\ -$$
Δᾶλον, ἐπεί σφιν Ἀπόλλων

$$-\ \cup\ \cup\ \ -\ \cup\ \cup\ -\ \overline{\wedge}\ \ \text{(or } -\cup\cup\ \overset{\smile}{}\text{?)}$$
δῶκεν ὁ χρυσοκόμας

$$-\ \ \cup\cup-\ \ \cup\cup\ \ -\ -$$
Ἀστερίας δέμας οἰκεῖν·

ἰήϊε Δάλι' Ἄπολλον·

Λατόος ἔνθα με παῖδες

$$-\ \cup\ -\ -|-\ \cup\ \cup-\ \ \cup\cup\ -\ \overset{\smile}{}$$
εὐμενεῖ δέξασθε νόῳ θεράποντα

ὑμέτερον κελαδεννᾷ

σὺν μελιγάρυι παι-
ᾶνος ἀγακλέος ὀμφᾷ.

In the second strophe it appears that the third line is separated from the fourth (θεράποντᾰ, an ending in a *syllaba anceps* and hiatus). In the first strophe this is not revealed. Conversely, the second strophe reveals also continuity between the penultimate line and the last.

It is possible that Anacreon, besides suggesting 'broken' Ionics in Aeschylus, gave a fresh impulse towards the composition of verse of the Glyconic and Pherecratean type. They are seen together in the lines which have been taken for a regular hymn to Artemis, but which Wilamowitz has shown to be rather a compliment to the people of Magnesia (*Sappho und S.*, p. 113). In this poem the longer stanza consists of four Glyconics followed by a Pherecratean: Catullus in his hymn to Diana has three Glyconics, as Anacreon has in other poems. Here, as in a similar verse to Dionysus, Anacreon begins with a shorter stanza, in which there are only two Glyconics:

γουνοῦμαί σ', ἐλαφηβόλε,
ξανθὴ παῖ Διός, ἀγρίων
δέσποιν' Ἄρτεμι θηρῶν.

That is, if we assume that $-\cup\cup$ *is* a dactyl:

$$-- \; -\cup\cup \; -\cup \; -$$
$$-- \; -\cup\cup \; -\cup \; -$$
$$-- \; -\cup\cup \; --.$$

Looking at the other specimens of Anacreon's composition in this form of verse we observe (a) the structure is 'hypermetric', the last syllable always long and followed by no *hiatus*[1] (cf. *σύμβουλος, τὸν ἐμὸν δ' ἔρωτ',* | *ὦ Δεύνυσε, δέχεσθαι* and *ἐλαφηβόλε* | *ξανθή*, lengthening before the double consonant *ξ*): (b) Anacreon has a strong preference for beginning with $--$, the 'spondaic basis', which Horace made invariable in metres of this type:[2] (c) the last line is catalectic or shorter by a syllable, in its rhythm very probably $-- \; -\cup\cup \; \smile - \; \wedge$, and coinciding in syllables with a syncopated or con-

---

[1] No *hiatus*, that is, within the stanza. There may be hiatus between one stanza and the next.

[2] A few of the extant lines show an iambus, $\cup -$ (*ἐγὼ δ' οὔτ' ἂν Ἀμαλθίης*, Fr. 8).

densed anapaestic line which Pherecrates, the comic poet, wrote κατὰ στίχον (*infra*, p. 254, footnote).[1]

Verse of this type was no doubt known to all the early poets, though there is no extant specimen by the Ionian, Archilochus. We have seen Sappho writing a stanza which consisted of two Glyconics and a line in which there is an additional dactyl:

> πόλλα καὶ τόδ' ἔειπέ μοι·
> 'ὤι μ' ὡς δεῖνα πεπόνθαμεν,
> Ψάπφ', ἦ μάν σ' ἀέκοισ' ἀπυλιμπάνω'

(which is one of the chief arguments for dactylic scansion, and from which it seemed easy to arrive at the 'Asclepiadean' type of 'Maecenas atavis edite regibus'). Besides being used in fixed stanzas by the Lesbian poets and by Anacreon, Glyconic verse was very frequently written by Pindar and by the dramatists, with numerous variations, such as resolution of a syllable or the transference of the dactyl to a different place in the line. The first Olympian ode begins with Glyconic + Pherecratean:

> ἄριστον μὲν ὕδωρ, ὁ δὲ | χρυσὸς αἰθόμενον πῦρ.
> ∪ − − ∪∪ − ∪ − | − ∪ − ∪∪ − ∪

Aeschylus makes less use of it than the other two tragic poets. His lyric composition is characterized by a liking for other things, for long dactylic groups, or systems of trochees with frequent syncopation, or the broken Ionics which he is said to have learned from Anacreon. But he does write Glyconics and Pherecrateans, sometimes alternating:

> Νῖσον ἀθανάτας τριχὸς
> νοσφίσασ' ἀπροβούλως
> πνέονθ' ἁ κυνόφρων ὕπνῳ.
> κιγχάνει δέ νιν Ἑρμῆς. (*Choeph.* 619–22.)

---

[1] It is strange to find Mr. White (*V. of Gr. Com.*, § 547) giving Pherecrates' lines with 'Aeolic' scansion, when their purport is to call attention to themselves as σύμπτυκτοι ἀνάπαιστοι.

Or as the closing cadences of a strophe:

> ὀμμάτων δ' ἐν ἀχηνίαις
> ἔρρει πᾶσ' Ἀφροδίτα.

Or

> τοὺς δ' ἄκραντος ἔχει νύξ.

He shows also a liking for certain variations or kindred forms, e.g.:

> γείνατο παῖδ' ἀμεμφῆ.
> δύσμαχα δ' ἐστὶ κρῖναι[1]

(which may be described as Pherecratean with the dactyl in the first place instead of the second). Like Euripides (*Her. Fur.* 419-22) he has a sequence of Pherecratean lines, with a penultimate Glyconic:

> νούσων δ' ἑσμὸς ἀπ' ἀστῶν
> ἵζοι κρατὸς ἀτερπής·
> εὐμενὴς δ' ὁ Λύκειος ἔσ-
> τω πάσᾳ νεολαίᾳ.   (*Suppl.* 684-7 = 694-7.)

(So also in the two preceding strophes, 639-42 = 652-5, and 663-6 = 674-7.)

Euripides shows some inclination to revert to Aeschylean enoplo-trochaics and Ionics; but apart from that the lyrics of the two younger dramatists are mainly of the Glyconic type.

The following are passages where Glyconics are written with considerable regularity:

Soph. *Antig.* 332 f.

πολλὰ τὰ δεινὰ κοὐδὲν ἀν-	– ⏑ ⏑ – ⏑ – ⏑ ⌞
θρώπου δεινότερον πέλει·	– – – ⏑ ⏑ – ⏑ – ∧
τοῦτο καὶ πολιοῦ πέραν	– ⏑ – ⏑ ⏑ – ⏑ – ∧
πόντου χειμερίῳ νότῳ	– – – ⏑ ⏑ – ⏑ –
χωρεῖ περιβρυχίοι-	⌞ – ⏑ – ⏑ ⏑ ⌞ (?)
σιν περῶν ὑπ' οἴδμασιν	– ⏑ – ⏑ – ⏑ – ∧

---

[1] Compare his liking for the Alcaic ending τὰν δυσάλωτον ἔλῃ τις ἀρχάν (– ⏑ ⏑ – ⏑ ⏑ – ⏑ – –), with two dactyls.

GREEK LYRIC VERSE

Oed. Col. 1211 f.

ὅστις τοῦ πλέονος μέρους	− − − ∪ ∪ − ∪ − ∧
χρῄζει τοῦ μετρίου παρεὶς	− − − ∪ ∪ − ∪ − ∧
ζώειν, σκαιοσύναν φυλάσ-	− − − ∪ ∪ ˏ − ∪ ⌊
σων ἐν ἐμοὶ κατάδηλος ἔσται	− ∪ ∪ − ∪ ∪ ˏ − ∪ − −

In *Oed. Tyr.* 1186–95 the strophe consists of groups (περίοδοι) of three, four and four lines, each group ending with a Pherecratean.

Oed. Col. 668 f.

εὐίππου, ξένε, τᾶσδε χώ-	− − − ∪ ∪ − ∪ ⌊
ρας ἵκου τὰ κράτιστα γᾶς ἔπαυλα,[1]	−⏓ − ∪ ∪ − ∪ − ∪ − ∪
670 τὸν ἀργῆτα Κολωνόν, ἔνθ'	∪ − − ∪ ∪ − ∪ ⌊
ἁ λίγεια μινύρεται	− ∪ − ∪ ∪ − ∪ − ∧
θαμίζουσα μάλιστ' ἀη-	∪ − − ∪ ∪ − ∪ ⌊
δὼν χλωραῖς ὑπὸ βάσσαις,	− − − ∪ ∪ − −
τὸν οἰνῶπα νέμουσα κισ-	∪ − − ∪ ∪ − ∪ ⌊
675 σὸν καὶ τὰν ἄβατον θεοῦ	− − − ∪ ∪ − ∪ − ∧
φυλλάδα μυριόκαρπον ἀνήλιον	− ∪ ∪ − ∪ ∪ − ∪ ∪ − ∪ ∪
ἀνήνεμόν τε πάντων	∪ − ∪ − ∪ ⌊ −
χειμώνων, ἵν' ὁ βακχιώ-	− − − ∪ ∪ − ∪ ⌊
τας ἀεὶ Διόνυσος ἐμβατεύει	−⏓ − ∪ ∪ − ∪ − ∪ − −
	(or ⌊ −)
680 θεαῖς ἀμφιπολῶν τιθήναις[2]	− − ∪ ∪ − ∪ − −
	(or ⌊ − ∧

Here line 676 is a dactylic tetrapody, a verse not unfrequently interposed among lines of other types (e.g. it is the penultimate line of the strophe in Alcman's παρθένιον), and the line that follows—as if to restore the balance, or to make the two lines together a brief deviation towards μέτρον ἐπισύνθετον—has no dactyl at all.

---

[1] A Phalaecean line, if this division of the lines is right. The penultimate line also is Phalaecean.

[2] = χρυσάνιος Ἀφροδίτα in the antistrophe. θεαῖς is one syllable

It will be observed that the line quite frequently ends in the middle of a word. There are passages where this occurs throughout or nearly so, e.g. Eur. *Ion.* 184–7. A less regular group of lines is seen in Soph. *Ajax*, 1217–22:

γενοί- μαν ἵν' ὑ-	∪ ⌴ – ∪ ⌴
λᾶεν ἔπεστι πόντ-	– ∪∪ – ∪ ⌴
ου πρόβλημ' ἁλίκλυστον ἄκ-	– ∪ – ∪∪ – ∪ ⌴
ραν ὑπὸ πλάκα Σουνίου,	– ∪ – ∪∪ – ∪ –
τὰς ἱερὰς ὅπως	– ∪∪ – ∪ –
προσείποιμεν Ἀθάνας	∪ – – ∪∪ – – (or ⌴ – ∧)

where only the third and fourth lines are normal Glyconics.

The combination of Glyconic with Pherecratean was sometimes treated as a line or στίχος and written κατὰ στίχον. It was so written by Anacreon, and a few lines of his are preserved. For the ordinary reader it is represented chiefly by one of the poems of Catullus:

(o colonia quae cupis | ponte ludere longo)

The Glyconic or Pherecratean line is not unfrequently 'acephalous'. *O.T.* 1195 οὐδὲν μακαρίζω is a good example, – – ∪∪ ⌴ – ∧. The other periods in the strophe end with a normal Pherecratean, so that here the long syllable is likely to be ⌴. This acephalous line is repeated in Aristophanes.

ὦ δῆμε, καλήν γ' ἔχεις	– – ∪∪ – ∪ –
ἀρχήν, ὅτι πάντες ἄν-	– – ∪∪ – ∪ –
θρωποι δεδίασί σ' ὥσ-	– – ∪∪ – ∪ –
περ ἄνδρα τύραννον.	∪ – ∪∪ – ⊻
ἀλλ' εὐπαράγωγος εἶ	– – ∪∪ – ∪ –
θωπευόμενός τε χαί-	– – ∪∪ – ∪ ⌴
ρεις κἀξαπατώμενος,	– – ∪∪ – ∪ –
πρὸς τόν τε λέγοντ' ἀεὶ	– – ∪∪ – ∪ –
κέχηνας, ὁ νοῦς δέ σου	∪ – ∪∪ – ∪ –
παρὼν ἀποδημεῖ	∪ – ∪∪ – ⊻[1]

[1] The strophe is repeated four times. The short syllable at the

Of these lyric systems some lend themselves more readily than others to the now fashionable quadrisyllabic method of scansion. Any Glyconic line of course does so ($\smile\smile - \smile$ | $\smile - \smile -$), once we are prepared to regard two short syllables coming together as belonging to different sections of the verse. εὐίππου, ξένε, τᾶσδε χώρας κτλ. fits the scheme fairly well, beginning with a heavy 'antispast' (the first syllable long) ($- - - \smile$ | $\smile - \smile -$, εὐίππου, ξέ|νε τᾶσδε χώ-), but it is disturbing to find a line of four unmistakable dactyls (676); ὦ δῆμε, καλήν γ' ἔχεις is 'acephalous', the first syllable of the antispast disappearing; the *clausula* -περ ἄνδρα τύραννον remains rather obscure, as does the first syllable short in κέχηνας, ὁ νοῦς δέ σου. The lyric from the *Ajax* is instructive, and perhaps furnishes a sort of clue to the nature of dochmii. The first and second lines are in syllables— whatever their time was—the two familiar types of dochmius; then follow two Glyconics, which answer to the second type of dochmius preceded by a disyllabic 'basis'. Next comes the second form of dochmius again, and the last line is Pherecratean. On the quadrisyllabic theory the first line will be antispast + syllable, which was actually one of the ancient descriptions of a dochmius; it consisted ἐξ ἀντισπάστου καὶ συλλαβῆς.

EXCURSUS

(b) *On the quadrisyllabic scansion of 'Dactylo-Epitrite' verse, on 'Iambic Syncopation', and on 'Ictus'.*

The type of metre which has often been called 'dactylo-epitrite' consisted, on that theory, of separate short groups of dactyls, interspersed with the 'epitritus', a metrical element which in syllables is $- \smile - \smile$. The 'epitritus' was so called by ancient

beginning of a line was unusual, it would seem, and the poet does not persist with it. It occurs three times in the first strophe, twice in the second, and not at all in the third and fourth.

metricians because its two parts were in the ratio 3 : 4. Whether that was so or not it is a convenient name for the group of syllables. The compound adjective 'dactylo-epitrite' is not ancient, but the parts of it are. Recent metricians have found a different structure in such verse, attested by ancient evidence (though the evidence does not really take us back to the musical score of Pindar or Aeschylus), and supplying, they claim, a better account of all the facts.

The opening of the third Olympian ode:

Τυνδαρίδαις τε φιλοξείνοις ἀδεῖν καλλιπλοκάμῳ θ' Ἑλένᾳ
κλεινὰν Ἀκράγαντα γεραίρων εὔχομαι

was analysed by J. H. Schmidt, W. Christ, and other metrical writers of the nineteenth century as follows:

$$-\cup\cup\ -\cup\cup\ --\ |\ -\cup\ --\ |\ -\cup\cup\ -\cup\cup\ -\bar{\wedge}$$
$$--\cup\cup\ -\cup\cup\ --\ |\ -\cup-.$$

They differed about details, and there was much discussion about the precise musical value of the syllables. Was the trochee lengthened in time to equal a dactyl, perhaps by being made ⌣ ∪ or ♩. ♪? These differences are comparatively unimportant, for recent metricians (notably Schröder in his edition of Pindar, and Blass in his edition of Bacchylides) have adopted a different analysis altogether:

$$-\cup\cup-\ |\ \cup\cup--\ |\ -\cup--\ |\ -\cup\cup-\ |\ \cup\cup-\bar{\wedge}$$
$$--\cup\cup\ |\ -\cup\cup-\ |\ --\cup-.$$

They call the metre 'enoplic' or 'enoplic-prosodiac', and the quadrisyllabic elements or bars are of the Ionic or choriambic type. The dactyls have vanished. What is the value of the analysis, and precisely how ancient is it?

The former method involves 'anacrusis', the latter dispenses with it. The word 'anacrusis' is not ancient, but it is still possible to argue for it. When Hermann invented it, did he hit upon a neater and simpler way of dealing with facts for which the Greeks had only a rather cumbrous and complicated terminology? Is it possible to say of him—as he himself said of Bentley's discovery of the digamma in Homer—that 'ipsam sanavit artem metricam'?[1]

---

[1] Compare what has been said above (p. 162) in regard to the possible derivation of Ionics from a trochaic dipody (while an iambic dipody

The nineteenth-century metricians were wrong in construing ordinary iambi and anapaests as trochees and dactyls with anacrusis. But it is not clear that the Greeks would not have welcomed the word anacrusis for other metres. In the case of the 'prosodiac-enoplic' type of verse the facts are obscure and complicated without it. In the line

τὸν παῖς ὁ Λατοῦς εὐρυμέδων τε Ποσειδάν

we are asked to recognize this structure,

$$--\cup-\,|\,--\cup\cup\,|\,-\cup\cup-\,|-,$$

so that the line is 'hypercatalectic'. But what is 'hypercatalexis'? It is a more difficult and obscure notion than 'anacrusis'. Probably neither was known to Aeschylus or Pindar. Further, this line when it was shorter by a syllable was called 'iambelegus'—'elegus' implying dactyls. Instead of 'anacrusis' a method of describing the line was to say that it began with an 'iambic penthemimeres'; and this seems to divide it rightly. It is the ancient—more cumbrous—equivalent for scansion with anacrusis. It begins with a group of five syllables (as the first two lines of an Alcaic stanza do), not with a group of four.

Another objection is a historical one. The choriambo-ionic scansion divorces the metre from similar lyrics which clearly consist of dactyls and trochees.

refuses to generate anything similar). The comparison there suggested between iambic scansion and Ptolemaic astronomy applies to the case— if this contention is sound—with curious accuracy. For Ptolemaic or geocentric astronomy was right *about the moon*. So iambic scansion was right for the iambic trimeter (and a few kindred forms of spoken verse), but not right about lyric verse. Compare also the modern treatment of rhythm in Latin prose with ancient theories on the subject. Zielinski's *Clauselgesetz* is based on extensive statistical labour, which the ancients did not attempt, and, whether we are prepared to accept his theory as final in every detail or not, it does arrive at a principle—an intelligible principle as to the number of syllables that are to be taken into account. How far back into the sentence are we to go? The ancient treatment as seen in Quintilian (ix, c. 4) is comparatively arbitrary and unregulated. Numerous metrical terms are applied to groups of syllables taken at haphazard. Zielinski's method is sound in the main, because the natural tendency of Latin was to a trochaeo-cretic movement: he says in effect, 'go back to what is characteristic of Latin prose rhythm, $-\cup-$'.

ὅσσας δ' εἷλε πόλεις πόρον
οὐ διαβὰς Ἅλυος ποταμοῖο
οὐδ' ἀφ' ἑστίας συθείς.

What is the 'epitritus' but the shortest trochaic κῶλον? And the enoplius but a group of dactyls, not the shortest possible, but a short and effective one? Can we imagine a poet—not in India or in Persia, but in Greece—inventing a metre which consists of a choriamb and an 'Ionicus a maiori'? Some of the quadrisyllabists themselves do not deny the relation to dactylo-trochaic lyrics. But if it is admitted, the choriambo-ionic scheme becomes merely a possible aspect of the group of syllables, a later interpretation or a special musical setting—a thing with which the ordinary reader need not concern himself.

Again, if we think of the 'prosodiac' as dactyls preceded by a syllable, we can understand why that syllable can be short, as it often is (ὁ τᾶς θεοῦ, ὃν Ψαμάθεια τίκτ' ἐπὶ ῥηγμῖνι πόντου). A 'prosodiac' is a 'paroemiac', and a paroemiac was part of a hexameter; it might be either ῥέχθὲν δέ τε νήπιος ἔγνω or παθὼν δέ τε νήπιος ἔγνω. In a famous lyric of Euripides the short syllable is prefixed to the first κῶλον only (ἄνω ποταμῶν ἱερῶν χωροῦσι παγαὶ κτλ.), not to the κῶλα that follow. It is difficult to believe that that colon alone began with an iambus and an anapaest, or alone was hypercatalectic (ἄνω ποτα|μῶν ἱερῶν | χωροῦσι πα|γαί). Similar things occur with other metres: a short syllable is prefixed to something so well known and constant that it is difficult to believe that its presence causes the whole to be transmuted or rearranged; e.g. Alcaeus's modification of a Sapphic line, ἰόπλοκ' ἄγνα μελλιχόμειδε Σάπφοι, or the short syllable before Ionics in Aes. *P. V.* 399.

But the choriambo-ionic enoplius claims to be attested by tradition, and it will be well to look at this evidence before proceeding further. Mr. White says (*Verse of Greek Comedy*, § 647): 'There is ample evidence that they'—the poets of the fifth century B.C.—'differentiated the prosodiac and enoplius from true anapaestic and dactylic cola.' 'Aristophanes himself testifies[1] as to the enoplius. Socrates in the *Clouds* (649 f.), in the first extant

---

[1] The passage has often been quoted and appealed to by other writers besides Mr. White.

SYNCOPATION AND ICTUS

literary reference to the enoplius, instructs Strepsiades that it is important for a gentleman in society to understand the difference between dactylic and enoplic verse. The two were different and yet so similar that an uninstructed person like Strepsiades might confuse them. Their differentiation is now not difficult. The enoplic dimeter $-\cup\cup-\cup\cup--$ differs from the dactylic tripody in metrical constitution.' The passage is :

> ἐπαίονθ' ὁποῖος ἐστὶ τῶν ῥυθμῶν
> κατ' ἐνόπλιον χὠποῖος αὖ κατὰ δάκτυλον.

What exactly does it prove? To argue from a passage in comedy is never a very safe thing to do, and here the chances are that what Socrates thinks so important is some preposterous piece of hair-splitting comparable in value to the measurement of ψυλλῶν ἴχνη. A dactylic lyric like ὦ πολύμοχθος Ἄρης, τί ποθ' αἵματι in the *Phoenissae* could presumably be scanned κατὰ δάκτυλον or κατὰ μονοποδίαν, and so could a hexameter (though a heroic hexameter could also be taken as two κῶλα divided and linked together by *caesura*). But a line like

> φαινομέναν δ' ἄρ' ἐς ἄταν σπεῦδεν ὅμιλος ἱκέσθαι

is neither of these things and not to be treated in either way. You must take it as—what? Something not dactylic at all? Not necessarily. It runs κατ' ἐνόπλιον. But Aristophanes would have written as he did even if an ἐνόπλιος was a group of three dactyls (the third spondaic in form). It is true that καθ' ἕνα δάκτυλον or κατὰ δάκτυλον ἕκαστον would have made a more logical contrast. That is the precise point at which it becomes unsafe to argue from a comic poet's phrase. The passage does not really prove anything about the internal constitution of an ἐνόπλιος in the fifth century. The Scholiast on the passage and ancient writers on metre, taken together, give us every possible view of the group of syllables $-\cup\cup-\cup\cup--$: there are four disyllabic feet ($-\cup\,|\,\cup-\,|\,\cup\cup\,|\,--$) or a choriamb and an Ionic, or the group is τὸ ἔχον δύο δακτύλους καὶ ἕνα σπονδεῖον. It is also said that two of them make a ἑξάμετρον κατ' ἐνόπλιον—the ἑξάμετρον, perhaps, which Strepsiades is to distinguish from a different sort of hexameter.

The next witness is Plato, in a well-known passage of the *Republic*, 400 B:[1] οἶμαι δέ με ἀκηκοέναι οὐ σαφῶς ἐνόπλιόν τέ τινα ὀνομάζοντος αὐτοῦ ξύνθετον καὶ δάκτυλον καὶ ἡρῷόν γε, οὐκ οἶδα ὅπως διακοσμοῦντος καὶ ἴσον ἄνω καὶ κάτω τιθέντος, εἰς βραχύ τε καὶ μακρὸν γιγνόμενον, καί, ὡς ἐγὼ οἶμαι, ἴαμβον καί τιν' ἄλλον τροχαῖον ὠνόμαζε, μήκη δὲ καὶ βραχύτητας προσῆπτε. This passage, like that in Aristophanes, is not one from which it will be safe to draw very precise inferences. It is casual in tone; the speaker is waiving aside the technicalities of the subject. So far as it does go, it does not seem to afford any very tangible support for the choriambo-ionic enoplius. 'ἴσον ἄνω καὶ κάτω' is a phrase that belongs to dactyls and anapaests, the γένος ἴσον ($\cup \cup = -$). The equality between a choriamb and an Ionic is not very likely to be in the speaker's mind (and which of these is ἄνω, which κάτω?). It is simply dactyls (or dactyls and anapaests) that he is thinking of in the first part of the sentence. Then he goes on to speak of iambi and trochees. An enoplius is something dactylic, one of *three* things. But we have already had three things in view: the dactyls of the *Phoenissae* ὦ πολύμοχθος Ἄρης (or, we might add, the unclosed, hypermetric dactyls of the type πολλάκι δ' ἐν κορύφαις ὀρέων, ὅκα, *supra*, p. 148), the heroic hexameter, and the hexameter κατ' ἐνόπλιον, φαινομέναν δ' ἄρ' ἐς ἄταν σπεύδεν ὅμιλος ἱκέσθαι. Blass (in his Preface to *Bacchylides*, p. xxxi) lays stress on the word ξύνθετος: a thing can be called σύνθετον or composite if it is made up of dissimilar parts (such as choriamb and Ionic). If putting like parts together were σύνθεσις, any and every rhythm would be σύνθετος. That is true; but it is not the only possible reason why a thing should be called σύνθετον. It might be so called because the parts were more distinct one from another than the parts of other things. And that would be the case here if we suppose that an ἐνόπλιος σύνθετος meant the combination of two simple ἐνόπλιοι. The *caesura* in a hexameter is a slight division: metrically, all that is required is the end of a word, though a strongly marked rhetorical pause or pause in this sense may coincide with it. The division between one line and the next

---

[1] Schröder says of this (*Pindar*, Appendix, p. 499) 'Platonis locum... procul habere satius erit'. 'Procul habere' is a good thing to do with a passage that does not prove what it is taken to prove.

SYNCOPATION AND ICTUS

in hypermetric dactyls must also be a slight one. But an enoplius has a marked closing cadence, the last foot is different from the others (like the end of a hexameter). The structure is σύνθετον because the parts have a fixed structure of their own. They can be easily seen and discriminated. Here ἐπισύνθετον comes into view as an adjective for a more complex building on the same principle.

The next piece of evidence is a passage in Hephaestion (c. xv) discussed by Mr. White (*V. of Gr. Com.*, § 630). It runs thus:

πρῶτος δὲ καὶ τούτοις (sc. ἐπισυνθέτοις) Ἀρχίλοχος κέχρηται· πῇ μὲν γὰρ ἐποίησεν ἔκ τε ἀναπαιστικοῦ ἐφθημιμεροῦς καὶ τροχαϊκοῦ ἡμιολίου τοῦ καλουμένου ἰθυφαλλικοῦ

Ἐρασμονίδη Χαρίλαε, χρῆμά τοι γελοῖον.

τοῦτο δὲ οἱ μετ' αὐτὸν οὐχ ὁμοίως αὐτῷ ἔγραψαν· οὗτος μὲν γὰρ τῇ τε τομῇ δι' ὅλου κέχρηται τοῦ ἐφθημιμεροῦς, καὶ σπονδείους παρέλαβεν ἐν τῷ ἀναπαιστικῷ κώλῳ, οἷον

ἀστῶν δ' οἱ μὲν κατόπισθεν ἦσαν· οἱ δὲ πολλοί.

οἱ δὲ μετ' αὐτὸν τῇ μὲν τομῇ ἀδιαφόρως ἐχρήσαντο, ὥσπερ Κρατῖνος

χαῖρ', ὦ μέγ' ἀχρειόγελως ὅμιλε, ταῖς ἐπίβδαις,
τῆς ἡμετέρας σοφίας κριτὴς ἄριστε πάντων,
εὐδαίμον' ἔτικτέ σε μήτηρ ἰκρίων ψόφησις.

ἐνταῦθα γὰρ ὁμοίως τὸ τρίτον μέτρον τέτμηται τοῖς Ἀρχιλοχείοις, τὰ δὲ πρὸ αὐτοῦ δύο πρὸ συλλαβῆς. καὶ μέντοι καὶ τοὺς σπονδείους παρῃτήσαντο τοὺς ἐν τῷ μέσῳ οἱ μετὰ τὸν Ἀρχίλοχον, οὐχ ὡς ἀναπαιστικὸν ἡγούμενοι, ἀλλὰ προσοδιακόν, τὸ ἐξ ἰωνικῆς καὶ χοριαμβικῆς, τῆς ἰωνικῆς καὶ βραχεῖαν τὴν πρώτην δεχομένης. What exactly does this passage tell us?

Archilochus wrote an often-quoted line Ἐρασμονίδη κτλ. In Archilochus himself there was always a τομή (*caesura* or *diaeresis*—the end of a word) before the last six syllables, which thus were trochaic (– ∪ – ∪ – –). But later poets (a very vague phrase) were not careful to have the τομή exactly there. Cratinus, for example, wrote the three lines χαῖρ' ὦ μέγ' κτλ., only the third of which is like Archilochus's line—ἰκρίων ψόφησις answers to χρῆμά τοι γελοῖον. In the others the division is a syllable earlier (χαῖρ', ὦ μέγ' ἀχρειόγελως | ὅμιλε, ταῖς ἐπίβδαις). Moreover they—'poets after Archilochus'—deprecated, or dispensed with, the spondees in the middle, as though regarding the first part not as anapaestic, but as prosodiac (the words are loosely set down—the meaning seems to be rather ὡς οὐκ ἀναπαιστικὸν ἡγούμενοι ἀλλὰ προσ.), prosodiac which consists of an Ionic and choriamb: (do not look at Ἐρασμονίδη and object to this, for) an Ionic *does* admit of a short syllable at the beginning. Later poets did not write μήτηρ in the middle of the line, as Cratinus did. They made the 'anapaestic' part stop a syllable earlier, apparently, presumably regarding it as prosodiac.

What does Mr. White elicit from the passage? 'Cratinus and the poets who followed him maintained and cultivated a fixed prosodiac form of this "tetrameter". They made it a real tetrameter, treating its division with indifference: χαῖρ' ὦ μέγ' ἀχρειόγελως κτλ., and regarding its first half not as anapaestic, but as prosodiac.' 'Cratinus and his successors, pleased with its rhythm, adopted a fixed form of the logaoedic period employed by Archilochus, *but gave it a different metrical constitution*:'— the italics are Mr. White's—'the first half was identified with the prosodiac, an ancient and well-known dimeter, the second was a catalectic iambic dimeter.'

'Cratinus and the poets who followed him'—so that Cratinus (senior to Aristophanes) launched the metre on new lines. But there is not a word about 'Cratinus and his followers'! οἱ μετ' αὐτὸν means οἱ μετ' Ἀρχίλοχον. The writer merely finds a useful illustration in lines of Cratinus. Poets later than Archilochus may mean anybody, possibly Callimachus and Theocritus. A group of poets is meant who refused to do what Cratinus obviously *did* do, to write a line with a spondee like μήτηρ in the middle of it. So far as the passage indicates anything it suggests that the prosodiac-enoplic reform or reconstruction was *later* than Cratinus. This is part of the 'ample evidence' for such a treatment of the verse by poets of the fifth century! (*V. of Greek Com.*, § 647.)

The passages show that ἐνόπλιος was a term in use in the fifth century, with some definite meaning. For the choriamb-ionic they seem to me to furnish no evidence at all. Nor does the word in itself suggest anything of the kind. It suggests martial exercises:

ἄγετ' ὦ Σπάρτας εὐάνδρου
κοῦροι πατέρων πολιατᾶν.

The second line is an enoplios with a syllable prefixed, or a 'prosodiac', and 'prosodiac' suggests marching—not to war, but in a procession, to a temple (πρόσοδοι μακάρων ἱερώταται, Ar. *Clouds*, 307).

If there are vulnerable points in the evidençe, if it is not absolutely cogent, the modern reader seems to be released from any strict and imperative obligation to spend time and toil in training his ear to follow a strange and alien rhythm, which may in the end prove to be a fiction of theorists. But we may now ask our next question, assuming that the schemes now in vogue have *some* basis, What is their nature and value?

Quadrisyllabic scansion, as we have seen, gives the following scheme for the lines of Pindar quoted above:

$$-\cup\cup-\ |\ \cup\cup--\ |\ -\cup--\ |\ -\cup\cup-\ |\ \cup\cup-$$
$$--\cup\cup\ |\ -\cup\cup-\ |\ --\cup-\ .$$

A rhythm is 'rising' (iambic) or 'falling' (trochaic), or presumably it may be neither (e.g. a choriambus). Thus the groups of syllables or bars or feet are (1) neither, (2) rising, (3) falling, (4) neither, (5) rising; and in the next line, (6) falling, (7) neither, (8) rising. It is not an easy thing to pass at once from a rising to a falling rhythm. The diversity or heterogeneity of this scheme is too great for reading; it seems plainly impossible that a reader could follow or render effectively such a thing. And what we want, for practical purposes, is to be able to read ancient poetry with some facility and pleasure, some perception of rhythm.

Here we shall of course be met by the answer or objection: 'It is not a scheme that is meant to be *read*; the groups of syllables are not ordinary Ionics or choriambi, they are simply equivalent groups of musical notes, without an *ictus*; your "rising" and "falling" rhythm perhaps involves an *ictus*, but we deny that there was any *ictus*, given by the voice, in Greek verse generally, and we deny it with special emphasis here. The verses were written to be sung to music (or rather, for the phrase "to music" would annoy Pratinas,[1] "with a musical accompaniment").'

Reserving for the present the question of *ictus*, we shall now

---

[1] τὰν ἀοιδὰν κατέστασε Πιερὶς βασίλειαν· ὁ δ' αὐλὸς ὕστερος χορευέτω· καὶ γάρ ἐσθ' ὑπηρέτας.

reflect: 'Then to *read* Pindar or Bacchylides is altogether illegitimate; we must close the volume—unless indeed we can train a chorus and have the poems rendered in song with music—and we must assume that the ancients never *read* Pindar at all, or read the text as prose (possibly—possibly Cicero[1] did so), *or* read it on simpler principles than those of this musical scheme.[2]

This brings us to Mr. White's central indictment of nineteenth-century Metrik. He holds that Apel, Schmidt, Christ, and others misapplied to melic verse simpler metrical principles which really belonged only to spoken verse (*Verse of Greek Comedy*, Introduction, p. xix f.). 'Iambic is the only rhythm that was used in spoken verse in Greek' (that is, in ψιλὴ λέξις in the strictest sense). 'Iambic, anapaestic, trochaic, and dactylic are the rhythms that were used in recitative rendering, but recitative does not signify in the least what we mean when we speak of an actor's reciting his lines. These are the four rhythms that modern poetry has developed. Both Greek and English, therefore, employ only simple disyllabic and trisyllabic rhythms in non-melic verse.[3] The Greeks, however, developed other rhythms, paeonic, Ionic, dochmiac, prosodiac-enoplic, Aeolic. With rare exceptions these rhythms were exclusively melic. The choruses of tragedy were sung. Only a highly imaginative mind can grasp the idea of reading dochmiac verse. The word "lyrical" has now a connotation far removed from its original Greek sense, and Bacchylides and Swinburne are not, in fact, poets of the same genre. If now the

[1] 'In versibus res est apertior, quamquam etiam a modis quibusdam cantu remoto soluta esse videtur oratio, maximeque id in optimo quoque eorum poetarum, qui λυρικοὶ a Graecis nominantur, quos cum cantu spoliaveris, nuda paene remanet oratio', Cic. *Orator*, § 183.

[2] There are pieces in 'enoplic-prosodiac' verse which cannot have been intended solely or chiefly for an elaborate choric performance, e. g. the verses in which Timocreon of Rhodes assailed Themistocles, or the later satirical moralizings of Cercidas which have recently come to light. Timocreon's contemporaries would not read his verse as prose.

[3] Ionics (ἀνακλώμενοι or Anacreontics) do exist in English ('all the might of Denmark's crówn', 'on the lófty British line'), and Ionic is a verse which, both in Greek and English, can be *read* quite easily and quite effectively, or at all events with a sufficient realization of its movement. But that matter is not relevant to the main argument here.

rhythms just named were not used in spoken verse in Greek, how credible and convincing is the allegation that the metrical structure of Aeolic verse must have been a form—a bastard form, at best— of the simple trochaic and dactylic rhythms that the Greek poets did employ in non-melic rendering, because we moderns cannot read Aeolic verse in any other manner! Regret that we cannot teach our pupils to render the *Odes* of Pindar as Greeks rendered them is an amiable sentiment, the resolution to read them even at the cost of reading them in the wrong fashion is prompted no doubt by a generous impulse, but neither has the least significance in the scientific determination of facts.'

Much that is said here is true and instructive, and the whole passage puts the issue in a very clear way. It might be pointed out further that when the Romans took to writing lyric verse for readers—as they clearly did, though the *carmen saeculare* and a few other things may have been actually sung—they regularized their structure in a very thorough way, 'stereotyping' a particular form of line and almost entirely excluding variations, thus making them easy for readers.[1] The Roman who tried Pindaric verse,

Pindarici fontis qui *non expalluit* haustus,

did not produce anything that was effective enough to survive (or to be mentioned in a survey of literature like Quintilian's in *Inst. Or.* x, c. i).

But the argument, perhaps, does not lead exactly in the direction that Mr. White supposes, and there is more than an 'amiable sentiment' involved. The question again thrusts itself upon us, 'How then did the ancients read Pindar and Bacchylides? Or did they never *read* them at all? And if the works of these poets could not be read—could not be produced, with artistic justification, except by a trained chorus with music—are we not bound to put them on the shelf, to exclude them from ordinary teaching and

[1] Easy also for composition by a verse-writer who is not also a musical composer. Could Alcaic verse be easily or even possibly written on a quadrisyllabic scheme: 'Non ante vul|gatas per ar|tes verba lo|quor socian|da chordis'? Are we quite prepared to believe that even a Greek poet and musician ever wrote it so with that scheme in his mind?

literary study altogether? Reading them as prose (even though Cicero possibly did it) cannot be justified.'

We are not absolutely limited, of course, to ψιλὴ λέξις. A reader can imagine the verse sung, though he could produce the sounds only in a very incomplete way. To prolong a syllable to three or four times, to make it τρίσημος or τετράσημος is a thing that lies beyond ψιλὴ λέξις, it is not natural to conversational utterance. But some sort of recitative or chant or half-chanting delivery is not excluded; it is not impossible for ordinary pupils or incomprehensible to them. So we may at least refuse to put on the shelf a number of lyrics of which the structure is simple and certain. We shall not exclude a trochaic lyric of Aeschylus because it has occasional syncopation:

$$\dot{\rho}υσίβωμον \text{ }^{\text{'}}Eλ\text{-}λά\text{-}νων \text{ } ἄγαλμα \text{ } δαιμόνων$$
$$(-\cup-\cup\mathrel{\llcorner}\mathrel{\llcorner}-\cup-\cup-\cup-\wedge).$$

What is the reasonable attitude, for an ordinary teacher, towards more difficult lyrical effects? Perhaps we may suppose him to say something like this: 'We do not wish to read Greek verse in a way that has no historical justification, or that would seriously misrepresent its effect. But our aim is not the strictly scientific one. We are prepared to be content with some approximate rendering, something short of scientific or archaeological precision. Further, we think that the importance of division by feet, for reading, is often exaggerated. It is important to know (and against the quadrisyllabic scansionists we are fairly sure of *that*) that Horace thought of his Alcaic line as beginning with a group of *five* syllables. Whether it is described as an ἰαμβικὸν πενθημιμερὲς or as two trochees with anacrusis does not affect the delivery. Calling it trochaic does not mean that we pronounce it "o—di pro —fanum", nor if we call it iambic is it to be pronounced "odi— profa—num". The ionic-choriambic-diiambic-ditrochaic scansion of Pindar may be only a musical arrangement—convenient for certain purposes—which does not bind the reader. In any case we are not prepared to accept or attempt these, for us, difficult arrangements except in so far as they are incontestably proved. In Roman imperial times—read for example Terentianus or Caesius Bassus on hendecasyllabics—metrical analysis was obviously a kind of ingenious game, chess-playing with syllables, and much of the metrical theory produced is complicated and useless lumber. We do not wish to be burdened with that, and therefore we scrutinize evidence closely. We do not think that your evidence does carry us back quite certainly to the fifth or sixth century. And the choriambic-ionic scansion is not always convincing. It is not entirely convincing when, as in the strophes of the fourth Pythian, we find among groups which *are ἐνόπλιοι* a group of syllables which we should call *four* dactylic feet (*three* dactyls and a spondee:

ἔνθα ποτὲ χρυσέων Διὸς αἰη(τῶν πάρεδρος).

$-\cup\cup-\ |\ \cup\cup-\cup\ |\ \cup--$ is not so convincing that we can welcome it with enthusiasm. Conversely, $-\cup\cup-$, which sometimes occurs, may be a *shorter* dactylic κῶλον rather than a choriambus. The dactylic scansion, which we are still inclined to retain (not being absolutely convinced about the other) does not *misdivide* Pindar's lines. The group of syllables that we take together is precisely the same, and we suggest that the two scansions are, for the ordinary reader, alike unreal, like the "iambic" and "trochaic" pronunciations of "odi profanum", i.e. he may adopt either without being seriously misled by it. You admit yourselves that the prosodiac and enoplius originated in, or grew out of, the dactylic or anapaestic paroemiac. The enoplius is an "acephalous" form of it. Mr. White says (§ 643): "The enoplius therefore is in origin a dactylic tripody of fixed form, but it differs from this tripody in metrical constitution"; and again (§ 647): "these poets" (the poets of the fifth century) "must have felt the anapaestic movement in the prosodiac and the dactylic in the enoplius." That is a good deal to admit. How do we know that a poet of the fifth or even fourth century (when the scansion you uphold had presumably gained ground) would not have told an ordinary reader who consulted him that the ionic-choriambic division was a musical arrangement or special treatment of the syllables with which he need not concern himself?'

The answer or retort to such a speech would perhaps be the following: 'There may be cases in which your dactylic scansion would not "seriously mislead" the reader. But discussion of them may be postponed; for we maintain that there are other cases where the reader *is* seriously misled by the dactylic or trochaic scansion, with anacrusis, which Apel, Schmidt & Co. have imposed upon you. There is the question of iambic catalexis and the Seikelos inscription, an inscription which, together with certain fragments of Aristoxenus, proves that you have been *protracting the wrong syllable*.'

This evidence is fully presented and discussed by Mr. White (p. 356 f., §§ 779-81), and it is unnecessary to enter into details about it here. The argument which follows (§§ 782-9), from the music of the two second-century hymns to Helios and Nemesis, is more complicated and subtle, but appears to be sound. We may take it that there is sound evidence for what may be called 'iambic syncopation', and it may be suggested that it would be convenient to make ⌐ (not ⌙) the symbol for it. The words with which the lyric of Seikelos (first century of the Christian era) begins, ὅσον ζῇς, are ∪ − ⌐, not ∪ ⌙ −.

This is not only shown by evidence. It is in itself reasonable, if iambic verse is to be separated from trochaic. The nineteenth-century metricians read iambic verse as trochaic with anacrusis, and consequently missed, or abolished, this effect. If a line really is iambic and begins with ∪ − ∪ −, we cannot take this as ∪ − ∪ ⌙. The second foot is an iambus; ∪ ⌙ is not intelligible at all. The syncope must be found in the following syllable.

πνοαὶ δ' ἀπὸ Στρυμόνος μολοῦσαι

is ∪ − ∪ − ⌐ ∪ − ∪ − ⌐, it is not ∪ ⁞ − ∪ ⌙ | − ∪ − ∪ ⌙ − ∧. The first syllable of Στρυμόνος, not the last of ἀπὸ, is prolonged. It is prolonged to the length of an iambus, so that the iambic movement can start again or proceed with -μονος μολοῦ-, and then the last syllable is protracted (the Seikelos inscription and the hymns seem to attest its protraction rather than the completion of the time by a pause).

Here then is a definite difference, and a quite important one. We cannot argue about it as we did about 'odi profanum'. Iambic and trochaic scansion give a notably different effect:

ἄναξ δ' ὁ πρέσβυς | τόδ' εἶπε φωνῶν
βαρεῖα μὲν κῆρ | τὸ μὴ πιθέσθαι.

SYNCOPATION AND ICTUS

It is certainly very different. It divides these lines conspicuously into two equal halves. Again, in *S. c. Th.* 293 we should have: ὑπερδέδοικεν λεχαίων δυσευνάτορας. Must we accept the principle as final, and learn to apply it and realize it throughout in the text of Aeschylus? And in all other poets who write anything that can be construed as iambic?[1]

Perhaps. But let us at least contemplate carefully the limits of our knowledge and run no risk of being too readily credulous.

Aeschylus wrote about a century and a half before Aristoxenus. We do not know what kind of metrical and musical notation, what terminology or ideas, existed in his day. They may have been very rudimentary. Grammatical terminology can hardly have existed at all. It is still incomplete in Aristotle. Yet Aeschylus writes correctly; there is very seldom anything that is obscure or confused; it is very seldom that we find anything like

ἐθρέψατ' οἰκητῆρας ... πιστοὺς ὅπως γένοισθε πρὸς χρέος τόδε.

Further, Aeschylus and other ancient writers sometimes have things of which modern grammar can give a better and clearer account than Greek grammarians could do.[2] It is possible that if we could summon Aeschylus as his Persians summoned Darius, and put questions to him, showing him modern musical notation for some of his verses, he would say, 'That expresses very much the effect that I intended, and expresses it more neatly and completely than the notation that I knew on earth.' Τρίμετρον and τετράμετρον would be current in his time, probably, as names for the iambic trimeter and trochaic tetrameter. He would think of the former as consisting of ἴαμβοι. What words would he use to describe the structure of a lyric like πνοαὶ δ' ἀπὸ Στρυμόνος μολοῦσαι? When he composed it with its music, would he divide it into bars and use symbols that indicated quantity, or only put musical notes above

---

[1] Mr. White, if one may argue from his notation, is not an ardent propagandist. In his metrical schemes he either does not indicate the protraction, or he puts a dot to indicate the missing time or syllable: ἐπαυχήσας δὲ τοῖς σοῖς λόγοις ∪ — . — . — ∪ — . — ∪ — (§ 73). This notation does not make it obvious to the eye which syllable, the preceding or the following one, is to be prolonged. ·

[2] For an illustration see *supra*, p. 132.

syllables? If he thought of it as consisting of 'feet', it is possible that he would use the word χορεῖος, which is certainly an early word and would be a convenient word for short *plus* long in either order, ∪ – or – ∪, or for lyric composition in alternate 'longs and shorts'.

If we try in this way to detach ourselves from notation and to imagine Aeschylus's procedure, further questions begin to suggest themselves. If a line began ∪ – ∪ ... (what we now call an 'iambic' beginning), did that necessitate 'iambic syncopation' throughout the verse and at the end of it? To illustrate the point from Aristophanes, in the lines:

> χρήσιμον μὲν οὐδὲν ἄλ-
> λως δὲ δειλὸν καὶ μέγα

we have no doubt trochaic syncopation, but in

> ζητοῦντες ἡνίκ' ἂν σὺ νι-
> κᾶς λέγων τὰς δίκας

we are to recognize iambic syncopation. It is quite certain that Aeschylus did not know the term *anacrusis* (which was invented by Hermann), but it is probable or all but equally certain that he did not know 'acephalous' either. Is it not possible that he would think of the rhythm of a line 'iambically' in one place, 'trochaically' in another, and thus be free to make *either* of two contiguous long syllables a protracted one?

When this possibility has been stated it opens up a further view. Can it be the real explanation of things which the nineteenth-century metricians explained by applying the method of modern music, with its invariable anacrusis and descending scansion? Στρυμόνος μολοῦσαι is a very familiar phrase—not iambic. Can it be that the line began as iambic and ended as trochaic? The iambic trimeter could easily be regarded as doing that, with its caesura:

> εὐάγγελος μέν, | ὥσπερ ἡ παροιμία,
> ἕως γένοιτο | μητρὸς εὐφρόνης πάρα.

'ὥσπερ ἡ παροιμία' presents itself to the ear rather as trochaic than iambic.[1]

---

[1] So in the scazon a trochaic movement may be said to 'set in' after a marked 'caesura', leading to the ending – ∪ ⌐ | – ⊻ :
  Suffenus iste, Vare, | quem probe nosti.

SYNCOPATION AND ICTUS

mea renidet | in domo lacunar

was actually described in later times as an iambic followed by a trochaic group. 'in domo lacunar' is the same phrase as Στρυμόνος μολοῦσαι. If πνοαὶ δ' ἀπό answers to 'mea renidet', would not the structure of the line demand that the suppressed or absorbed time should be absorbed by the first *comma* or group of syllables and not by the second? In a similar way the second part of a hexameter could be thought of as anapaestic. The paroemiac (ῥεχθὲν δέ τε νήπιος ἔγνω) coincides with a catalectic anapaestic dimeter. In later times at all events there was no shrinking from such analysis. When Aristophanes was composing anapaestic tetrameters, did he in bringing a line to a close stop to reflect whether it was dactylic or anapaestic?

ἥκιστ', ἀλλ' οὐράνιαι νεφέλαι, μεγάλαι θεαὶ ἀνδράσιν ἀργοῖς.

It is a hexameter from οὐράνιαι onwards, and we shall be justified in waiting for very cogent evidence before we begin to contemplate the scansion:

λέξω τοίνυν τὴν ἀρχαίαν παιδείαν ὡς διέκειτο (or ∪ ⏜ ?)
ὅτ' ἐγὼ τὰ δίκαια λέγων ἤνθουν καὶ σωφροσύνη 'νενόμιστο.

The provisional conclusion or contention which we seem to arrive at from this discussion is that, while iambic syncopation appears to be a proved fact, we are not yet prepared to admit that all verses which appear to have an iambic beginning were thought of as 'iambic' by the poet—we do not know that Aeschylus would have called his lyrics either iambic or trochaic—or were thought of as iambic throughout, for this purpose of syncopation.

The question of reading lyric verse involves the question of *ictus*, which we postponed. Mr. White follows various metricians of recent times in denying that there was any voice-ictus or stress-ictus —a voice-ictus can hardly have been anything but a slight stress— in ancient Greek verse (*V. of Gr. Com.*, Intr., pp. xxiii, xxiv, § 28). There is no ancient evidence for it, only for beating time with the hand or wand or foot. He quotes M. Kawczynski: 'Or il me paraît inadmissible de faire exécuter aux anciens par la bouche ce qu'ils faisaient avec le pied.' But Greek poetry was far more often choric or supported by music than ours is. Mr. White has told us that no metre but the iambic trimeter was delivered in ψιλὴ λέξις. Such beating of time was far more familiar to them than to us. But what if there is no conductor's wand or dancer's foot available or obtainable? Must not *something* be done 'par la bouche' to replace it? Does a long string of short syllables become necessarily amorphous, *scopae solutae*, unless we can beat the floor or move a hand, unless we can make a movement which the hearer can hear or see? What if he is in the next room and cannot see us? Does that make it *impossible* to read to him resolved anapaests:

κακοφάτιδα βοάν, κακομέλετον ἰάν,

six short syllables and a long one, ∪ ∪ ∪ ∪ ∪ ∪ —, which would be rendered at once intelligible by the very slightest rise of the voice on the third of them?

νέφος ἐμὸν ἀπότροπον, ἐπιπλόμενον ἄφατον

can be read as resolved anapaests (νέφος ἐμον ἀποτρόπον), but the context shows it to be dochmiac and the incidence of *ictus* would be different—what it would be in a dochmius is one of the things about which we have no quite certain information. It is not only in cases like this, where there are short syllables throughout, that *ictus* is called for in reading. It is plainly important that when a heavy trochee or iambus takes by resolution the shape ∪ ∪ — or — ∪ ∪, the apparent anapaest and dactyl should be distinguished by ictus from the real anapaest and dactyl of anapaestic and dactylic verse. They are ∪́ ∪ > and > ∪́ ∪, not equivalent in time to the true anapaest and dactyl, for the long is an irrational, not a normal long. Whether we mark both short syllables with the ictus or only one of them (∪́ ∪́ — or ∪́ ∪ —) seems unimportant. For reading, it would suffice that the very slight stress required should be heard on the first syllable; both syllables would accompany the downward stroke of a conductor's wand or of the foot. The structure of Greek verse was given by quantity, and when such verse was sung, with music, or gesture and movement (σχήματα), or both, there would seem to be no need for a stress of the voice also. In that sense we may admit it to be true that 'there was no *ictus* in Greek verse'. But when these adjuncts are

SYNCOPATION AND ICTUS

removed, either *ictus* is *something* audible or the structure of the verse must be lost.[1]

The bearing of this on the main subject of this excursus is to strengthen the contention that the Ionic-choriambic-diiambic-ditrochaic scansion would be impossible for a reader, ancient or modern.

[1] In Latin the whole question of *ictus* becomes a different one. The conditions were different in at least three ways: (1) The Latin accent was different from the Greek accent, stress not pitch, and so more like what *ictus* had to be when given by the voice; (2) it was regular in its incidence on words, following a uniform and simple law; (3) the Romans more often wrote verse for readers.

CHAPTER II

THE HISTORY OF METRE AT ROME

THE history of verse at Rome falls into three great phases or stages, of the first of which we have only a dim and distant view: (1) Saturnian verse, (2) verse of the Republican period, (3) verse of the Imperial age (some of its features disclose themselves before the end of the Republic). To these might be added a fourth, the later time when accent indubitably asserts itself as a principle of verse composition. But the latter of these periods is beyond the scope of this book; it connects itself with the Middle Ages when verse could be written like 'díes írae, díes illa' ('díes' replacing 'dĭēs') or like

> ád Marónis Maúsoléum
> dúctus fúdit súper éum
> píae rórem lácrimáe

(where '-éum' rhymes with 'éum' and presumably had a similar sound).

Ancient Greek verse is consistently quantitative throughout, as far as we know it (till accent begins to assert itself in the first or second century after Christ). At a quite early time it has shaken off alliteration. There are alliterative phrases occasionally in Homer, such as νηήσας εὖ νῆας or τὸ γὰρ γέρας ἐστὶ γερόντων, and proverbs show a tendency to it (κακοῦ κόρακος κακὸν ᾠόν), but there is nothing at all resembling the alliteration of Old Italian or Old English verse. Further, if there was a period when the less conspicuous part of a foot was 'free' and might be one syllable or two (– or ᴗ or ᴗᴗ), the earliest verse we know has regulated very strictly such variation. There is hardly any question of a trochee in an epic hexameter (though a beginning like πολλὰ λισσομένη has been taken to be an indication of such a thing); no question of a Sapphic line's beginning with – – or – ᴗ ᴗ; no spondee in the 'even' places of an iambic line. The verse of the Lesbian poets does seem, it is true, to admit the substitution of one group of four syllables for another. The most curious example of this is in a quite recently recovered poem of Alcaeus, the verse of which is that known to readers of Horace as the Lesser Asclepiadean. The four syllables which follow the 'basis' may be not only – ᴗ ᴗ –, but also ᴗ – – ᴗ or ᴗ – – – or ᴗ – ᴗ –. But this variation is regulated in its incidence. It is admitted in every second line, the alternate lines being strictly Asclepiadean (*Oxyrhynchus Papyri*, vol. x, pp. 73–5).

Very different are the beginnings of verse in Italy. The *Versus Faunius* or *Saturnius* shows no such strict regulation and definiteness of form. It is multiform, if not irregular, in the highest degree—Caesius Bassus says that it varied so much 'ut vix invenerim apud Naevium quos pro exemplo ponerem'—and it has been the subject of much discussion. Was it a genuine Italian verse, independent of Greek verse, in its origin at all events, if perhaps influenced by it later? Was it strictly quantitative, or much affected by accent, or wholly accentual? Which theory will best account for the greatest number of the extant lines? Ancient metricians (quite justifiably, as far as our evidence goes) quoted as a normal Saturnian, if any one form could be regarded as normal, the line:

dabunt malum Metelli Naevio poetae.

The accentual theory scans this

        dábunt málum Metélli | Naévio poétae.

There are three accents in the first part of the line, and two in the second: both parts begin with a trochaic or 'falling' effect, the first syllable being accented. Scanned by quantity the verse resembles

  The queen was in her parlour eating bread and honey,

which Macaulay quoted to illustrate it in the Preface to his *Lays*. It is

$$\cup - \cup - \cup - - \;|\; - \cup - \cup - \overset{\cup}{-}.$$

The quantitative theory makes the verse 'iambic', the movement is a 'rising' one, at all events in the first part of the line; though of course we may describe the whole—for a modern inquirer, and without asserting that the ancients felt it so or felt it so throughout—as consisting of two trochaic tripodies preceded by an anacrusis. The accentual theory of the verse has somewhat lost ground in recent years. Leo threw the weight of his authority into the 'quantitative' scale. The issue cannot here be discussed at length. There is certainly some difficulty in supposing that Livius and Naevius composed at the same time [1]—though in different works—two kinds of verse which are so different in principle. As to the vital matter of accounting for extant lines—there are about 170 in all—it may be said briefly that, while the quantitative theory leaves many lines unexplained or very hard to explain, the accentual view explained *too many*: i.e. it did not account for them convincingly, it was too complaisant or flexible in its scheme.

  The verse certainly consists of two parts. There is almost

---

[1] Livius perhaps began by translating the *Odyssey* into Saturnians, producing plays later, but there is quite sufficient evidence that Naevius wrote his *Bellum Punicum* in his old age, *after* he had produced many dramas.

a.ways some sort of pause or division about the middle of it.
It is also pervaded by alliteration, a feature of Old Italian
poetry which long survived, finding its way into the hexameter
and other metres of Greek origin. In these two features it
bears a marked resemblance to Old English verse, such as was
written by Langland or whoever was the author of *Piers
Plowman*:

> I was weori of wandringe | and wente me to reste
> Under a brod banke | bi a bourne syde.

In the English verse alliteration is regular: a letter or sound
occurs twice in the first half of the verse and once in the
second. This was not the case in Saturnians, though now
and again the alliteration in a Saturnian does conform to
English rule:[1]

> magnam domum decoremque | ditem vexarant.

There was a revival of verse of this kind in the West of England
in the latter half of the fourteenth century. During the same
period Chaucer and other poets were writing verse of a different
kind, characterized by rhyme and by a regular rhythm (iambic)
derived from French verse.[2] Thus there would seem to be in
England in 1350-1400 a state of things as regards metre very
closely resembling the conditions at Rome in the third century
B.C. Does this analogy support the view that Saturnians were
accentual? Does it make it much easier to believe that

---

[1] Now and again, also, a Saturnian shows what is said to be a feature
of early Celtic verse, the 'binding' of the beginning of the second
hemistich with the end of the first by alliteration:

> superbiter *con*temptim | *con*terit legiones.

[2] Mr. Bridges' poem on 'Christmas Eve' is a very subtle reproduction
of what might have been written between 1350 and 1400, for the new
tendencies are not excluded altogether. Rhyme and rhythm both
appear in it:

> The cónstelláted soúnds || ran sprínkling ón earth's flóor
> As the dark vaúlt abóve || with stars was spángled o'ér.

accentual verse and verse that was quantitative in its basis
were written at the same time? Perhaps it helps a little
towards such a conclusion. But it would be highly unsafe
to take it as evidence or to give it any serious weight. For
there are considerable differences. It does not appear that
the *same poet* ever wrote both, in the distinct and wholly
separate—consistently separate—way in which Naevius wrote
his Saturnians and his dramatic metres derived from the
Greek. There had been some confusion of the two in
Layamon. Of Langland Prof. Saintsbury says, 'He knows
the new metre quite well enough to have written it had he
chosen, certainly well enough (which is perhaps even a higher
degree) to avoid falling into it constantly when he does not
choose, though its irresistibleness traps him now and then'
(*History of English Prosody*, vol. i, p. 181). A second differ-
ence between the two cases is even more important. It is not
suggested—there are no indications—that the same word would
be pronounced differently, or would tend to be delivered differ-
ently, in the two forms of verse. 'weori' and 'wandringe', the
words in themselves, sounded alike whether they occurred in
the verse of Langland or in the verse of Chaucer. Alliteration
and rhythm were different devices for dealing with the *same*
linguistic material. But it is not so in Naevius, if Saturnians
were accentual. 'dábunt málum', if the verse is accentual, are
in falling rhythm: the first syllable of two is the syllable that
is conspicuous or that counts. If the verse is quantitative,
the syllables make two iambi, $\cup - \cup -$. Could the same
material be treated so differently by the same poet at the same
time? It cannot be said to be impossible. But the English
analogy does not make it much more probable, in any very
definite way. If we are to look for an analogy, we might
perhaps point rather to the time when the edifice of quanti-
tative verse was crumbling, the time when Hilarius could write
in trochaics 'níhil ultra vox honoris afferebat desuper', or

Augustine 'gĕnus autem mixtum piscis', while Claudian could write quantitative verse with a correctness scarcely inferior to Ovid's.[1] The converse, it might be argued, is equally conceivable, a time when accent was waning and quantity gaining ground. But the two cases are not exactly on the same level. The accent that was gaining ground in the fourth century was an undoubted feature of the real, living speech of the people, and literary verse was or had become an artificial thing. In the time of Andronicus and Naevius, quantitative verse was no doubt in a sense artificial. It was cultivated by men of letters who knew Greek. But it succeeded and prevailed—succeeded even on the stage, for popular audiences. Could it have done so if it was a superstructure of an artificial kind with no real foundations in the Latin language? Mr. Bridges and others have tried to make English verse quantitative; they have produced some curious and beautiful pieces that have an interest for scholars, but they have not altered the main current of English verse. Why did Ennius succeed where Mr. Bridges and his predecessors have failed?

That is the issue—what has been said is rather a statement of the issue than a necessarily final argument. There are things which the accentualists could adduce on the other side. They could say: 'If the experiment succeeded, it was largely because the incidence of accent in Latin was such as to make coincidence of ictus and accent a thing easily achieved.' They might argue also that the morphology of Latin points to a quite strong stress accent in early times, Nómasios, for example, becoming Numisius or Numerius. And they could point to the fact, or probability, that owing to the practical and unimaginative bent of the Old Italian character, no great and

---

[1] Claudian (if the text at the place is sound) lapsed once and once only into a colloquial or non-classical quantity:

ipsum etiam ferĭtura Iovem   (*De R. Pros.* iii. 359);
ferĭtura is a good example of the Law of Breves Breviantes.

widely known poems had been written in the native form of verse. Ennius had not, like Mr. Bridges, a Shakespeare or a Milton before him.

The recent and still rather tentative science of 'Comparative Metric' has of course included Saturnians in its view, and has endeavoured to bring them into relation to a supposed Indo-European form of verse. That form is a verse of sixteen syllables, 8 + 8, which gradually took iambic or choriambic shape at its close; the half of it became o o o o ⏑ – ⏑ o (where o stands for an indeterminate syllable, short or long). To relate to this a verse which has the look of being two tripodies—one of them conspicuously trochaic—does not seem an easy matter, but it can be done. The Greek tetrameter, iambic or trochaic, made its second half catalectic, while the first half remained complete. The long line was thus an artistic structure; it did not end twice in the same way. But the Saturnian cut short and condensed *both* halves at the end, while also making the second 'acephalous'. The original scheme would be

⏑ – ⏑ – ⏑ – ⏑ – ⏑ – ⏑ – ⏑ – ⏑ –

(of course not in this strict form: for ⏑, a long syllable or two shorts would freely be admitted). The Saturnian is

⏑ – ⏑ – ⏑ – ⌞ | ∧ – ⏑ – ⏑ – ⌞ (or – ⏑ – ⏑ ⌞ –)

novém Iovís concórdés | fíliaé sorórés.[1]

[1] The iambic dimeter is seen in

The king was in his counting-house | counting out his money,

and the treatment of verse of this type by English poets is sometimes instructive, or at all events suggestive, for the interpretation of Saturnians. The occurrence of a compound word or of two monosyllables at the end of a half-line shows how natural and obvious is the effect of syncopation there,

únder yónder béech-trée | síngle ón the greén swárd.

Meredith has also syncopation in other places:

the whíte stár hóvers
Lów óver dim fields | frésh with bloómy déw.

Both parts of the line end in the same way, and the double syncopation tends to separate them. At the end of the first, hiatus and *syllaba anceps* naturally occur:

> virum mihi, Camenă, | insece versutum (P. Liv. 1.)[1]

(Livius's rendering of ἄνδρα μοι ἔννεπε, Μοῦσα—he addresses the Italian goddess of song),

> subigit omnem Loucanam | obsidesque abdoucit.
> (I. 405. 6.)

Hiatus has been thought to occur also at the end of each dipody, as in

> topper citi : ad aedes | venimus Circaë,

but it certainly occurs also within a dipody or after one foot

> postquam avem aspexit | in templo Anchisa.

The quantitative scheme, it must be admitted, requires many licences to make it workable; so many that its claim to be a real scheme becomes rather doubtful. The second part of the Saturnian line has an obvious resemblance to certain phrases which existed in a quite definite shape in Greek verse. It coincides in syllables with

> veris et Favoni,

the second κῶλον in one of Horace's Archilochian metres (*Odes* i. 4), and also with the second part of a line which Horace writes in *Odes* ii. 18

> mea renidet | in domo lacunar—

In the first of these lines, and in others,

> Knees and tresses folded | to slip and ripple idly,

the arrangement of words seems to make the second part begin with an anacrusis (or, if we prefer that description, an acephalous iambic phrase recovers its first syllable), as in Saturnians we have *in éxpeditiónem* or *Románm rediit triúmphans*.

[1] References are to Diehl's *Altlateinische Inschriften* (I.) and *Poetae Romani veteres* (P.) in the Bonn 'Kleine Texte'.

a line which requires only the insertion of an iambus (e.g. 'quidem' after 'mea') to make it a regular Saturnian. That part of the Saturnian coincided so often with a well-known Greek verse was no doubt one of the things which caused the Roman metricians to treat it as quantitative. If the writers of it wrote it as quantitative, they were negligent of its proper rhythmical effect. In a trochaic phrase like 'in domo lacunar' it is not unlikely that the penultimate syllable was τρίχρονος or τρίσημος ⌣ = ∪∪∪), and this would forbid its resolution into two shorts. This the Roman writers of Saturnians ignored or had forgotten. They sometimes resolve the syllable, as Plautus resolves the penultimate syllable of an iambic septenarius.

One of the most certain variations in the Saturnian is a further syncope, the suppression of another syllable, so that instead of −∪ −∪ −− we have −∪ ⌣− −−. With the first half normal, this results in coincidence with a choriambus:

−⌣⌣ −⌣
Amulius divisque gratulabatur.[1]

Another curious and clearly recognizable variation is the substitution of trochee for iambus. The substitution of a choriambus for two iambi—which means the substitution of a trochee for the first—appears to occur in English iambics, as when a blank verse begins 'Purples the east ...'. It is found also in the Greek trimeter, and though it is very rare (*supra*, p. 86), one or two of the instances may have been known to Milton. But in the extant Saturnians choriambi are very few, and many other appearances of trochees have to be reckoned with. In the line

immolabat auream | victimam pulcram (P. Naev. 2.)

[1] The cadence of the scazon is the most frequent ending for a period in oratorical prose (−∪−−−). It is notable that other Saturnian forms coincide with favourite prose-endings: 'maxume mereto' −∪− ∪∪∪, 'donūm dănūnt Hērcŏlī' (Zielinski's double cretic), 'terra pestem teneto' (the 'Asiatic' clausula, −∪− −∪−⌣). Clearly these were things that appealed to the Italian ear whether in verse or prose.

the whole of the first part is trochaic, *auream* taking the place of *Metelli*. But – ᴗ – may take the place of 'Metelli' *without any change in the preceding feet*

$$- - \mid \cup - \mid - \cup - \quad - \cup \llcorner \cup \cup -$$
donum danunt Hercolei | maxume mereto (I. 65. 4.)

and the converse of this seems to occur in the old incantation (P. *carm. vetust.* 6)

$$- \cup - - \quad \cup - -$$
Terra pestem teneto
Salus hic maneto ($\cup \llcorner - \cup - - ?$).

So in Naevius 18

$$- \cup - - \quad \cup - -$$
deinde pollens sagittis | inclutus Arquitenens ($- \cup \cup \llcorner \cup \cup - ?$)

There are numerous other variations, some slight, some perplexing in the extreme. Among the slighter is the admission of an anapaest for an iambus, or of a dactyl for a trochee ('conterit legiones', P. Naev. 31). A few lines appear to have no diaeresis in the middle—a word does not end at the end of the first part. There are two examples in the dedicatory inscription of a Guild of Cooks:

opiparum ad vitam quolun|dam festosque dies

(I. 86. 2.)

a line which seems to begin with $\cup \cup \cup - \underline{\prime} - \cup -$, where the cretic may be compared with *Hercoli* quoted above.[1]

---

[1] The ending *festosque dies* or *-dam festosque dies* ($- - \cup \cup -$) is strange, on any quantitative theory, and the more so because it would have been so easy to make it answer to the norm (if there was a norm) by making it *-dam diesque festos* (= *Naevio poetae*). The exact date of the inscription is not known. If the cooks were in Sardinia before 204, cooking for Roman officers, it is a curious coincidence that there was in the army (perhaps as a petty officer in an auxiliary cohort) a man from Rudiae who was to be famous as a poet. But it would be fanciful to suggest that the cooks employed Ennius to write the verses for them. Ennius no doubt could write Saturnians, though he disparaged them later when he competed with Naevius in epic poetry (*Annales* vii, init.). His

The fifth line is:

ququei (= coqui) huc (= hoc) dederunt impera|toribus summis,

where the second part of the line seems to show the syncopation already illustrated ('-toribus summis', $-\cup\mathrel{\llcorner}--$). If so, the first part is a complete iambic dimeter, which might be quoted by the holders of the Indo-European theory. They might point also to forms of the second part of the line, such as

> imperator dedicat   (I. 66. 5.)
> in expeditionem   (P. Naev. 20.)

which together might be held to point to 'in expeditionibus' as a possible form.[1] But probably these are accidental vagaries rather than reversions conscious or unconscious to a primitive type. Against them must be set the most perplexing variations of all, when the second part of the line assumes so attenuated a form

> parisuma fuit [2]
> fuisse virum

that one is tempted to resume the accentual theory and suppose that the principle of the second. part was simply that there must be accents in it.

Upon the primitive Italian versification there supervened— overlapping it considerably—the verse of the early drama.

Hedyphagetica (and his gout!) could be adduced as showing an interest in the art of the cooks.

[1] The ancient metricians cited half a dozen different forms of Greek verse as answering to various forms of the Saturnian. One of these makes the first part an iambic dimeter:

> turdis edacibus dolos | comparas amice.

In nearly all of these schemes the *second* part is the same, $-\cup-\cup-\underset{\smile}{}$ ('Naevio poetae'). An iambic dimeter there, we may infer, was unknown, or at all events unfamiliar.

[2] *parisuma fuit* is not quite so difficult as *fuisse virum*, perhaps, for *fuit* (*fuvit*) may be *fūit*.

The nature and history of this have been briefly considered above (pp. 79 f.). It may be taken as established that this verse took some account of accent : that can hardly be doubted by any careful reader of Prof. Lindsay's Appendix to his larger edition of the *Captivi*. And with this regard for accent are connected the deviations from the Greek restrictions. Livius and Naevius made words like 'dábunt' or 'málum' iambic, not trochaic, and they had to face some deviation of ictus from accent, especially in certain parts of the line, such as the beginning and the end of a senarius :

> utinám ne in nemore . . .
> vectí petebant.

A word of one or of three syllables immediately started a movement natural to Latin in which accent and ictus largely coincided. *O di ímmortáles* was a natural beginning for an iambic line, *immórtalés di* was an effect to be avoided ; *labórans, quaérens, párcens, illi serviens* was iambic throughout for the Roman ear, though there is a short syllable only in the first foot and the last. In trochaic verse the difficulties were less, and popular verse as we have seen was often trochaic (*supra*, p. 103):

> Gállos Cáesar ín triúmphum dúxit, ídem in cúriam.

Ennius originated a different movement in his hexameters, in which the deviations from Greek quantitative principles were very slight. But the other kind of verse flourished and advanced in the drama, and hexameters for long made little progress towards Greek finish. A new movement towards precision and euphony begins only within the last fifty years of the Republic, with Cicero, Laevius, and Catullus. The versification of the Republican period is characterized on the whole by the neglect of Greek restrictions. Certain new restrictions and compensations were introduced, no doubt, which belonged specially to Latin. But the general fact remains. It depends on the point of view whether we say that this Roman verse has greater freedom and naturalness, or greater licence and irregularity.

In the time of Augustus and his successors the Roman handling of Greek metres was very different. Apart from comedy, probably, and the Fables of Phaedrus certainly, there was very little that the strictest Hellenist could call licence or irregularity. On the contrary, the Greek would have to acknowledge that Latin versification was stricter than his own. He would find tragic verse in which the fifth foot was *always* a spondee : in lyric verse of the Glyconic, Asclepiadean, and hendecasyllabic type, the first two syllables *always* both long, never ∪ – or – ∪ (which Catullus had admitted) : the heroic hexameter almost always ending in a word of two or three syllables, very rarely in a monosyllable, very rarely in a word of four syllables, and still more rarely in one of five : the elegiac pentameter nearly always ending in a word of two syllables : and many other limitations of the same kind. In this period, as in the earlier one, the Romans modify Greek forms of verse to suit their own language. But now the modifications are *within* Greek rules and involve hardly any transgression of them. New laws are imposed. Horace enacts a number of new rules for his lyric metres, sometimes obeying them with absolute uniformity, sometimes deviating once or twice from his rule, as if to show that it is after all only an enactment of his own, as when he once in an early ode begins a Glyconic line with – ∪

ignis Iliacas domos

and twice neglects the diaeresis which he imposed upon Alcaics

spectandus in cer|tamine Martio.

Horace's rules, as far as we know, were regarded by his successors as absolutely binding. Statius was not free to write an Alcaic line like that.

For this tendency in later Roman versification more than one cause can be assigned. There is first the very general cause that the Romans were related to the Greeks as Statius, when he wrote Alcaics, to Horace. In the form of their poetry they were imitators, and the imitator or successor cannot take the same liberties that were taken by his master. What in the predecessor were the pleasing vagaries or experiments of genius are in the imitator only licence or negligence. Greek and Latin verse composition at the present day is subject to this principle. Nobody proposes to allow a schoolboy to write a pentameter like

quam modo qui me unum atque unicum amicum habuit.

The hexameter he is expected to attempt is the Virgilian or Ovidian, his elegiac couplet is to be modelled upon Ovid, or at all events upon nothing earlier than Propertius or Tibullus. Of every form of verse at Rome it may be said, in Aristotle's words, that πολλὰς μεταβολὰς μεταβαλοῦσα ἐπαύσατο ἐπεὶ ἔσχε τὴν αὐτῆς φύσιν. Of course the modern composer does sometimes try to write verse exactly in the vein of Lucretius or Catullus. But that is a *tour de force* or a special kind of literary exercise. The ancient poet or verse-writer was not an imitator in the same degree, and did not set about his work in that way. It was not only at Rome that this principle operated : Callimachus and Apollonius had prepared the way for Virgil by avoiding many of the features of Homeric verse ; they did not allow themselves the freer and looser movement of many Homeric lines, only the more euphonious and well-balanced were retained.

A second cause was undoubtedly the nature of the Latin language, its fibre or texture, and in particular the nature and incidence of its accent. A stress accent, even though slight, came into competition with the ictus or beat of the verse, as the Greek accent did not do. It is probable, though perhaps not provable, that this was the reason why in hexameters an ending like

nec mi pretiúm dederitis

was avoided. Whether such changes were made consciously or half-consciously or from a vague and almost unconscious feeling for euphony, it is difficult to say. It seems certain that the more complex and variable types of Greek lyric were found to be unworkable in Latin. The language could not be poured into moulds so exact and so elaborate. The reader could not follow so subtle a structure, partly because the Latin accent would lead him astray. The Latin accent also had perplexing effects upon quantity. There is practically nothing in Greek that resembles 'domí mánsit' or 'ex Graécis bónïs Latinas'.[1] Even in the Augustan age, when the sense for quantity and for metrical form had been highly developed, the reader probably demanded some well-known and recurrent metrical scheme to guide him. Horace, when he was asked by Augustus to compose a hymn for the Ludi Saeculares, must have been tempted to choose some Pindaric form. But he chooses one of the Lesbian stanzas which he had already practised and 'standardized'. He does not even take the Alcaic stanza, which he had used with conspicuous success for political and religious themes. He selects the Sapphic stanza, with its three

---

[1] The incidence of accent in Greek was different and much more varied, and even if it happened to fall similarly on a group of syllables, being a musical accent or pitch-accent, it had not the same power to affect quantity. In Greek verse quantity was rigid. It is sometimes said that Greek varies its quantities more than Latin, and Martial gave currency to the idea when he wrote:

Graeci, quibus est nihil negatum
et quos Ἄρες Ἄρες decet sonare.

But in the same dialect and in the same period quantity is not variable to any appreciable extent. Attic tragedy had ξεῖνος and μοῦνος beside ξένος and μόνος, but the speech of tragedy is composite, and these forms were Ionic or Old Attic.

AT ROME

lines all exactly alike and the fourth extremely simple. And he chooses this with Greek precedent against him, for the fixed and recurrent short stanza of the Lesbian 'individualistic' lyric had had no place in such public celebrations.

The third cause was a metrical theory which had become current at Rome in Horace's time. It was set out by Varro, and afterwards by Caesius Bassus. It has been traced back to Heraclides Ponticus, and it may have been invented or developed by him. We shall have to consider it further in dealing with Horace's lyrics. It was a theory of the origin and derivation of metres. They were supposed to have sprung from certain simple verse forms, especially the hexameter and the iambic trimeter. The trochaic tetrameter was also required. A hexameter like

$$\text{Κούρητές τ' ἐμάχοντο καὶ}$$
$$\text{Αἰτωλοὶ μενεχάρμαι}$$

gave birth to the Glyconic and Pherecratean lines. A 'hendecasyllabic' line was accounted for in a similar way. It followed that the first two syllables should both be long. A Sapphic line contained the beginning of a trochaic tetrameter:

$$-\ \cup |-\ \ -|-$$
integer vitae,

and since the Romans and the Latin language had a liking for spondees and long syllables,[1] the Roman lyric poet was ready to enact that the second foot must be a spondee.

---

[1] It seems probable, though it might be difficult to prove, that Latin supplied spondees in greater profusion than Greek. It is not difficult to recall terminations that are heavier in Latin, showing either a long syllable or a syllable closed by a consonant where Greek has something less: *corpus*, σῶμᾰ, *monti, montem, montes,* ἀνδρί, ἄνδρᾰ, ἄνδρες, ἄνδρᾰς, *solvebas, solvi, solvisti,* ἔλυες, ἔλυσᾰ, λέλυκᾰ, ἔλυσᾰς, *feriebas, feriebatur*, ἔτυπτες, ἐτύπτετο. No doubt there are also cases of the converse, such as ναύτης, *naută,* σελήνη, *lună.*

All this theory and practice began at Rome before the Empire, in the last days of the Republic. Catullus, it is true, does not adopt the theory in his Sapphics and hendecasyllabics.[1] But it was known in his time, and he and his friends (preceded by Laevius and Cicero) were cultivating a more exact and refined versification than had hitherto been attempted. This they learned largely from the poets of the Alexandrian age, from Callimachus or Euphorion. Alexandrian poetry never attained to the highest levels, and after Apollonius it became feebler and more frigid. But Rome was a different place from Egypt or Syria,

> quas sub perpetuis tenuerunt fata tyrannis.

It was still a free State in Catullus's time (though freedom was gravely menaced), and it had great traditions of freedom and self-respect, a national life and spirit which in the next generation resulted in poetry such as had not been written for some four centuries—since the great age of Athens came to an end with Euripides.

This greater poetry of Rome and Italy begins, for us, with the *Georgics* (completed and read to Octavian at Atella in 29 B.C.). It is not likely that what Varius had produced was of great importance; Ennius had been national in spirit, but crude and rugged in form; Lucretius's subject had not been specially Roman, and his verse fell short of consistent finish and harmony.

The century which preceded the *Georgics* was a period of very varied literary activity at Rome and of very varied experiments in metre. In the last three decades of the second century B.C. Lucilius was writing his *Saturae*, in which after experiments with other metres (iambic and trochaic, written of

---

[1] Some of his hendecasyllabic poems have only — — as the 'basis', e.g. Nos. V, IX, X. In these he may have been deliberately following the Heraclidean precept.

course in the Roman fashion, and a few elegiacs) he made a free and rather formless hexameter the vehicle of his satire, creating a type of satire—in hexameters throughout—of which Quintilian could say 'tota nostra est'; Accius was carrying on the work of Ennius and Pacuvius in tragedy, writing verse which was even more defiantly Roman in its frequent spondees than the verse of Ennius (*supra*, p. 89); and comedy was dealing with Roman or Italian scenes in the *Togata*, to be presently succeeded by the *Atellana*—both of these in verse substantially similar to that of Plautus. Even these coarser and more national forms of comedy had to compete in popular favour (as Terentian comedy earlier had had to compete) with boxing-matches or gladiatorial shows, which now received the recognition of the State. In the general life and politics of the time, Roman or Italian, anti-Hellenic tendencies are represented by Marius, the peasant-soldier of Arpinum, whose rival Sulla was much more Hellenist and cosmopolitan.

Roman tendencies and native ideas did not hold the field. Beside them there was much study and effort more or less inspired by Greece, and especially by Alexandria and Pergamum. Accius wrote various forms of verse, outside his tragedies. Whether he wrote any Saturnians is doubtful.[1] He certainly wrote Sotadean verse, which had more vogue at Rome than the modern reader realizes ('Ionic a maiore' in the form of a catalectic tetrapody,

$$--\cup\cup\,|\,--\cup\cup\,|\,--\cup\cup\,|\,--),$$

and he used this Sotadean verse as a vehicle for discourse on poetry and literary topics. Eratosthenes had dealt with the history of comedy in verse, and Horace's alleged predecessor, Neoptolemus of Parium, with the principles of poetry

---

[1] It was maintained by Leo, but the evidence is not quite conclusive. This was part of his case for the quantitative nature of Saturnians. If Accius wrote them, some sort of continuity of tradition comes into view: Accius—Varro—Caesius Bassus.

in general. At Rome, besides Accius, there were Volcacius Sedigitus and Porcius Licinus. From the former we have what was an Alexandrian thing, a 'canon' of poets, the well-known lines in which Roman comic poets are marshalled in order of merit, Caecilius coming first and Plautus second:

> Plautus secundus facile exsuperat ceteros ;

Licinus dealt with the history of poetry in verse:

> Punico bello secundo Musa pinnato gradu
> intulit se bellicosam in Romuli gentem feram.

'Musa' is Ennius's goddess of Greek or Graeco-Roman song, not the 'Camena' whom Andronicus had addressed in the first line of his Saturnian *Odyssey*; and Licinus is nearer the truth than Horace with his 'post Punica bella'. The two trochaic lines of Licinus show no violation of Greek rule: there is no spondee in the first, third, or fifth place.[1]

In the first three decades of the next century (100–70 B.C.) a new movement begins in Roman poetry. To that time belongs Cicero's version in Latin hexameters of the Φαινόμενα of Aratus, which, as he tells us himself, he wrote when he was 'admodum adulescentulus', a phrase which points to 90–85 B.C. or, if it exaggerates his youthfulness, to 80 at latest. The hexameter has undergone a great change. Straggling and unpruned in Ennius, it is here coerced into a shape not greatly different from that of the Augustan age. How far the change was due to Cicero himself it is difficult to say, for only scanty fragments of the verse of this time have survived, and still more scanty evidence for dating them. To these years probably belong Matius's rendering of the *Iliad*, and an earlier *Moretum* in verse much looser than that of the *Moretum* which came to be ascribed to Virgil. Apart from hexameters, Catulus presents

---

[1] In the twelve lines, however, in which Licinus deals with the career and death of Terence, the versification is less strict.

an example of a Roman of rank amusing himself with the composition of epigrams in an Alexandrian vein:[1]

>constiteram exorientem Auroram forte salutans,
>   cum subito a laeva Roscius exoritur, etc.;

and there are the romantic effusions and metrical excursions of Laevius, commonly assigned to this time, though the date and personality of Laevius are somewhat obscure and ill-attested. In Laevius metrical and poetical experiment seems to be a kind of pastime, the fanciful and artificial occupation of hours of leisure, composition such as is depicted a little later by Catullus:

>scribens versiculos uterque nostrum
>ludebat numero modo hoc, modo illo,
>reddens mutua per iocum atque vinum
>ut convenerat esse delicatos.

The extreme of artificiality is seen in the Alexandrian attempt, after the example of Dosiadas, to write a poem in lines of such regulated length as to present to the eye on the page the figure of an altar or an axe or other object. The surviving fragments of Laevius reveal also experiments in the precis composition of Ionics, and a curiously romantic and eccentric treatment of old Greek stories in iambic dimeters, along with a new vein of fancy in titles, double compounds such as Protesilaudamia and Sirenocirca. Laodamia wonders whether her long-absent lord has fallen under the spell of some enchantress in Asia, decked out in Lydian gold and gems:

>   aut
>nunc quaepiam alia de Ilio
>Asiatico ornatu adfluens
>aut Sardiano aut Lydio,
>fulgens decore et gratia
>pellicuit?

[1] Mainly Alexandrian, though there are earlier examples, one or two of them attributed to Plato.

Andromache has twined a wreath for Hector:

> tu, Andromacha, per ludum manu
> lascivola ac tenellula
> capiti meo trepidans libens,
> insolita plexti munera.

We are far from Homer and Homer's spirit when Andromache's hand is 'lascivola ac tenellula', and these *molliculi versus* of a *tener poeta*[1] are metrically careful and exact; they run smoothly, and the second foot is a pure iambus. In his liking for this metre Laevius anticipates the taste of later centuries and reminds us of the age of Prudentius and early Christian poetry. In diction as in metre he had a tendency to curious refinements, to what is unfamiliar, bizarre, or *recherché*, (Aul. Gell. xix. 7. 4).

Thus Laevius, if his work is rightly placed about 80 B.C., was a forerunner of the group of young poets whom Cicero called 'cantores Euphorionis', out of whose number Asinius Pollio and Cornelius Gallus (whom Cicero perhaps had in mind when he spoke of Euphorion) survived to see the Augustan age. In their hands and in their time (roughly 65–45 B.C.) poetry at Rome was what it would quite naturally be in a period of great political agitation and social unrest. It was either violently political and personal, plunging into the midst of the unrest and agitation, as in Catullus's verses on Caesar:

> socer generque, perdidistis omnia;

or it dealt with the most remote and romantic stories, such as were collected for Gallus by Parthenius in his Ἐρωτικὰ

---

[1] Catullus's phrase for his friend Caecilius. There were precedents for the lyric treatment of Homeric stories in Alcman, Stesichorus, and Sappho. The Andromache fragment recalls the recently recovered poem on the wedding of Hector and Andromache, attributed (though not with certainty) to Sappho.

παθήματα, as in Catullus's *Peleus and Thetis*, Calvus's *Io*, Cinna's *Smyrna*, and the extant *Ciris*, which later was attributed to Virgil, who was then a youth. Lucretius stood aloof from the tempests of the time in a different spirit, preaching with grave earnestness the creed of Epicurus, which was to set men free from unrest and ambition, from the fear of gods and the fear of death. But we are here concerned with the metrical qualities of all this poetry, not with its spirit or its themes.

Both in its iambic and its romantic vein the poetry of the 'cantores' was characterized by a high degree of finish and exactness and even artificiality. To write a poem in purely iambic feet throughout (as Catullus did in his *Phaselus* and in his most venomous attack on Caesar, No. XXIX) was something of a *tour de force*, especially in the somewhat heavy and spondaic language of Latium. The workmanship was the workmanship of Callimachus,[1] and the choice of metres was more or less Alexandrian, only now and again deviating into direct imitation of Sappho. Callimachus had used the 'scazon' or 'choriambus' extensively in his Fables, as a recently recovered papyrus has enabled us to realize. In their treatment of the hexameter the 'cantores' showed similar smoothness and finish. They decried Ennius, and agreed with Callimachus in deprecating the long and ambitious epic or κυκλικὸν ποίημα. They cultivated poetic diction (though they have still a number of prosaic words and phrases which Augustan poetry rejected), and they spent great pains in polishing the cadence of their lines. Elision is infrequent, though sometimes rather harsh when it does occur. They have an Alexandrian liking, which

---

[1] Not, specially, of Archilochus. Horace had some justification when he wrote:

> Parios ego primus iambos
> ostendi Latio, numeros animosque secutus
> Archilochi.

Catullus, no doubt, had something of the *animus*: perhaps more of it than Horace.

Cicero did not share, for the σπονδειάζων, seen in Catullus's poem, in the *Ciris* (to a less degree), in the anonymous passage (no doubt rightly assigned to a 'cantor Euphorionis') (Bährens, *Fr. Poet. Lat.*, p. 327)

> tuque Lycaonio prognata e semine nymphe,
> quam gelido raptam de vertice Nonacrenae,

and in the scanty fragments of Varro Atacinus, who may be said to stand between them and Virgil or to represent the transition from them to the Augustan age:

> hortantes 'o Phoebe' et 'ieie' conclamarant.

These are minor features of their verse. Its general character is that it has a certain monotony in cadence and heaviness in construction. The monotony arises from the too frequent use of a type of line, quite effective in itself, which is in evidence at the very opening of Catullus's poem:

> Peliaco quondam prognátae vértice pínus
> dicuntur liquidas Neptúni násse per úndas.[1]

Accent and ictus coincide three times. The heaviness of construction consists in the frequent extension of a grammatical period or sentence over many lines, its subordinate clauses or *cola* often occupying a whole hexameter each. The oratorical period is dominant; the structure of the language has not yet been adapted to verse. The sense too often ends with the end of the line. The frequency with which it does so has been investigated. The result is to show it happening about twice as often in Catullus as in Virgil. The inquirer Drachmann (in *Hermes*, vol. 43) gives figures for the ending of periods, sentences, and subordinate clauses. The figures for sentences will suffice for our present purpose. They are: Cicero, *Aratea*, 50·3 per cent.; Catullus LXVI, 50·8 per cent.; Lucretius, about

---

[1] Observe in this line how Catullus's Alexandrianism betrays itself in 'dicuntur' (κλείονται, φατίζεται). The story is not a reality to the poet; he thinks of it as a myth.

50 per cent.; *Ciris*, 51·3 per cent.; *Culex*, 41·3 per cent.; *Georgics*, 34·8 per cent.; *Aeneid*, 27·7 per cent. (These figures must be taken as only approximate, for they are based not on a survey of the whole texts, but on tracts of two or three hundred lines.) Very often the subordinate clause which occupies a whole line is participial:

caerula verrentes abiegnis aequora palmis, (Catullus.)
coccina non teneris pedibus Sicyonia servans,

(*Ciris*, 169.)

a thing which Virgil and the Augustan poets admitted very sparingly. The present participle in the nominative—especially if it came at the end of the line, and was preceded by the principal verb—seems to have been particularly disliked; in the *Eclogues*, which usher in a new era, there is only one example of it—one in 829 lines—and that is an echo of Lucretius:

florentes ferulas et grandia lilia quassans.

(*Ecl.* x. 25 : Lucr. iv. 587.)

What remained for Virgil to do, and what he did—perhaps Varro Atacinus helped—was to recast the language of poetry, to pour it into different moulds, to break it up into shorter sentences which either occupied about half a line or at all events stopped at a caesura, usually the penthemimeral or hephthemimeral. This was a thing which never had to be done for Greek, in historical times; the Homeric poet or succession of poets had achieved this mastery of sentence-construction in verse. But this was not the whole of Virgil's secret. The other part of it was to vary the division of the line in such a way that a whole group of lines gained harmony and coherence. Instead of a long grammatical sentence with its clauses occupying lines of verse, we have now a poetic fabric or structure, a paragraph held together by metrical or rhythmical variations. The caesura shifts or swings this way and that, in a way that could often be represented by a curved line. Verses formed by one sentence, in which the caesura is very slight and rather metrical than rhetorical, do occur. But they are not heaped together. Such a verse often stands very effectively as the first or last of a group.

> nec vero hae sine sorte datae, | sine iudice sedes:
> quaesitor Minos | urnam movet; ⋮ ille silentum
> conciliumque vocat | vitasque et crimina discit.
> proxima deinde tenent | maesti loca, ⋮ qui sibi letum
> insontes peperere manu | lucemque perosi
> proiecere animas; | quam vellent aethere in alto
> nunc et pauperiem et | duros perferre labores!
> fas obstat, ⋮ tristique | palus | inamabilis unda
> alligat ⋮ et novies | Styx interfusa coercet.[1]

The achievement of the Augustan age lay partly in the mastery of metre, partly in things which lie *extra artem metricam*, the treatment in a new spirit of larger themes— themes of national significance, or of graver human importance than the abnormal adventures and passions of Io, Smyrna, or Scylla. The *Georgics* is at once the encomium of Italy and the epic of Man's relations with Nature; the *Aeneid* the epic of a far-reaching purpose of the gods, worked out through the fortunes and efforts of a strong but submissive personality— strong at least in the outcome, for such weakness as Aeneas shows belongs to the earlier part of his career and does not reappear after his meeting with the shade of Anchises in the world of ghosts. These things belong to the history of Roman poetry, not to the history of metre. In the Augustan age several

---

[1] In analysing a group of Virgilian lines, it is desirable to have a different symbol for what we have seen to be the vital caesura, and for divisions which, though not vital, have yet considerable metrical and rhetorical importance. The symbol for the latter might be used for a division which is sometimes the vital one, but is not so in a particular line. The first of the lines quoted above perhaps has a subordinate trochaic division: 'sine sorte ⋮ datae |'.

forms of verse were brought to maturity, were regulated and more or less finally 'standardized'. One of these was the elegiac (*supra*, p. 53). Tragic verse was probably written by Varius and Ovid in a strict and hellenized form differing little from the verse of Seneca. Horace gave new grace and finish to the Lucilian hexameter of satire, while preserving its conversational ease and variety. And Horace set himself to be the Alcaeus of Latium and to annex for Rome a new province of lyric poetry, or rather several provinces, for his lyric had more than one vein, it could be moral or patriotic, erotic or convivial. The metres of Horace will be treated in a separate chapter, but it may be useful to summarize here the changes which he made in the forms of verse he adopted. They are changes characteristic of the Roman craftsman. The Roman had an aptitude for law and for framing definite regulations, and Horace was the νομοθέτης for lyric verse after his time. The historian of poetry may speak of the secret of lyric verse being lost with Horace and the moulds broken,[1] but what Horace did—from the metrician's point of view—was to impart to the moulds a rigidity that was unbreakable. In the metres of the *Odes*, there are no variable syllables, no places where the poet may put a short or a long as he pleases. And this regularity is obtained by enacting that where the metre admits a long syllable that syllable shall *always* be long. In some metres this had a greater effect than in others. It made Alcaics capable of a Roman *gravitas* which eminently suited such patriotic odes as the first six of Book III. Secondly, Horace laid it down that certain places in a line *must* be marked by the end of a word. In Asclepiadean metres it was the end of the first, or of the first and second, 'choriambus'. In Sapphics, and in the first two lines of an Alcaic stanza, the result was to give the lines a more complex structure, they ceased to be

---

[1] Mr. J. W. Mackail in his sketch of *Latin Literature*.

single *cola* and became lines consisting of two parts, divided by a caesura and a diaeresis, as in the hexameter and pentameter, respectively. It should be added that, though Horace's regulations were not broken by later poets, most of them were once or twice departed from by Horace himself, as if he wished to show that he knew quite well that the verse had been different and that these restrictions were self-imposed.

The more important metres were so effectually 'standardized' in the Augustan age that very little that is new in principle is met with after that time. The historian of verse in the Imperial age would have to deal with a few new phenomena, such as the vogue of 'Faliscan' verse

(quando flagella iugas, ita iuga, $-\cup\cup-\cup\cup-\mid\cup\cup\cup-$),

unimportant for literature, or the occasional use of Anacreontics, as in Hadrian's epitaph for his horse. And if he went far enough or aimed at completeness he would have to deal with what is indeed new and in fact revolutionary in principle—the encroachments of accent and the rise of accentual verse. But this does not come within the scope of a text-book of classical metre. It is rather a prelude to the metrical history of later centuries. In its beginnings, moreover, it is peculiarly entangled and perplexing. Accent supplants quantity sporadically, at long intervals (as in Hilarius), or the verse is half invaded by it, or (as in Commodianus) there is a strange mixture of accent and pseudo-quantity—things which happen also in Greek verse at Byzantium.

CHAPTER III

THE LYRIC METRES OF HORACE

I. Introductory

THE following pages on Horatian lyrics were written before the rest of this book and without reference to it, as has been explained in the Preface. I have not rewritten them, or altered them materially, for it is here in particular that some repetition may be justified or at all events excused. The *Odes* of Horace are read in all schools where classics are taught at all, but at the present day, unfortunately, many of the pupils do not know Greek.

The pages, however, were not written for readers entirely ignorant of Greek. Greek is occasionally quoted, and Greek theory and practice are touched upon. To what extent this should be done—for the student of Horace—is a somewhat difficult matter. He ought to have some idea of the form in which Horatian metres were composed by Sappho and Alcaeus, but he is not deeply concerned with the nature and rhythmical structure which the metres had in these early days, and he is still more slightly concerned with theories of an 'Indo-European verse' from which they are supposed to be derived. It is more important to explain to him (so far as there is any evidence for it) what views Horace himself probably held about the verse he was writing. This means touching upon the Varronian theory of the derivation of metres, the metrical notions of

Caesius Bassus (who cannot have known Horace, but who was perhaps born early enough to know Ovid), and the metrical practice of Seneca in lyric composition. In arrangement, I follow here also the threefold classification of metres which comes from the Greeks. It seems inevitable—there *are* only three ways of combining feet in metrical groups—and it has two great advantages in that it at once leads the learner from the simpler to the more complex and follows the chronological order in which Horace probably mastered the forms of verse which he wrote.

It seems obvious that the common practice of taking up some one book of the *Odes* and reading it continuously cannot result in introducing the pupil to Horatian metre in any easy or simple way. If it is the Second Book or the Third, he will begin with *Alcaics*; if it is the First, the variety and complexity will be too great. Another method of dealing with the *Odes* would be that the teacher should make his own selection from them, beginning with what is metrically simple. So, too, in reading Pindar, it is better to begin, say, with the fourth Pythian than with the first Olympian ode. If this method were adopted, and applied to spheres other than metre, the result would be that instead of reading perhaps two books of the *Odes* from beginning to end, the Class or Form would read all that are of conspicuous interest and importance. The pupil should have a plain text of the whole of Horace (so that passages in the *Satires* or *Epistles* could be looked up) or at all events an edition of the *Odes* and *Epodes*, such as Mr. Page's. Initiation into metre should come first; for a Horatian ode read unmetrically or as prose is an absurdity, more likely to destroy the pupil's sense of literary form than to foster it. The selection will therefore begin with a group of poems read mainly for their metre. To suggest such a metrical group is all that is strictly relevant here, and beyond the sphere of metre each teacher will have his own preferences and will prefer to make his own selection. But, in order to adumbrate the method as a whole, I venture to append a selection of poems arranged in other groups. In the metrical group the pupil should be required to learn by heart, and very thoroughly, several lines of each form of verse. In simpler metres two lines may suffice. In Sapphic or Alcaic verse he should be required to learn and to recite correctly several stanzas. In suggesting a group of poems to be read for their metre, I have endeavoured to select things which have an intrinsic interest also, but which might have been written by Horace at any time —which are undated, and do not fall into any chronological arrangement of his lyrics.

Metrical Selection.

I.

Odes I. vii ('Laudabunt alii') } dactylic.
„ IV. vii ('Di ffugere nives')
Epodes ii ('Beatus ille') iambic.
Odes III. xii ('Miserarum est') Ionic.

II.

Epodes xiii ('Horrida tempestas').
Odes I. iv ('Solvitur acris hiems').

III.

Odes I. xii ('Quem virum aut heroa') Sapphic.
„ II. xiii ('Ille et nefasto') Alcaic.
„ IV. viii ('Donarem pateras')
„ I. xi ('Tu ne quaesieris') } Asclepiadean.
„ I. iii ('Sic te diva')
„ I. xiv ('O navis referent')

Poems of historical interest

(in order of time).

Epodes xvi ('Altera iam teritur.' To be compared with Virg. *Ecl.* iv. About 40 B.C.?).

Epodes vii ('Quo, quo scelesti.' An early protest against civil war).
,, ix ('Quando repostum.' Actium).

Odes I. xxxvii ('Nunc est bibendum.' Conquest of Egypt).
,, I. xxxi ('Quid dedicatum.' Temple of Apollo, 28 B.C.).
,, II. xv ('Iam pauca aratro.' Selfish luxury of the age).
,, III. ii ('Angustam amice.' Virtues called for under the new government).
,, III. iii ('Iustum et tenacem.' Troy not to be refounded).
,, III. v ('Caelo tonantem.' Lessons of history, Regulus).
,, III. vi ('Delicta maiorum.' Corruption of the age).
,, III. xiv ('Herculis ritu.' Augustus in Spain).
,, III. xxiv ('Intactis opulentior.' The demand for moral legislation; a thankless task, l. 30, 'clarus postgenitis').

Carmen Saeculare (l. 17, hopes of success—legislation attempted).

Odes IV. v ('Divis orte bonis') } Successful reform.
,, IV. xv ('Phoebus volentem')
,, IV. iv and xiv (Successes of Drusus and Tiberius).

Horace as a Poet.

His poetic art.

Odes I. i ('Maecenas atavis.' The poet's vocation).
,, I. xxxii ('Poscimur. si quid.' Alcaeus).
,, III. xxx ('Exegi monumentum').
,, IV. ii (Pindar. 'Operosa parvus | carmina fingo').
,, IV. iii ('Quem tu Melpomene.' Recognition).

Anacreontea. Poems of Love and Wine.

   Odes I. v ('Quis multa gracilis').
     ,,   I. xxii ('Integer vitae').
     ,,   III. ix ('Donec gratus eram tibi').
     ,,   III. vii ('Quid fles, Asterie.' A novel in a nutshell).
     ,,   III. xxvii (Europa. A lyric with a narrative and dramatic element).
     ,,   III. xxi ('O nata mecum').

A Poet of Nature and the Country.

   Odes III. xiii ('O fons Bandusiae').
     ,,   III. xviii ('Faune, Nympharum').
     ,,   III. xxiii ('Caelo supinas.' Phidyle).

Hymns to gods.

   Odes I. x (Mercury. Mythological).
     ,,   I. xxi (To Apollo and Diana, the tutelar divinities of Augustus. To be compared with Catullus, xxxiv).
     ,,   I. xxxiv ('Parcus deorum cultor.' A declaration of belief; not, perhaps, what he would say in a satire or epistle).
     ,,   II. xix ('Bacchum in remotis.' A more subtle study. Ecstasy subsiding into tranquillity; a delineation of the κάθαρσις of ἐνθουσιασμός).

Poems of friendship.

   Odes I. xxiv ('Quis desiderio.' On the death of Quintilius).
     ,,   II. i ('Motum ex Metello.' Pollio).
     ,,   II. vii ('O saepe mecum.' Philippi).
     ,,   II. ix ('Non semper imbres.' To Valgius, deprecating plaintive elegies).
     ,,   II. xvii ('Cur me querelis.' Maecenas).

Poems on the philosophy of life.

   Odes II. iii ('Aequam memento').
     ,,   II. x ('Rectius vives, Licini').
     ,,   II. xviii ('Non ebur nec aureum').
     ,,   III. i (The poet's creed).

This selection includes 55 poems out of 121. It is only tentative; other selections could be made. But if the pupil read these pieces he would certainly get some idea of the scope and quality of Horace's poetry; and of the pieces that are excluded, many would quite certainly be excluded by any selecting hand. The Metrical Selection includes a few poems which would also come under one or other of the subsequent heads (the first and second, for example, are poems of Nature or Natural Scenery).

II. Homogeneous Metres

(μέτρα μονοειδῆ)

By a homogeneous metre is meant one which uses the same foot—or rather the same type or εἶδος of foot—throughout. Such a metre is the dactylic hexameter; for the spondee that occurs in it is not a different type of foot—a long syllable takes the place of two shorts, that is all. Such also is the iambic trimeter; for here also the spondee is not to be thought of as an alien or dissimilar element.

i. *Dactylic.*

Horace uses the hexameter as an alternate line, the first of a couplet. A poem written in hexameters throughout could hardly count as a 'lyric'. The second line is sometimes iambic or in part iambic: that arrangement belongs to Section III (*infra*). When the second line is dactylic, the couplet, and the metre of the whole poem, come under our present head 'Homogeneous'.

First, a word about the nature of Horace's hexameter. The student is perhaps tempted to dismiss it without consideration: 'Hexameter? Oh, that is the metre we know in Virgil.' This is a great mistake, and will result in failure to appreciate Horace's metrical art. A lyric hexameter and an epic hexameter are very different things. There is nothing in Horace's hexameters at all resembling such things as

>   monstrum horrendum, informe, ingens

or

>   omnia praecepi atque animo mecum ante peregi.

Here in one line are three elisions ('monstr(um)', 'horrend(um)', 'inform(e)'—'praecep(i)', 'atqu(e)', 'mec(um)'). A lyric line must have a lighter and more rapid movement, and the rapidity is achieved mainly by the avoidance of elision. In Horace's lyric hexameters an elision occurs on the average about once in every twelve lines. In the *Aeneid* they are about six times as numerous, one occurring in every two lines.[1] The lyric hexameter runs swiftly and smoothly to its close; and, further, rapidity is given to a passage or group of lines by variety of pause: sometimes a strong pause occurs within a line, and a slight one, or none, at the end of it, e.g.:

---

[1] There are 123 hexameters in the *Odes* and *Epodes*, and in them there are ten elisions. Of the ten, three are elisions of the short *e* of *neque*, and it is not certain that Horace did not write *nec*. In the *Eclogues*—which are lyric and dramatic in character, not epic or heroic—elisions are less frequent than in the *Aeneid*. In several eclogues an elision occurs at the rate of one to every three lines; in others they are still less frequent (in *Ecl.* vii, one to eight lines). It is a very rare thing in the *Eclogues* to find two elisions in the same line. When Seneca uses the hexameter in lyrical passages of tragedy he has no elisions at all (*Med.* 110-15, *Oed.* 407 f.).

THE LYRIC METRES

> ... seu te fulgentia signis
> castra tenent | seu densa tenebit
> Tiburis umbra tui. | Teucer Salamina patremque
> cum fugeret | tamen uda Lyaeo
> tempora populea fertur vinxisse corona.
>
> (*Odes* i. 7. 19–23.)

The caesura is usually of a very normal sort, in the middle of the third or fourth foot (penthemimeral—coming after the fifth half-foot, as in 'Tiburis umbra tui'—or hepthemimeral, after the seventh). Horace does *not* (as one might perhaps expect him to do) make much use of the 'trochaic' caesura, which divides a dactyl thus: $-\cup\,|\,\cup$

> naturae verique. sed omnes una manet nox.
>
> (i. 28. 15.)[1]

Two purely dactylic metres are used by Horace. (a) In *Odes* i. 7 and 28 a hexameter is followed by a shorter dactylic line of four feet (tetrameter). The shorter, like the longer, ends in a spondee, and is similar in its general effect. It shows greater freedom in its termination; it may end with a word of four syllables, or with two disyllables (*morituro, nihil ultra, Venusinae, nocituram,* etc.). The hexameter conforms to what may be called the general norm of the Virgilian or Ovidian hexameter, i.e. a quadrisyllabic ending occurs usually in the shape of a Greek proper name (*Rhodon aut Mўtilēnēn, comes Ōriōnis*). (b) In *Odes* iv. 7 the couplet consists of a hexameter followed by what may conveniently be called a dactylic tripody catalectic, $-\cup\cup\,-\cup\cup\,-$, the group of syllables which forms the second half of a 'pentameter'; more accurately, or more rhythmically, written $-\cup\cup\,-\cup\cup\,-\bar{\wedge}$; i.e. the third dactyl is incomplete, only half of it is expressed in

---

[1] It is the comparative frequency of the 'trochaic' caesura in Homer that gives to the Homeric hexameter its rapid movement.

sound, and the rest of its time (equal to the duration of one long syllable) is a pause or space of silence. There is only one elision in the whole poem (or none at all, if we read *nec* for *neque* in l. 25). The shorter line does not conform in its termination to the norm of the Ovidian pentameter; there is no overwhelming preference for an ending in a word of two syllables (*quae dederis animo, fecerit arbitria*—only six lines out of fourteen have a disyllabic ending).[1]

ii. *Iambic.*

In one of the *Epodes* (xvi) Horace writes, as the second line of a couplet, a line consisting of pure iambic feet throughout

$$\cup - \cup - \cup - \cup - \cup - \cup -.$$

With these light and rapid iambi are associated hexameters in which no elision occurs; in the iambic lines there are only four elisions (two cases of '*neque*', and elision of the final syllables of *ratem* and *gregem* (ll. 24 and 62). Thus the poem as a whole has in an eminent degree the ease and rapidity of movement which we have already observed in Horace's dactylic verse. Catullus had written the same form of iambic verse (in iv, 'Phaselus ille quem videtis hospites'). Neither poet admits so much as a tribrach or resolved iambus, a thing which could be done without adding any weight to the line.

A verse written with this degree of strictness and regularity is an artificial thing, and Catullus perhaps learned it from the poets of Alexandria.[2] Horace, however, appears to have

---

[1] This metre is the nearest approach that Horace makes to elegiac verse. He does not write that; he seems to prefer to attach to a hexameter anything rather than a pentameter. There are indications that he was not in sympathy with Propertius, and when he addresses Tibullus (i. 33) and Valgius (ii. 9) it is to deprecate the plaintive tone of the elegy. Suetonius says that he had seen elegiac poems that were said to be Horace's, but he thought them spurious.

[2] In Archilochus and in the Attic drama a line consisting of pure

thought that it was the original form of the iambic trimeter, and that spondees were admitted later (*Ars Poet.* 255-8):

> tardior ut paullo graviorque veniret ad aures,
> spondeos stabiles in iura paterna recepit
> commodus et patiens, non ut de sede secunda
> cederet aut quarta socialiter.

The iambus, with good-natured courtesy and tolerance, allowed spondees to come in, but not to the extent of vacating in their favour the second or fourth place in the line. The view is unhistorical, but it gives us briefly the structure of an iambic line. It is assumed as a matter of course that the iambus did not vacate the sixth and last place. Even in the verse of Plautus and Terence he does not do that. What account can be given of this arrangement? A genuine spondee is not equal to an iambus; it is a foot of four times ($--=\cup\cup\cup\cup$), not of three. No poet would deliberately set about constructing a line out of elements or bars so unequal as these.

A clue is supplied by the Greek name of the metre—Trimeter. The Romans called it a *Senarius*, with less understanding of its nature. In calling it a trimeter the Greek was thinking of a dipody as the μέτρον or constituent or unit of measurement. It is a line of three dipodies. Now in the group $\cup-\cup-$ there is one syllable which can be lengthened, which may be allowed to be somewhat heavier, without impairing the general effect. That is the first syllable; the dipody may be $--\cup-$.[1] The *second* foot must be a pure

iambi, with no spondee, does of course occur from time to time. Such a line is also found in lyric systems (e. g. ἄγουσά τ' ἀντίφερνον Ἰλίῳ φθοράν, Aes. *Agam.* 406). What is new in Catullus is the use of it throughout a poem, line after line (κατὰ στίχον).

[1] Rhythmically, or when the verse was sung, the syllable probably had not the time of a normal long. The time may have been $1\frac{1}{2}:2$, not $2:2$. For such a syllable some metricians have used the symbol $>$ ($>-$, a spondee which could be combined with iambi; $->$, a heavy trochee or trochaic spondee). Or the time may have been $1\frac{1}{2}:1\frac{1}{2}$.

iambus. In trochaic verse the converse is seen. It is the last syllable of the dipody that may be heavier; it is the first foot that must be a pure trochee. If we try the experiment of inverting the order in either case, we shall see that this is inevitable. If the second iambus were allowed to be heavy, the dipody would present the appearance of $\smile - - -$, a short syllable and three longs, an amorphous thing. So, if the first trochee were heavy, the syllables would be $- - - \smile$, again a thing that has no obvious rhythm or easily recognizable structure. The trochaic dipody, with this option in the last syllable ($- \smile - \overset{\smile}{-}$) is an element in many forms of verse. We shall meet with it again in lyric measures, and shall there find that a further step was possible—to enact that the last syllable of the four *must* be heavy or long.

It remains to describe briefly the chief forms of Horatian iambi and their characteristics.

In one poem (*Ep.* xvii) he uses the trimeter throughout, line after line (κατὰ στίχον), with the normal option of a spondee in the first, third, and fifth places.[1]

In the first ten epodes he uses the same line as an alternate one, putting after it the shorter dimeter (of four feet, *quaternarius*). Such a line was called an ἐπῳδός, whence the name *epodi* for the whole collection of pieces.

(*a*) The caesura is usually conspicuous and highly normal, in the third or fourth foot:

[1] In lines 11-12 of this poem Horace has a metrical effect which recalls the older tragedians, Ennius or Pacuvius :

> unxere matres Iliae addictum feris
> alitibus atque canibus homicidam Hectorem.

Several of the old tragedies were on subjects taken from the story of Troy. Though Horace speaks of them elsewhere with no great admiration, thinking their versification heavy and cumbrous, the mention of Hector recalls them to his mind, and in the second of these lines, without violating his own stricter canons, he writes a line in the manner of Ennius.

beatus ille | qui procul negotiis.
minatus urbi vincla | quae detraxerat.

(β) A tribrach is admitted, i.e. the long syllable may be resolved. When the long is so resolved, the two short syllables must be in the same word:

pavidumquĕ lĕpŏrem et advenam laqueo gruem

(observe that the ordinary accent on the first syllable of 'léporem' helps the effect, coinciding with the *ictus* of a resolved iambus; ∪⊥ becomes ∪ ∪∪). Thus in the line

aut amite levi rara tendit retia

metre at once determines that the words are 'amite levi;
$$\cup\cup\cup--$$
$$--|\cup\cup\cup|-$$
for the scansion 'aut amite levi' would divide a tribrach wrongly.

(γ) There are a few instances of what seems to be an anapaest in the fifth place (so *laqueo* in a line just quoted):

priusque terra sidet inferius mari.
nunc gloriantis quamlibet mulierculam.

But all of them are open to a doubt: it is possible to pronounce 'inferyus', 'mulyerculam'. It is not clear that Horace meant to admit an anapaest in the fifth foot at all.

(δ) Horace's iambi do not conform to the rule known as 'Porson's Canon'.

The rule is that if the last word in a line is in form a 'cretic' foot (−∪−, *Tusculi*), and if the preceding word is one of more than one syllable, then the syllable immediately preceding the 'cretic' must be short.

Thus the rule is *not* broken in the line:

furorne caecus an rapit | vis acrior

but it is broken in lines like:

non ut superni villa | candens | Tusculi.

Such lines are very rare in the Greek drama, and where they do occur, attempts have been made to remove them by conjectural emendation.[1] When the rule is violated, the line is weighted towards the end, an effect which seems to have pleased the Romans. It is used by Horace in a special way, to weight the end of the couplet. In the first ten epodes there are 366 lines, 183 trimeters, and 183 dimeters. In the trimeters the Porsonian rule is broken seventeen times; in the dimeters—that is, at the end of the couplet—seventy-four times. In the trimeters the effect occurs on the average once in eleven lines, in the dimeters nearly twice in every five lines.[2]

(ε) If we consider the number of lines in which the penultimate foot is a spondee, we find a similar result and a similar contrast between the trimeter and dimeter. Out of 183 trimeters 97 have that ending; of the 183 dimeters only 16 (or 15) have *not* a spondee in the third place; as many as 167 are spondaic. But even in trimeters Horace has

---

[1] A famous instance is the first line of the *Ion* of Euripides:

Ἄτλας ὁ χαλκέοισι νώτοις οὐρανόν

emended by writing νώτοις χαλκέοισιν. In

... Ἀριώμαρδος Σάρδεσιν,

Aes. *Pers.* 321, a proper name justifies the deviation from rule.

[2] As against these seventy-four cases, there are only six certain examples of the type:

pernicis uxŏr Apuli,

where the line ends in a word of three syllables, and the Porsonian rule is *not* violated. Therefore in the line v. 100:

et Esquilinae alites

the probability is quite 12 to 1 that Horace meant 'Esquilināe alites', i.e. there is no shortening (a thing which belonged to dactylic verse in Greek, not to iambic), but rather what is seen in Virgil's line

Glaucō et Panopeae et Inoo Melicertae

(where Panopeǎe is an instance of what it is *not* safe to assume in Horatian or highly hellenized iambics).

a penultimate spondee more often than the Greek tragic poets; the percentage in his verses is 53, in theirs about 40.[1] Roman tragedy, we shall not be surprised to find, is heavier still in its penultimate feet. In Seneca's tragedies the spondee seems to be compulsory (with the alternative of an anapaest); examples of iambi in the fifth place are very rare and doubtful.

One other form of iambic verse remains to be mentioned—the 'catalectic' line, which is the second of the couplet in *Odes* ii. 18:

> non ebur nec aureum
> mea renidet in domo lacunar.

This couplet is a 'homogeneous' metre, though the first line is a trochaic ($-\cup-\cup-\cup-\wedge$); a trochee is a foot of the same kind or type as an iambus, its parts being in the same ratio of 2 : 1. But it is not certain that the first line would be thought of as trochaic. It was called Εὐριπίδειον (or ληκύθιον sometimes, from the scene in Aristophanes, *Frogs* 1200 f.). It was part of an iambic line, from the penthemimeral caesura onwards. Further, it is a question whether iambic or trochaic scansion is preferable for the second line. Taken as trochaic, with a preliminary syllable or 'anacrusis', the line is:

$$\underline{\cup} \mid -\cup-\underline{\cup}-\cup-\cup\underline{\ \ }-\wedge$$

This scansion gives the more intelligible account of the closing cadence; the penultimate syllable is one of three times ($=\cup\cup\cup$ or $=$ a whole trochee), and the last syllable is part of a trochee—a trochee catalectic.[2] The line, however, begins with an iambic movement, and it is not impossible that Horace thought of it as made up of two parts:

---

[1] This is based on a survey of about 500 lines of tragedy.
[2] The last syllable of *lacunar* is short in prosody, but the last syllable of a line is a *syllaba anceps*, i.e. may be reckoned metrically as long.

mea renidet | in domo lacunar.¹

'mea renidet' is the first part of an iambic line, the two-and-a-half feet that come before one of the chief pauses. 'in domo lacunar', $-\cup-\cup-\overset{\smile}{-}$ or $-\cup-\cup\llcorner-\wedge$ is a well-known metrical group or phrase; and it is a phrase which Horace appends to a group of dactyls in an ode (i. 4) in which the second line of the couplet is the line we are now considering. It is only in these two odes that Horace uses this metrical phrase; the other ode is not 'homogeneous' and belongs to Section III.²

iii. *Ionic.*

The only other 'homogeneous' metre written by Horace is the Ionic verse of *Odes* iii. 12. This is so regular and simple in form that little need be said of it. The foot is the *Ionicus a minore*, $\cup\cup--$, and the poem consists of four stanzas, each containing ten *Ionici*. Within the stanza the grouping seems to be $4+4+2$, but this is more doubtful. The end of a foot is usually marked by the end of a word, an arrangement which has a somewhat monotonous effect. Catullus used this metre in a very different way in the 'Attis' (see p. 163).

[1] This view is found in Terentianus Maurus:

sequens epodos | cum parte iambi tres habet trochaeos.

[2] The pause after the fifth syllable is quite distinct in every line of i. 4 ('regumque turres. o beate Sesti'). It is a curious fact that Horace's line wants only the addition of one iambus to make it a normal Saturnian:

mea ⟨quidem⟩ renidet | in domo lacunar
dabunt malum Metelli | Naevio poetae.

Perhaps the *horridus numerus* of the *carmina Livi*, enforced by the cane of Orbilius, made a deeper impression upon his mind than he cares to admit. It may be noted also that there are a few Saturnians which have as their first part syllables answering to *non ebur nec aureum* (in Naevius, 'immolabat auream'; 'qui suis astutiis' ($-\cup---\cup-$) in t e verses o he 'Collegium Coquorum').

III. Archilochian or Parian Metres

(μέτρα ἐπισύνθετα)

Archilochus of Paros, in the seventh century B.C., wrote both iambic poems and elegies. Horace is a professed follower of his, and claims to have been the first to present his 'iambi' to the Roman reader:

> Parios ego primus iambos
> ostendi Latio, numeros animosque secutus
> Archilochi.   (*Epp.* i. 19. 23.)

The claim at first sight seems a little unjust to Catullus, who certainly had something of the spirit or 'animi' of Archilochus. But as regards the 'numeri' it is strictly justified. Catullus writes the 'scazon' mainly (which belonged to Hipponax, not to Archilochus), very seldom the ordinary trimeter, in more than one poem the rigid form of verse which admitted no spondee, and nowhere the combination of trimeter with dimeter in a couplet, which Horace uses regularly in his *Epodes*.

But Archilochus not only wrote iambic and elegiac poems separately; he also combined the two forms of metre in the same verse or couplet, and here, too, Horace probably had a valid claim to be the first to introduce Archilochian 'numeri' at Rome. Greater variety, piquancy, or complexity was given to a verse by combining in it different metres. But what Archilochus did was not to fuse or mix up different types of feet. To put a dactyl and a trochee in the same group or κῶλον was a thing which belonged not to him, but to the Aeolian or Lesbian school of poets. What Archilochus did was to set down a *group* of iambi or trochees beside a group of dactyls. The groups were *internally* homogeneous; it was only the whole verse or couplet that combined unlike elements. The simplest example of such an arrangement is a hexameter followed by an iambic trimeter (*Epode* xvi):

> altera iam teritur bellis civilibus aetas,
> suis et ipsa Roma viribus ruit.

But the groups combined may be shorter than these, and the transition from one movement to another more frequent:

> ∪ − ∪ − − − ∪ − | − ∪∪ − ∪∪ −
> nivesque deducunt Iovem. | nunc mare nunc siluae

(iambic dimeter followed by a dactylic tripody catalectic).

Here the reader may be disposed to ask: ' Is this last example a *verse* made up of two *groups* or κῶλα, or is it two verses? What do you mean by verse and by κῶλον?' One thing that can be said with some certainty in answer is that for a group, phrase, or κῶλον there was an upward limit of length; e.g. for dactyls the limit was four. A series of more than four dactyls is not one phrase but two.[1] Is there also a downward limit for a ' verse'? 'Verse' is a looser term, and perhaps not much would be gained by making it a strict one. A simple κῶλον or phrase may be a 'verse', e.g. it would be inconvenient to be debarred from speaking of an iambic dimeter as a 'verse'. The phrases

> nivesque deducunt Iovem
> nunc mare nunc siluae

are long enough to serve as separate verses. They may be written in one line if the poet or the editor wishes to suggest that they are to be taken very closely together, with only a slight pause between them. Another question is possible: 'Is there a downward limit for a κῶλον?' e.g. do the *two*

[1] A hexameter consists of two κῶλα, not exactly equal in length, linked together by the device of the caesura.

dactyls in the last line of an Alcaic stanza make a κῶλον? But this question does not yet concern us; for in his Archilochian metres Horace uses no phrase shorter than three dactyls or four iambi.

The Archilochian metres present no great difficulties or problems. We may classify them by taking first those in which there is least complexity:

(1) A dactylic hexameter of the rapid, lyric type described in Section II, followed by an iambic trimeter which also moves rapidly, having in it no spondees. *Epode* xvi. There are no elisions in the hexameters, and in the iambi they are very few and slight.

(2) *Epodes* xiv and xv. Hexameter followed by iambic dimeter. The dimeter has the characteristics already noted as belonging to it when it follows an iambic trimeter; a liking for a spondee in the fifth place, and ready admission of an ending like 'adhaerens bracchiis', which does not conform to the Porsonian rule.

(3) A hexameter followed by a line of which the second half is the second half of an elegiac 'pentameter', while the first half is an iambic dimeter. They *are* 'halves' in time or rhythm, for an iambic dimeter and a dactylic tripody alike have twelve *morae* or *tempora* (each is a δωδεκάσημον or δωδεκάχρονον μέγεθος). We have seen that each is long enough to count as a separate verse. Further, they *are* written as separate verses; for at the end of the first (as is *not* the case in an elegiac pentameter) a *syllaba anceps* is admitted (*Epode* xiii):

  ∪ –∪ – –– ∪⌣ – ∪ ∪ – ∪ –⏞
  reducet in sedem vice. | nunc et Achaemenio
  levare diris pectoră | sollicitudinibus
  findunt Scamandri flumină | lubricus et Simois.

Like the dactylic tripody catalectic in *Odes* iv. 7, the second κῶλον shows no preference for the Ovidian disyllabic ending. Out of nine lines, five end in a word of three syllables ('silŭae', l. 2; 'genua', l. 4, &c.).

In one Archilochian metre the iambic part comes first:

(4) An iambic trimeter (admitting spondees in the usual places) followed by a dactylic tripody catalectic and an iambic dimeter. Some of the lines can be construed as a complete dactylic tripody followed by a trochaic dimeter catalectic (*Epode* xi):

$$-\cup\cup\ -\ \cup\ \cup-\ -\ |\ -\cup\ -\ -\ -\ \cup\stackrel{\cup}{-}\wedge$$
fabula quanta fui, con viviorum et paenitet.

But that this is not what Horace meant is shown both by *syllaba anceps*:

Inachia furerĕ | silvis honorem decutit

and by hiatus:

fervidiore mero | arcana promorat loco.

All the dimeters but one have a spondee in the third place, and several of them are also non-Porsonian.

(5) In *Odes* i. 4, the first line consists of a dactylic tetrameter, followed by a trochaic κῶλον of three feet (originally no doubt of four, but we cannot be sure that Horace meant it to be read so):

$$-\cup\ -\cup\ --\quad \text{or}\quad -\cup\ -\cup\ \llcorner\ -\wedge.$$

The second line is one which has been already discussed (p. 236). In the first line no hiatus occurs between the dactylic and the trochaic part; the two parts are not 'asynartete' or detached, as in the case in the compound lines of *Epodes* xi and xiii.

IV. METRES OF THE 'AEOLIAN' OR 'LESBIAN' TYPE

(μέτρα μικτά)

When a dactyl and a trochee occur in juxtaposition within what is undoubtedly one phrase or κῶλον, we have a type of metre clearly different from the two preceding kinds. The κῶλον is now internally heterogeneous.[1]

Verse of this kind was probably as old as Archilochus, and perhaps much older; for it would seem to belong to quite primitive minstrelsy to make the less conspicuous part of a foot consist indifferently of one short syllable or of two. But it is in the Lesbian poets, a little later than Archilochus, that it first appears in an artistic shape and finds a place in literature. This Lesbian or Aeolian verse perhaps retained one feature of its origin; some forms of it began with two syllables which seem to be subject to no restriction; they may be − − or ∪ − or − ∪ or ∪ ∪ − or even ∪ ∪. This so-called 'basis' or 'basis Aeolica' is in Horace strictly regulated. It is uniformly a spondee.[2]

But, it may be asked, how are we to draw a line between this type of metre and the 'Parian' type? This is the question which we postponed—how *short* may a κῶλον be? If *two* consecutive feet are alike, are we to regard them as a κῶλον and so make the metre Parian? Perhaps it is

---

[1] The term 'Logaoedic' for metre of this kind has fallen into discredit, but some designation is wanted for the class: μικτὸν μέτρον is a convenient and simple term. It is not to be understood as meaning that the feet were of different *length*. When a dactyl was used along with trochees it may have been more rapid, its time equivalent to ∪ ∪ ∪.

[2] With *one* exception in *Odes* i. 15. 36 ('ignis Iliacas domos': it is difficult to believe that the prosody of *ignis* could be *ignīs* and not *ignĭs*). Perhaps an early ode, written before Horace had finally fixed his metrical scheme.

best to postpone the question again, or dismiss it with only an approximate answer; it would be fairly accurate to say that at least three feet must be alike, to be treated as a separate κῶλον. We have seen that no κῶλον in Horace's Parian metres is less than that.

We may approach the matter in a different way by enumerating some of the elements, or groups of syllables, which are met with in the non-Parian metres.

(a) There is first the 'basis' just mentioned, in Horace always − − (found in Asclepiadean, Glyconic, and Pherecratean lines). That it should be separated in some way from the rest of the line seems to be indicated by the occurrence of lines in which it is absent:

δεῦτέ νυν ἅβραι Χάριτες καλλίκομοί τε Μοῦσαι

(which is otherwise very like 'nullam, Vare, sacra', &c. *Odes* i. 18).

(b) Another important element is the trochaic dipody, − ∪ − ∪ or − ∪ − −. The second of these forms, with the last syllable long, is, or coincides with, the Pindaric 'epitritus', and it has been suggested that in the third line of the Alcaic stanza Horace has a Pindaric effect in view, though the metre he is writing is a very different one.[1]

(c) With this we may associate ⊻ − ∪ − −, that is, epitritus with anacrusis, or the first two and a half feet of an iambic trimeter (ἰαμβικὸν πενθημιμερές).

(d) The syllables − ∪ ∪ −, sometimes reckoned as a 'choriambus', are also a dactylic dimeter catalectic.

(e) − ∪ ∪ − ∪ − may be described as an Aeolic tripody. In *Odes* i. 8, it is longer by a syllable:

[1] The 'epitritus' in Pindar is regularly used in metres of the 'Parian' type. The name 'epitritus' comes from measuring the length of its component parts, − ∪ and − − (∪ ∪ ∪ and ∪ ∪ ∪ ∪), 3 : 4. Adjectives compounded with ἐπι- express the ratio of $n+1$ to n (ἐπόγδοος, 9 : 8, &c.).

Lydia dic per omnes,

a line or group which originally and musically was probably a tetrapody, $-\cup\cup\ -\cup\ \llcorner\ -\wedge$. Here it occurs at the beginning and end of a couplet, with (b) + (d) intervening

hoc deos ve're Sybarin, $-\cup\ --\ |\ -\cup\ \cup-$.

These are nearly all the elements that are required for the construction of Horace's non-Parian metres. (e) may be thought of as a κῶλον, but for other and shorter groups of syllables Caesius Bassus, who wrote on metre not long after Horace's time, supplies another convenient word, κόμμα, *incisum*; κόμμα is a block or cut-off portion—(c) is a portion of an iambic trimeter. It is probable that Horace himself thought of such *commata* and that he was guided in so doing by a metrical theory to which Varro had given currency at Rome. According to this theory the primary metres were the dactylic hexameter, the iambic trimeter, and the trochaic tetrameter. Other metres were supposed to have been arrived at by combining portions of these. Thus the 'hendecasyllabic' line, which Catullus uses and Horace does not use, could be regarded as consisting of a part of a hexameter + part of a trimeter:

$$- \ -|- \ \cup\cup|- \ \ | \ \ \cup- \ | \ \cup-\underset{\smile}{}$$
cui dono lepidum | novum libellum.

But if this was its nature, the first two syllables should both be long, for an iambus or a trochee cannot form part of a hexameter. Hence, perhaps, Horace's regular spondaic 'basis'; so, too, in Martial and Statius a hendecasyllabic line always begins with two long syllables. It can hardly be doubted that the influence of this theory is one of the causes why a Horatian line is often so different in effect from the corresponding line in Sappho or Alcaeus. The Greek line runs lightly as a single whole, whereas Horace's line is made up of two *commata*.

The metres that we have now to consider fall under the three heads of Alcaic, Sapphic, and Asclepiadean, the last of these carrying with it the similar but shorter Glyconic and Pherecratean lines.

i. *The Alcaic Stanza.*

The Alcaic stanza is constructed, out of the elements specified above, in the following way: The first two lines consist of (c)+(e); the third line of (c)+(b); while the last line is an extended form of (e), beginning with two dactyls instead of one, and completing its last foot, instead of being catalectic. The effect of the whole becomes more apparent if instead of (c) we write (b) with anacrusis. The stanza then runs

$$\smile (b) + (e)$$
$$\smile (b) + (e)$$
$$\smile (b) + (b)$$
$$E$$

The fourth line is a larger form of (e), without anacrusis. Thus the third and fourth lines repeat on a larger scale the movement which is found in each of the first two lines; using simpler symbols we may describe the stanza as a b a b A B. It is this structure that gives to the third line its peculiar weight and significance; it has often been observed that the effect of a Horatian Alcaic stanza depends largely on that line. It is a weighty line, similar to Pindar's 'epitrite', with the fifth syllable always long. In the first two lines, we may say, this movement maintains itself for about half the line; then a dactyl breaks in upon it, but without maintaining itself—a trochee follows; in the third line the 'epitrite' movement holds out twice as long, the dactylic invasion is staved off longer; then in the fourth line the dactyl rushes in in greater force—this time there are two dactyls instead of one, and then trochees reappear in a somewhat fuller form than in the first and second lines.

To recognize this as the real movement of Horace's stanzas involves ruling out certain views of it which have sometimes been held. We must refuse to believe that the first and second lines end in two dactyls.[1] And we shall not be inclined to accept a 'choriambic' or 'Ionic' scansion, which makes the stanza end thus:

$$| -$$
sacerdos

$$- \cup \cup |- \quad \cup \cup - | \cup - -$$
virginibus puerisque canto.

The chief features of Horace's stanza, as compared with Alcaeus's, are that in the first two lines he has a *diaeresis* at a fixed place, and that he makes the fourth syllable of the group $- \cup - \overset{\smile}{}$ regularly long.[2] The first two lines thus

---

[1] If Horace himself thought that they did, which is perhaps not impossible, he must have held also that a long final syllable could count as short. But it is difficult to believe that he so thought or felt about

ne forte credas interitura, qu$\overline{ae}$
longe sonantem natus ad Aufidum ...

A *syllaba anceps* in the sense of a short syllable that counted as long is common enough. The converse is more difficult and doubtful. A final dactyl belongs properly to lines which are 'hypermetric', e. g.:

πολλάκι δ' ἐν κορυφαῖς ὀρέων ὅκἄ
θεοῖσιν ἅδῃ πολύφαμος ἑορτά κτλ. (Alcman.)

(Compare the verses of Ibycus quoted above, p. 123, where the final dactyl occurs in a group of lines meant to be hypermetric, and *not* in a contiguous group.) The view that a long could count as a short, put in circulation by Heraclides Ponticus or some other theorist, perhaps misled Seneca into writing a cretic where he ought to have had a dactyl: *Oed.* 449 f., in a passage of seventeen lines he has five heavy endings—

vivaces hederas rem$\bar{u}$s t$\breve{e}$n$\breve{e}$t
summa ligat vitis carchesia.

[2] From this rule Horace departs only *once*, in *Odes* iii:

si non perir$\breve{e}$t inmiserabilis
captiva pubes.

So rare a thing has naturally caused editors to doubt about the text, and become more complex structures ; and an air of Roman *gravitas* is lent to the whole, which makes the verse an appropriate vehicle for the moral and patriotic reflections of *Odes* iii. 1-4. The *diaeresis* gives to the first and second lines an effect like that of the elegiac pentameter (which does not necessarily have dactyls in its first part, only in the second). Horace introduces it with great regularity; there are only two lines in which it is wholly absent (i. 37. 14 'mentemque lymphatam Mareotico'; iv. 14. 17 'spectandus in certamine Martio'); in three others the *diaeresis* is marked by the slight pause or division between the parts of a compound word ('antehac nefas de|promere Caecubum, i. 37. 5).

In certain types of verse, such as the elegiac pentameter, the end of a κῶλον or κόμμα or metrical section is regularly marked by the end of a word. Apart from such structures, a line or κῶλον usually tends to *avoid* any marked agreement between words and metrical elements. Thus a hexameter has its marked pause (*caesura*) within a metrical foot, not at the end of it; and the *parts* of a pentameter illustrate the principle, though the whole does not (e.g. 'lucida | sidera | nox' is inadmissible). Coincidence between word and foot is perhaps most frequent in trochaic tetrameters:

quaeque silvas quaeque lucos quaeque montes incolunt.

---

to suggest emendations (e. g. *perires*, followed by vocative). But it is Horace's way to deviate now and again from a self-imposed rule, as if he said to us, 'I know quite well that the metre as Alcaeus wrote it admits something different, but I choose to make certain long syllables regular because it suits the Latin language, and makes the verse more uniform and therefore easier for the reader to appreciate'. Seneca probably took the same view, and thought of this *comma* as ᝷ — ∪ — ᝷. He has the fifth syllable short more often than Horace, when he uses the phrase as a detached brick or *tessera* in piecing together a lyric: *Oed.* 752 'effudit armă'; *Agam.* 861 'Aurora movĭt ad solitas vices'; *ibid.* 916 'latravit orĕ'.

In the third and fourth lines of his stanza Horace usually avoids it. A line like:

    Alcaee | plectro | dura | navis (ii. 13. 27.)

is very rare, and Mr. Page points out that in five of the eight instances the penultimate word is repeated at the beginning of the next line:

      dura navis,
    dura fugae mala, dura belli,

and that in one of the other three a special effect of sound seems to be intended ('pronos relabi posse rivos'). The three long syllables of the line are very frequently in one word:

     – – –
   audita Musarum sacerdos.

In the fourth line the prevalent *caesura* is shown in

   virginibus | puerisque canto.

The 'trochaic' division of the second dactyl is much rarer

    – ∪ | ∪
   interiore nota Falerni.

One other question requires an answer—that of what is called synapheia (συνάφεια, from συναφής) or 'hypermetron', continuity of scansion between one line and the next. Virgil admits this effect in hexameters, but not very frequently:

    turres et tecta Latinorum
   ardua cernebant iuvenes.

It was regular in anapaests; and naturally frequent in any group of short lyric lines, for a break coming at short intervals would give to the whole an effect of disconnexion.[1] A line is

---

[1] The continuity of utterance involved caused 'hypermetric' systems to have in Greek the name πνῖγος. A good example occurs in Eurip. *Ion* 184-7:

   οὐκ ἐν ταῖς ζαθέαις Ἀθά-
   ναις εὐκίονες ἦσαν αὐ-
   λαὶ θεῶν μόνον, οὐδ' ἀγυι-
   άτιδες θεραπεῖαι.

detached from the line that follows it when it ends with a *syllaba anceps* or when there is no elision between them. On the other hand, the absence of elision and of a *syllaba anceps* does not *prove* that a hypermetric effect was intended, though, if they are absent throughout a whole poem, there is a strong presumption that the poet wrote the piece or the stanzas of it on the 'hypermetric' principle. 'Hypermetron' is positively revealed when there *is* elision or when a word runs on into the second line. In the Alcaic stanza Horace does not bind himself to a hypermetric structure. Mr. Page collects eighteen instances of *hiatus* or the absence of elision (all in the first three books—none in the fourth); there are about as many instances of *syllaba anceps* in the first book alone, e.g.:

> hic tibi copiā | manabit·
> quanta laborabas Charybdĭ | digne puer, &c.

Unmistakable 'hypermetron' occurs chiefly between the third and fourth lines of the stanza. There are only two instances of elision:

> nos in aetern|um exilium impositura   (ii. 3. 27.)
> delabentis Etrusc|um in mare.   (iii. 29. 35.)

In one instance the third line ends in a preposition:

> retusum in | Massagetas.   (i. 35. 39.)

In eight it ends with *et*, preceded by elision:

> barbarorum et | purpurei.   (i. 35. 11.)

Similarly, but without elision (once):

> depone sub lauru mea nec | parce cadis.   (ii. 7. 19.)

Thus there are twelve cases of unmistakable or all but certain continuity; to set against them, only one instance of a similar thing between the first and second lines:

> fuge quaerere et | quem Fors dierum.   (i. 9. 13.)

Catullus has the similar ending:

> saltuumque reconditorum
> amniumque sonantum.   (xxxiv. 11-12.)

ii. *The Sapphic Stanza.*

The so-called 'longer Sapphic' has already been explained (*Odes* i. 8 'Lydia, dic, per omnes'; see p. 244). We are now concerned with the shorter and more familiar Sapphic, which Horace uses very frequently and which had been attempted by Catullus.

The Aeolian line written by Sappho may be thought of as a line of five trochaic feet, light in its movement, in which the writer exercises once the option of making the lighter part of the foot consist of two syllables instead of one. This, as we have seen, was perhaps a feature of very primitive verse, but in Sappho's verse it is strictly regulated; it occurs in the third foot, and nowhere else. Its occurrence in the second place gives a 'Phalaecean' line

φίλταθ' Ἁρμόδι', οὔ τί που τέθνηκας.

The quadrisyllabic or choriambic scansion adopted by some recent metricians divides a Sapphic line thus:

$$-\cup-\overset{\smile}{-}\ |\ -\cup\cup-\ |\ \cup-\overset{\smile}{-}.$$

In either case it begins with a trochaic dipody, and here, as in the Alcaic stanza, Horace makes the fourth syllable invariably long, $-\cup--$. At the end of the line also he obviously has a preference for this effect. Most lines end with a completed spondee $\overset{-\ \cup}{\ \ }$. An ending like 'diuque | laetus intersis' is infrequent.[1]

Sappho's verses now and again, but only now and again have a pause after the fifth syllable:

καὶ γὰρ αἰ φεύγει | ταχέως διώξει.

[1] And '-que' may be a *syllaba anceps*. Horace has no line like Sappho's

πύκνα δινεῦντες πτέρ' ἀπ' ὠράνω αἴθε-
ρος διὰ μέσσω,

where the last foot can hardly be anything but a trochee.

For reasons which can only be conjectured, not certainly ascertained, Horace had a special liking for this type of line. In the third book he has it throughout; in the first occasionally, and in the second twice, he has a pause which answers to the 'trochaic' or 'Homeric' caesura in the hexameter, dividing a dactyl thus, $-\cup\mid\cup$:

Mercuri, facunde | nepos Atlantis.

In the fourth book and in the *Carmen Saec.* he admits it more freely. But even there the great majority of lines have a caesura resembling the chief caesura of the Latin hexameter. It may be that the hexameter was in his mind. The result was to make the line a more complex thing, constructed of two parts, just as the 'diaeresis' in the first two lines of the Alcaic stanza gave an effect like that of the elegiac pentameter. But, apart from the analogy of the hexameter, Horace was probably influenced by the metrical theory already mentioned (p. 244). According to this theory of the derivation of metres, a Sapphic line consisted of the beginning of a trochaic line ($-\cup-\overset{\smile}{-}$, two and a half feet) and the beginning of an iambic one ($\cup\cup-\cup--$, again two and a half feet; an anapaest is of course admissible in the first place in a senarius). He may have meant to make this structure obvious. Catullus followed Sappho, and bound himself by no such rule. He has the Horatian caesura quite frequently, but he also has lines without either of Horace's pauses:

seu Sacas sagittiferosque Persas.[1]

After Horace, the Horatian caesura becomes normal and invariable. Sapphic lines are regularly written with a caesura after the fifth syllable. This can be seen in Statius (*Silvae* iv. 7) and in the lyrical parts of Seneca's tragedies (e. g. *Medea* 579–669). Further, in his freer lyric compositions,

---

[1] Catullus, it will be observed, also admits a trochee in the second place, 'seu Sacas sä-', 'pauca nūntĭate'; but he does not have it very often.

Seneca uses the two portions of a Horatian Sapphic separately; for him the two 'commata' are detachable metrical units or phrases, which can be used like bricks for building a different structure. Sometimes, for example, he inverts their order:

> niveique lactis | candidos fontes.   (*Oed.* 495.)

Sometimes he repeats the first part:

> nomen alternis | stella quae mutat,   (*Agam.* 820.)

or the second:

> vetuitque collo | pereunte nasci.   (*Ibid.* 836.)

He deals with Alcaic *commata* in the same way, sometimes combining Alcaic and Sapphic:

> procella Fortunae | movet aut iniqui.   (*Ibid.* 594.)

Further, the metrical theory seems to appear in the fact that in place of the two short syllables in a Sapphic he admits ∪ or –:

> roscidae noctis iussitque Phoebum
> nullus hunc terror | něc impotentis
> praebuit saevis tinxitque crudos
> vicit acceptis | cūm fulsit armis;

for an iambic senarius does not necessarily, or even very frequently, begin with an anapaest.

When the place of the caesura was once fixed, in a Latin Sapphic, the incidence of accents was to a large extent determined:

> quále porténtum néque militáris
> Daúnias látis álit aesculétis
> nec Iubae téllus génerat leónum
>   arida nutrix.

'quále porténtum', 'Daúnias látis'—the words may vary in length, but the principles of Latin accentuation put the accent on the same syllable. The regularity is interfered with only when a word of *one* syllable occurs in certain positions, as is seen in the third of these lines, 'nec Iúbae' (in 'póne sub cúrru' there is no such disturbance). The ode to which the lines belong (i. 22 'Integer vitae') has been set to music in modern times on the basis of accent:

Ínteger vítae scélerisque púrus,

and, further, it has even been advanced as a theory that Horace wrote with this accentual scheme in view. Conscious observation of accent in *one* of the many elaborate forms of Greek lyric which Horace cultivates is not in itself a very probable thing. Some feeling for Latin accent, it is true, seems to be required to explain the modifications which certain Greek metres underwent on being transferred to Latin. But it is difficult to believe that the attention to accent was deliberate.

The line which closes a Sapphic stanza, known as *Adoneus*, requires little discussion. Its scheme is $-\cup\cup-\asymp$, dactyl and spondee. It may be noted that its form resembles the end of a Virgilian or Augustan hexameter; it consists usually of words of two, or three, syllables ('terruit urbem', 'augur Apollo'). The exceptions are: 'Fabriciumque', 'Mercuriusque', 'militiaeque', 'est hederae vis', 'Bellerophonten', 'seu Genitalis', and several lines of the type 'se quoque fugit', 'te duce, Caesar', 'cum bove pagus'.

In regard to synapheia or hypermetron, the facts are very much the same as in Alcaic verse. Horace does not bind himself to continuity of scansion, but has it not unfrequently. It appears that when there is hiatus between one line and the next, the final syllable is never a short vowel, but always a long one, or *um* or *em* ('insecutae | Orphea silvae'; 'leonum | arida nutrix'). Here we see again Horace's preference for $-\cup--$ as compared with $-\cup-\cup$. Close connexion between the third and fourth line is indicated by effects like 'nigroqu|e invidet Orco' (though this occurs also in other places of the stanza) and more clearly by division of a word between them, 'Iove non probante ux|orius amnis' (not found in other places).

iii. *Asclepiadean Metres.*

Glyconic and Pherecratean. The Lesser and Greater Asclepiadean.

If we prefix to the 'Aeolic tripody' described above, the usual disyllabic 'basis', the result is a 'Glyconic' line: $\underline{\smile}\,\underline{\smile}\mid-\smile\smile\,-\smile-$. This may be interpreted as trochaic, with a rapid dactyl taking the place of one of the trochees $(-\smile\mid-\smile\smile\mid-\smile\mid-\wedge)$. On the other or quadrisyllabic interpretation it is $\underline{\smile}\,\underline{\smile}\,-\smile\mid\smile-\,\smile-$:

$$\smile\,-\,-\,\breve{\smile}\mid\smile-\,\smile-$$
ἄριστον μὲν | ὕδωρ ὁ δὲ

(Pindar, *Ol.* i. 1.)

(antispast + diiambus). But it is difficult to believe that the two short syllables do not go together, and that they form part of a dactyl is indicated by the occurrence in Greek of shortenings which belong to dactylic verse (κείσομαῖ before a vowel). The 'Pherecratean' line is shorter by a syllable;[1] probably what happens is that a penultimate trochee takes the form of a single protracted syllable:

$$\underline{\smile}\,\underline{\smile}\mid-\smile\smile\mid\sqcup\mid-\wedge$$

This line was eminently suited to be the last of a group or stanza, and a good example of the arrangement is preserved from Anacreon:

---

[1] The fifth-century comic poet Pherecrates devised a type of anapaestic metre which coincided in syllables with the lyric verse we are considering:

ἄνδρες, πρόσσχετε τὸν νοῦν
ἐξευρήματι καινῷ
συμπτύκτοις ἀναπαίστοις.

This may have been $-\,\angle\mid\sqcup\mid\smile\smile-\mid-\overline{\wedge}$. How the name came to be given to the lyric verse is unknown.

> γουνοῦμαί σ' ἐλαφηβόλε
> ξανθὴ παῖ Διός, ἀγρίων
> δέσποιν', Ἄρτεμι, θηρῶν.

Anacreon writes this verse with synapheia or hypermetrically (e.g. ἐλαφηβόλε̄ | ξανθὴ). This stanza was used by Catullus in his 'Hymn to Diana', and in his 'Epithalamium' (in the former there are three Glyconic lines in the stanza, in the latter four):

> silvarumque virentium
> saltuumque reconditor-
>   um] amniumque sonantum.

The metre was also used by tragic and comic poets (e.g. the passage from Euripides quoted above, p. 248, note). But Horace would have none of it. Was he avoiding the tracks of Catullus?

> libera per vacuum posui vestigia princeps,
> non aliena meo pressi pede.

Not only does he avoid this stanza, but he uses the Pherecratean line *not* as the last of a group, but as the third of four. With Horace, the Glyconic becomes a closing line; in the verse of

> quis multa gracilis te puer in rosa,

Pherecratean precedes it, in other odes it follows a group of three Asclepiadeans; or, again (as in i. 3), it precedes, in a dipody, a line which is not shorter than itself, like the Pherecratean, but the lesser Asclepiadean, which is longer.

In all metres of this type Horace made the 'basis' consist regularly of two long syllables. Catullus did not. Following the greater freedom of the early Greek poets he admits a trochee or an iambus, and he gives rapidity of movement to his 'Epithalamium' by making the initial trochee very frequent. Horace's practice was probably due to a metrical theory which elicited from a single hexameter both the Glyconic and Pherecratean lines:

> cui non dictus Hylas puer
> aut Latonia Delos

(when Virgil's hexameter is thus cut into two separate verses, the last syllable of 'puer' can be taken as a *syllaba anceps*).

The 'Asclepiadean' metres may safely be regarded as extensions or expansions of the Glyconic.[1] The Aeolic tripody $-\cup\cup-\cup-$, *dulce decus meum*, may be thought of as postponed by the interposition of an incomplete form of it, thus:

> O et [dulce decus] dulce decus meum

and the incompletion or postponement may occur twice:

> nullam, Vare, sacra vite prius severis arborem,

that is

> nullam severis arb- severis arb- severis arborem.

But this fictitious example introduces what Horace avoids, the severance of a word at the end of the 'choriambus' or choriambic group of syllables, $-\cup\cup-$. Horace's scheme is illustrated rather by

> quae nunc oppositis debilitat pumicibus mare

converted into

> quae nunc pumicibus pumicibus pumicibus mare.

In Alcaeus and Catullus the severance of a word is not avoided:

> μηδὲν ἄλλο φυτεύ-σῃς πρότερον δένδριον ἀμπέλω.

> nec facta impia fal-lacum hominum caelicolis placent.

Whatever scheme of scansion Horace had in mind, he must

---

[1] The name may be derived from Asclepiades of Samos, the elegiac poet contemporary with Philetas. But there seems to be no other evidence for his use of the verse. Presumably he, or another poet of the same name, used it extensively, κατὰ στίχον. But extant passages of Alcaeus show that he also had written it κατὰ στίχον.

OF HORACE

have felt that to carry a word over this point would involve a prolongation of a syllable, a thing which is unnatural except when verse is actually sung. The lyric poet is of course in theory a singer throughout, but except in the *Carmen Saeculare*, and perhaps in one or two other pieces, Horace is really writing for readers. So he makes the end of a 'choriambus' coincide with the end of a word, so that instead of a prolongation there may be a short pause.[1] If such a difficulty was felt the inference would seem to be that the choriambus, whatever may have been the description of it in ancient metrical or musical notation, was not simply $-\cup\cup-$, but rather $-\cup\cup\mathrel{\llcorner}$ or $-\cup\cup-\wedge$. Thus we seem to have a definite justification for adopting the 'trochaic' or modern or rationalizing method of scansion. But it is not safe to say, 'This *was* the ancient notation'. Probably it was not; quite possibly, however, if we could put this notation before an ancient metrician or musician he would say: 'I see; that is a good method of notation: it was not ours, but it seems in many ways better, simpler, and more consistent.'

Horace observes with considerable strictness the rule which he has adopted for the 'choriambus' in Asclepiadean verse. In a few instances he admits, instead of the end of a word, the end of a prefix or part of a compound word:

> arcanique fides prodiga per-lucidior vitro.[2]
> dum flagrantia de-torquet ad oscula.

---

[1] It seems fairly clear that it is for the same reason that the first half of an elegiac 'pentameter' ends with the end of a word. Elegiac verse was a metre which at an early date came to be merely read and not necessarily sung.

[2] Pompeius (157. 5 к) declares that Horace's *perlucidior vitro* shows the separable compound with *per* 'very', e.g. 'per pol saepe peccas' (Plaut.). It is quite likely that this *per* was more detached or detachable than other prefixes. But it is hardly credible that Horace intended it here. To compare an adj. with the prefix *per* is a solecism. It is a virtual superlative; *per*beatis*simus* belongs to vulgar Latin.

This resembles his deviations from the rule of the diaeresis in Alcaic lines:

> utrumque nostrum in|credibili modo

(*supra*, p. 247). In Alcaics he twice goes further than this:

> mentemque lympha|tam Mareotico.

In Asclepiadeans the only similar thing occurs in iv. 8:

> non incendia Car|thaginis impiae.

The text of this ode has been a subject of much discussion, but there is no good reason for denying this line to Horace. Metrical rules were often stretched or relaxed when a proper name had to be introduced. Further it may be said to be Horace's general practice to break once or twice a rule which he has imposed upon himself, as if he were saying, 'I reserve my freedom; I write as I do quite deliberately and I know that the verse can be written otherwise'.

V. Schemes of Horace's Lyric Metres

(in the order in which they have been dealt with above).

1. Μέτρα μονοειδῆ.

Dactylic.

(a) i. 7 and 28.

$$-\overline{\cup\cup} \mid -\overline{\cup\cup} \mid -\overline{\cup\cup} \mid -\overline{\cup\cup} \mid -\cup\cup \mid -\underset{\smile}{-}{}^{1}$$
$$-\overline{\cup\cup} \mid -\overline{\cup\cup} \mid -\cup\cup \mid -\underset{\smile}{-}$$

(b) iv. 7.

$$-\overline{\cup\cup} \mid -\overline{\cup\cup} \mid -\overline{\cup\cup} \mid -\overline{\cup\cup} \mid -\cup\cup \mid -\underset{\smile}{-}$$
$$-\cup\cup \mid -\cup\cup \mid -\overline{\wedge}$$

---

[1] The last syllable may be marked $\underset{\smile}{-}$ from the point of view of prosody. It is often actually a short syllable. Metrically the last foot is $--\frown$.

A spondee in the fifth foot is so rare that it has not been indicated in the scheme. It is rare also in the third foot of the second line ('mensorem cohibent, Archyta,' *Odes* i. 28. 2).

OF HORACE

Iambic.

(a) *Epode* xvii.

$\;\underline{\smile}\,\underline{\smile\smile}\;|\;\smile\,\underline{\smile\smile}\;|\;\underline{\smile}\,\underline{\smile\smile}\;|\;\smile\,\underline{\smile\smile}\;|\;\underline{\smile}\,-\;|\;\smile\,-$

(b) *Epodes* i–x.

$\;\underline{\smile\smile}-\;|$
$\underline{\smile}\,\underline{\smile\smile}\;\Big|\;\smile\,\underline{\smile\smile}\;|\;\underline{\smile}\,\underline{\smile\smile}\;|\;\smile\,-\;|\;\underline{\smile}\,-\;|\;\smile\,-$
$\underline{\smile}\,\underline{\smile\smile}\;|\;\smile\,-\;|\;\underline{\smile}\,-\;|\;\smile\,-$

(c) ii. 18 (the first line perhaps 'trochaic').

$-\smile\;-\smile\;-\smile\;-\wedge$
$\underline{\smile}\,-\;|\;\smile\,-\;|\;\underline{\smile}\,-\;|\;\smile\,-\;|\;\smile\,-\;|\;-$
(or $\underline{\smile}\,-\;|\;\smile\,-\;|\;\underline{\smile}\,\|\,-\smile\;|\,-\smile\;|\,\sqcup\,|\,-\wedge$)

Ionic.

iii. 12.

$\smile\smile\,--\;|\;\smile\smile\,--\;|\;\smile\smile\,--\;|\;\smile\smile\,--$
$\smile\smile\,--\;|\;\smile\smile\,--\;|\;\smile\smile\,--\;|\;\smile\smile\,--$
$\smile\smile\,--\;|\;\smile\smile\,--$

2. Μέτρα ἐπισύνθετα.

('Parian.')

(1) *Epode* xvi.

$-\,\underline{\smile\smile}\;|\;-\,\underline{\smile\smile}\;|\;-\,\underline{\smile\smile}\;|\;-\,\underline{\smile\smile}\;|\;-\smile\smile\;|\;--$ [1]
$\smile\,-\;|\;\smile\,-\;|\;\smile\,-\;|\;\smile\,-\;|\;\smile\,-$

(2) *Epodes* xiv and xv.

$-\,\underline{\smile\smile}\;|\;-\,\underline{\smile\smile}\;|\;-\,\underline{\smile\smile}\;|\;-\,\underline{\smile\smile}\;|\;-\smile\smile\;|\;--$
$\underline{\smile}\,\underline{\smile\smile}\;|\;\smile\,-\;|\;\underline{\smile}\,-\;|\;\smile\,-$

(3) *Epode* xiii.

$-\,\underline{\smile\smile}\;|\;-\,\underline{\smile\smile}\;|\;-\,\underline{\smile\smile}\;|\;-\,\underline{\smile\smile}\;|\;-\smile\smile\;|\;--$ [1]
$\underline{\smile}\,-\;|\;\smile\,-\;|\;\underline{\smile}\,-\;|\;\smile\,\underline{\smile}\;\|\;-\smile\smile\;|\;-\smile\smile\;|\;-\overline{\wedge}$

(4) *Epode* xi.

$\underline{\smile}\,\underline{\smile\smile}\;|\;\smile\,-\;|\;\underline{\smile}\,-\;|\;\smile\,-\;|\;\underline{\smile}\,-\;|\;\smile\,-$
$-\smile\smile\;|\;-\smile\smile\;|\;-\overline{\wedge}\;\|\;\underline{\smile}\,-\;|\;\smile\,-\;|\;\underline{\smile}\,-\;|\;\smile\,-$

---

[1] The fifth foot is twice a spondee (l. 17 and l. 29) in Epode xvi, once a spondee in Epode xlii (l. 9).

THE LYRIC METRES OF HORACE

(5) *Odes* i. 4.

$-\cup\cup\ |\ -\cup\cup\ |\ -\cup\cup\ |\ -\cup\cup\ \|\ -\cup\ -\cup\ --$
$\smile-\ |\ \cup-\ |\ \smile-\ |\ \cup-\ |\ \cup-\ |\ -$
(or $\smile-\ |\ \cup-\ |\ \smile\ \|\ -\cup\ |\ -\cup\ |\ -\ |\ -\wedge$)

3. Μέτρα μικτά.

i. *The Alcaic Stanza.*

$\smile\ -\cup\ --\ |\ -\cup\cup\ -\cup\ -$
$\smile\ -\cup\ --\ |\ -\cup\cup\ -\cup\ -$
$\smile\ -\cup\ --\ -\cup\ -\smile$
$-\cup\cup\ -\cup\cup\ -\cup\ -\smile$

ii. *The Sapphic Stanza.*

$-\cup\ --\ -\ \vdots\ \cup\cup\ -\cup\ -\smile\ (ter)$ [1]
$-\cup\cup\ -\smile$ (Adoneus)

The longer Sapphic, *Odes* i. 8.

$-\cup\cup\ -\cup\ --$
$-\cup\ --\ |\ -\cup\cup\ -\ |\ -\cup\cup\ -\cup\ --$

iii. '*Asclepiadean*' *metres* (including Glyconic and Pherecratean).

Horace uses the following forms:

(a) $--\ -\cup\cup\ -\smile$ (Pherecratean)
(b) $--\ -\cup\cup\ -\cup\ -$ (Glyconic)
(c) $--\ -\cup\cup\ -\ -\cup\cup\ -\cup\ \smile$ (Lesser Asclepiadean)
(d) $--\ -\cup\cup\ -\ -\cup\cup\ -\ -\cup\cup\ -\cup\ -$ (Greater Asclepiadean)

(c) and (d) are written κατὰ στίχον—the same line throughout—in a few odes (i. 1, iii. 30, iv. 8: i. 11, 18, iv. 12): a) and (b) only in combination with other lines. The stanzas used are as follows:

Odes i. 3, (b) + (c).
„ 5, (c) (c) (a) (b).
„ 6, (c) *ter* + (b).

---

[1] Sometimes, but not often

$-\cup\ --\ -\cup\ \vdots\ \cup\ -\cup\ -\cup.$

APPENDIX

(A)

GLOSSARY OF SOME METRICAL TERMS

Accent is sometimes used in the sense of *ictus*. This is a dangerous usage, which may lead to serious confusion of ideas.

Neither accent, in its proper sense, nor quantity is a merely metrical phenomenon. They are things existing in actual speech, outside metre altogether. Either may form the basis of verse. The poet arranges words in such a way that accented syllables (or long syllables) come at regular intervals, satisfying his sense of rhythm. The metrician describes this when it has been done; he furnishes the outline or scheme of the verse. Sometimes the poet is also a metrician, and tells us what scheme he had in mind; sometimes he is not, and we do not know for certain how he would have described his work. In the words that the poet puts together the accented or long syllables are already fixed by current usage. Accent may mean that certain syllables are pronounced on a higher note, differing in musical pitch (as was the case in Greek), or that certain syllables are pronounced more loudly, with a greater effort of the voice (a 'stress' accent, as in modern Greek and English). When accent is the basis of verse, accent and ictus normally coincide.

While it is substantially true that accent and quantity exist already for the poet, it may be admitted that metrical study and the practice of poets sometimes make a difference to the language for an educated ear. Quantity may be regulated, emphasized, elicited. The early poets, and Ennius in particular, did this for the Latin language. They developed what was quantitative in it. Mr. Bridges and others have tried to do this for English, with less success. 'Hīs pleăsŭre īn hăppĭnēss' is a hemistich that depreciates the English accent and involves the rules for 'quantity by position', that *nh* makes a syllable long, and *pp*—a double consonant—means a short syllable. Neither rule is altogether convincing for the English ear.

Anacrusis (from ἀνακρούω, 'strike up', strike a preliminary note on the lyre): a term, unknown to the ancient poets, invented in modern times to designate what is very familiar in modern music, a note or syllable which precedes the first actual bar of the measure. Whether such a syllable should be recognized is not an important question for Latin versification; in Horatian metre the question of anacrusis arises only in the case of the first three lines of an Alcaic stanza.

Theoretically, a verse with anacrusis is also catalectic, and the syllable which appears at the beginning is equal to the syllable lost at the end, e.g. a trochaic line should, in theory, have a short syllable as anacrusis: $\smile \mid -\smile-\smile-\smile- \wedge$. But there seem to be undoubted instances of verses with anacrusis which are *not* catalectic, e. g. Aes. *Prom.* 135:

σύθην δ' ἀπέδιλος ὄχῳ πτερωτῷ

(= the fourth line of an Alcaic stanza, with a short syllable prefixed). If the third line of an Alcaic stanza has an anacrusis it has it without catalexis.

The word, and the idea, seem to be required for certain forms of strictly lyrical Greek verse. It is a mistake to apply the notion to such verse as spoken senarii, and to construe these as trochees with anacrusis. (The notion of anacrusis is not out of harmony with ancient ideas. Trochaic and iambic verse were the same 'in rhythm', the ratio of the parts of the foot was the same, 2 : 1. What did occur to the ancients was the converse idea that an iambic verse might be 'acephalous', or lack its first syllable.)

Aphaeresis is used for the converse of elision: the following vowel, not the preceding one, is 'taken away' (ἀφαιρεῖται), and has no place in the metrical scheme, as in μὴ 'γώ for μὴ ἐγώ. Latin elided a long vowel freely, and had practically no use for aphaeresis.

Arsis and **Thesis**. The Greeks meant by arsis the lifting of the foot in the march or dance, and by thesis the downward movement. In an anapaest the two short syllables accompany the former movement, the long syllable the latter:

arsis | thesis
$\smile \smile$ | $-$

Hence for the Greeks the long syllable in a dactyl, anapaest, iambus, &c., is the thesis, the rest of the foot the arsis.

A different use of the terms grew up in Roman imperial times, and after that yet another usage, which has been the prevalent one with modern metricians—the *voice* and not the foot came to be thought of, and hence *arsis* and *thesis* exchanged meanings. The long syllable in the anapaest came to be called the arsis. 'Rise' and 'fall' in English, and 'Hebung' and 'Senkung' in German, have been adopted as terms answering to this use of arsis and thesis. In view of these equivalents it would be a mistake to revive the Greek use of the words.

Asynartete (ἀσυνάρτητος, συναρτᾶν, fasten together): Horace's line:

$\smile - \mid \smile - \mid - - \mid \smile \stackrel{\smile}{-}$
reducet in sedem vice. | nunc et Achaemenio

is asynartete; it would have been 'synartete' if he had made it a rule that the last syllable of the iambic part must always be an actual long syllable, and that it may not be followed by a hiatus. An elegiac pentameter is 'synartete'. In Horace's line there is a rupture of continuity; the two parts or κῶλα are not 'fastened together' or closely attached. The short syllable of 'vicĕ' counts as a long, with a pause after it.

Basis: (1) a step in march or dance, the lifting and lowering of the foot, arsis+thesis. The term belongs chiefly to anapaests. (2) Basis or 'basis Aeolica' is used to designate what is something not unlike an anacrusis, except that it consists of two syllables or a whole foot. In Horace, and in poets after him who use metres to which it belongs (e.g. Statius and Martial in hendecasyllabics), it is always two long syllables or a spondee (one exception, *Odes* i. 15. 36). In the early Greek poets it may be − ∪ or ∪ −, and occasionally it is ∪ ∪ − or ∪ ∪ (Catullus admits − ∪ and ∪ −).

Brachycatalectic: it is doubtful whether this term has any utility at all, and at all events it is of no use for Horace.

Bucolic: belonging to herdsmen (βουκόλοι) or to the songs of herdsmen (Pastorals, *Bucolica*). The hexameters of Theocritus very frequently have a division at the end of the fourth foot, and this was called the bucolic diaeresis:

ἡ κατὰ Πηνειῶ καλὰ τέμπεα | ἡ κατὰ Πίνδω
nam neque Parnassi vobis iuga, nam neque Pindi

(the end of a word is not enough. 'Peliaco quondam prognatae vertice pinus' is not a bucolic line. To make a line 'bucolic' in any useful sense of the term there must be a more or less marked rhetorical pause or pause in the sense).

Caesura (τομή): a cutting or severance, a break or division of a verse which does not coincide with the end of a metrical foot (some writers use the word to include also a division which does coincide with a metrical ending, but it seems expedient to call that by a different name, diaeresis). A hexameter must have a caesura, it may not fall into two equal parts. A line written by Ennius:

spernitur orator bonus, horridu' miles amatur,

is defective, and not to be imitated. A senarius also must have a caesura, a pause *not* at the end of the third foot, but in the third or fourth foot. Aeschylus's line:

Θρᾴκην περάσαντες | μόγις πολλῷ πόνῳ

may have been meant to depict a slow and halting march.

Catalexis, catalectic (καταλήγω, stop, come to an end, break off): catalexis takes place, and the line is catalectic, when instead of a syllable or syllables uttered by the voice there is a pause of silence answering to them in duration. The last foot is incomplete (in sound, not in time). Thus, when dactylic verse is catalectic, two short syllables (= one long) are dropped (or are unrepresented in sound): $-\cup\cup-\cup\cup-\overline{\wedge}$. (See 'Pause.')

Colon (κῶλον): a 'phrase' or coherent group of feet, sometimes forming in itself a 'verse' (στίχος, *versus*), sometimes part of a verse. A hexameter and a pentameter are 'verses' consisting of two *cola*. But sometimes the distinction between a 'colon' and a 'verse' is rather arbitrary or conventional. An 'asynartete' verse

(reducet in sedem vicĕ. | nunc et Achaemenio)

might appear as two lines or *versus*, if the poet or his editor so determined:

>reducet in sedem vice.
>nunc et Achaemenio.

Comma (κόμμα, *incisum*): a term used in rhetoric for a group of words shorter than a κῶλον, and also used by Caesius Bassus in metre.

It is convenient to use it for a group of syllables which have not the length and independence of a κῶλον, but yet do form a separable group, e.g. the first five syllables of a Sapphic line, $-\cup--$, which is a 'comma' or severed portion, of a trochaic line. But the parts into which a hexameter is divided by the 'caesura' should not be called commata. A dactylic hexameter is not one κῶλον made up of two commata, but a line, *versus* or στίχος, made up of two κῶλα.

Crasis (κρᾶσις, κεράννυμι) takes place when a vowel at the end of a word is not elided before a following vowel, but fused with it. Thus if καί could suffer elision, καὶ ἐγώ would be κ'ἐγώ ($\cup -$; but with καί crasis is the rule, and the result is a spondee, not an iambus (κἀγώ, $--$).

'Cyclic' dactyl: a term which rests on a very doubtful passage in Dionysius, where there is mention of a special kind of anapaest 'which they call κύκλιος' (if κύκλιος is right, an anapaest belonging to the dithyramb and its κύκλιος χορός would be meant: 'cyclic' answers to κυκλικός, and would connect the foot with epic poetry).

It was used by J. H. H. Schmidt and other metricians of last century to denote a dactyl shorter and more rapid than a normal one, answering in time to a trochee, and capable of being combined with trochees. The symbol $\frown\cup$ was used for it, and the time was supposed to be ♩♪♩. The theory was that a normal long syllable could be replaced by slightly shorter syllable with a very short one attached to it, $\frown\cup$ for $-$. (When a dactyl is divided by caesura, as in the Horatian Sapphic, ♩ ♫ seems more probable.) Such a dactyl could be described as a δάκτυλος τρίχρονος or τρίσημος.

APPENDIX

Diaeresis: a break, word-ending, or division which coincides with the end of a foot or a metrical group. It is convenient to have a term other than caesura for such a division as that in the middle of an elegiac pentameter or a trochaic tetrameter:

$$\acute{-} \cup - \underset{\smile}{-} \acute{-} \cup - \underset{\smile}{-} \mid \acute{-} \cup - \underset{\smile}{-} \acute{-} \cup - \wedge.$$

Horace's break in the first two lines of an Alcaic stanza is also to be described as a diaeresis. The syllables $\underset{\smile}{-} - \cup - -$, with which the line begins, were perhaps thought of as part of an iambic senarius; but the break would be a 'caesura' only if what followed were the rest of an iambic verse—whereas a quite different effect follows, beginning with a dactyl. The scansion 'odí | profán|um vúlg|us et árc|eó' (iambic, of a kind, throughout) is not to be thought of.

Diiambus and **Ditrochaeus** (δίς) are terms sometimes used for an iambic or trochaic dipody ($\underset{\smile}{-} - \cup -$ and $- \cup - \underset{\smile}{-}$). (Cic. and Quint. used 'dichoreus' for $- \cup - \underset{\smile}{-}$, and meant by *trochaeus* what we call a 'tribrach'.)

Dimeter: a term used for a group of *four* feet (tetrapody) in certain kinds of verse: i.e. the unit of measurement is not one foot, but a pair or dipody. Iambic and trochaic verse were so divided and described by the Greeks (see p. 232). A line of four anapaests also was called a dimeter; but a line of four dactyls was called a tetrameter.

Dipody, tripody, tetrapody, pentapody, hexapody are words used for a phrase or verse measured by the number of single feet that it contains: dipody a group of two πόδες, tripody one of three. Hexapody, if in use, would answer to senarius.

Elision (*elidere*, force out, thrust out): a vowel 'elided' before a following vowel was 'thrust out' of the metre or metrical scheme. For metre 'elision' is a term that expresses the fact better and more clearly than the Greek word συναλοιφή. The vowel did not count metrically, though it is not to be supposed that it was altogether inaudible or entirely omitted by the voice.[1]

In Greek it was chiefly the short vowels α, ε, ο that were treated in this way. Latin went much further, and regularly elided vowels long or short, and also final syllables in *m*. Thus in *regnō ŏberat* the long *o* has no place in the metre, it is the following *ŏ* that counts ($- \cup \cup \underset{\smile}{-}$). See *Hiatus*.

Epitritus (πούς ἐπίτριτος, a foot divided in the ratio 4:3): a name for the group of syllables $- \cup - -$ ($\cup \cup \cup \mid \cup \cup \cup \cup$), a trochaic dipody or 'ditrochaeus', ending with the heavier syllable which was allowed in that place. Whether the time was really 3+4 and the 'foot' ἑπτάσημος is a very disputable matter.

---

[1] Forms like *animadverto, magnŏpere, domitio* (= *domum itio*, homecoming) seem to point to great attenuation of the vowel or of *um*.

The term is chiefly used for an element in those odes of Pindar that are sometimes called 'dactylo-epitrite' (a form of metre used also by the tragedians), where it is combined with what on one theory is a dactylic κῶλον (usually $-\cup\cup\ -\cup\cup\ --$), and on another a choriambic and Ionic group ($-\cup\cup-\ |\ \cup\cup\ --$).

Hiatus: a verse *hiat*, there is a break or 'gap' in it when a vowel is not elided before a following vowel: 'Glāucō | ēt Pănŏpēaĕ ĕt Inoo Melicertae.' 'Glauc' et, Panope' et' is the normal, continuous scansion in Latin, but here the vowels stand side by side; between them, instead of a consonant, there is nothing, a 'gap' or 'rift'.

Hiatus is of two kinds, both exemplified in this line of Virgil. (1) The preceding vowel retains its length, (2) it is shortened. (2) is a regular practice in Greek dactylic verse, but it seems to have also had some root in Latin. 'Ĭtă mĕ | dī ămēnt, lĕpĭde āccĭpĭmŭr (Plautus), ān quī ămant' (Virg. *Eclogues*), probably answering to actual facts of pronunciation.

Latin verse admitted both kinds very sparingly. Virgil's 'insulāe Ionio in magno' is explained by the fact that a word of Cretic form ($-\cup-$, īnsŭlāe) was not allowed to suffer elision in heroic verse. In Greek epic verse hiatus is more frequent, and when short syllables follow a long it is admitted very freely (Πηληιάδεω Ἀχιλῆος, in *Il*. i. 1).

Hypercatalectic. See 'Brachycatalectic' and 'Anacrusis'. 'Acephalous' and 'Hypercatalexis' were ancient terms used to account for things which the modern notion of 'anacrusis' often explains in a simpler way.

Hypermetron or synapheia: metrical continuity between one line and the next (συνάφεια, contact, absence of any metrical severance or interruption). This is found chiefly in anapaests and in some Glyconic stanzas (see p. 248). The last syllable is not a *syllaba anceps*, and elision takes place if the next line begins with a vowel. The end of a line may fall within a word. In Horace's lyrics, as in most metres, this effect is permissive, not imperative. In some forms of verse it is very rare; Sophocles now and again has elision at the end of an iambic line, σὺν οἷς τ' | οὐ χρῆν ὁμιλῶν, and Laevius in iambic dimeters writes:

> saurae, inlices bicodulae, hin-
> nientium dulcedines.

In an epigram of Simonides it is used to bring an intractable name into an elegiac couplet:

> ἦ μέγ' Ἀθηναίοισι φάος γένεθ', ἡνίκ' Ἀριστο-
> γείτων Ἵππαρχον κτεῖνε καὶ Ἁρμόδιος.

Horace has it occasionally in this, the most unmistakable form of it ('nequé purpura ve|nale neque auro').

It might be convenient to use 'hypermetron' for metrical continuity between one *line* and the next, and 'synapheia' for continuity between two κῶλα which make up a line.

Ictus, 'beat'. Horace uses the word when he imagines himself to be training a chorus:

> Lesbium servate pedem meique
> pollicis ictum.

In this sense it is a movement of the hand or foot, accompanying the metre, but outside of it. In 'pavidumque leporem' (p. 234) the ictus of a resolved iambus is on the first syllable of 'leporem' (∪ ∪∪ taking the place of ∪ −). On that syllable falls also the ordinary accent of the Latin word 'léporem'. The ictus marks the 'arsis' of a foot. But very often it falls on a syllable which is not accented. It is a matter of dispute what an ictus was. Was it made audible? Was it of the nature of a slight stress accent? In 'arma virumque cano' the first syllable of 'cáno' is the syllable on which the ordinary accent falls; the ictus falls on the second. How then was 'cánó' pronounced here? How was 'Itáliám' pronounced in the next line? That is a question to which no very definite or certain answer can be given. To read Latin verse well is a difficult thing, at all events for us. Perhaps the following remarks may safely be made about it: (*a*) the metrical structure must not be obscured, it must be felt, and made sensible to the hearer, even if this sometimes involves dropping or attenuating the ordinary accent; (*b*) when the ictus falls on a long syllable a reader or reciter whose native language is English, with its tendency to make a strong stress accent the chief form of emphasis, should endeavour to make the syllable really *long* (prolonged, not made loud), without thinking about an 'ictus' apart from that; (*c*) when the ictus falls on a short syllable he will find that, in Latin, it usually coincides with an ordinary accent (as in 'pavidumque leporem'), so that he need not think about it in this case either.

Lyric. The word 'lyric' is used in two senses, a wider and a narrower one. In its wider sense (as in the title 'Bergk's *Poetae Lyrici Graeci*) a lyric poem is any poem which does not narrate, as an epic does, or put characters and action on the stage, as a drama does, but gives expression to the feelings or thoughts of the poet (or of the poet and his friends, or the poet and his countrymen, as in a lament or a song of victory). In this wide sense it includes elegiac and iambic (abusive or personal) poems. In the narrower sense, which is the ancient one, it means a poem to be sung to music, a song—for which 'melic' poem is sometimes used.

Elegiac and iambic poems had at first a musical accompaniment, but at a quite early date they came to be merely spoken or recited. So they fall clearly within the sphere of 'metre' or *Metrik*; no syllable has more than the time of an ordinary long. It is otherwise with 'melic' poems. Some Greek lyrics were meant *only* to be sung, not to be read at all. In dealing with these *Metrik* is really encroaching upon, or borrowing ideas from, the province of rhythm or music.

Metre, *Metrik*, Μετρική: μετρική is a branch of ῥυθμική, metre is rhythm manifested in a particular medium or ὕλη, namely, articulate syllables or speech. We may think of ῥυθμική as a highly abstract, central inquiry, which provides empty forms or time-spaces, of a certain length and subdivided in one way or another, to be rendered visible or audible by some kind of movement or sound, e. g. ὀρχηστική deals with rhythm as revealed by the movements of a dancer (σχήματα). *Metrik* deals with rhythm as it is worked out in detail in spoken syllables. So Quintilian remarks that dactyl and anapaest are the same in rhythm: 'for rhythm it does not matter whether the two short syllables precede or follow the long'. Metre has sometimes meant a rather mechanical way of describing certain groups of syllables, regardless of their rhythm. Thus a dochmius ($\cup--\cup-$) can be described as consisting ἐξ ἀντισπάστου καὶ συλλαβῆς, $\cup--\cup\,|\,-$, but this is a purely metrical description. For rhythm or music it had to be regarded as a ποὺς ὀκτάσημος (βαίνονται δὲ οἱ ῥυθμοί, τὰ δὲ μέτρα διαιρεῖται, οὐχὶ βαίνεται). In modern times writers on classical verse have usually not been content with a merely descriptive or mechanical system.

Pause (Λεῖμμα, κενὸς χρόνος): the space or interval which is not occupied by sound at the end of a catalectic verse. The symbol in common use for a pause is the initial letter of Λεῖμμα. Without any addition this denotes a pause equal to a short syllable (κενὸς βραχύς). Longer pauses are denoted by adding a symbol of length: thus $\overline{\wedge}$ is a pause equal to $\cup\cup$ or $-$ (κενὸς δίχρονος, or, in the language of music, δίσημος), $\overline{\overline{\wedge}}$ a pause equal to $\cup\cup\cup$ or $-\cup$ (κενὸς τρίχρονος). Only $\wedge$ and $\overline{\wedge}$ are required for Horatian metres ($\overline{\wedge}$ in the case of 'arboribusque comae').

It is difficult to avoid using the word 'pause' for another thing, a slighter and less measurable pause, e. g. the 'bucolic' pause in 'omnia vel medium fiant mare. vivite, silvae'. This is a rhetorical pause or pause required by the sense, and as such outside metre; but it determines the metrical type of line—the line is one with a marked *diaeresis* after the fourth foot.

Prosody is a word which in its origin is not well suited to express what is commonly meant by it; the Greek word προσῳδία meant accent, and the Greek accent was a musical or pitch accent (πρὸς-ᾴδειν).

'Prosody' is now used in two ways:

(1) Sometimes it is used very widely and loosely, to include much of what belongs to metre, *Metrik*, or μετρική.

(2) In relation to Latin and Greek it has a narrower meaning, and a quite useful one. *Metrik* tells us how short and long

syllables are arranged in the various kinds of verse; prosody tells us what actual syllables are short and long, or competent to occupy these places. Thus the distinction between 'lĕvis' and 'lēvis' belongs to prosody. So, again, it is a matter of prosody that the final syllable of 'mihĭ, tibĭ, sibĭ' is *either* short or long. But if we proceed to ask, 'When is it long?' the answer is no longer strictly within the bounds of 'prosody'. Metre is involved, for the fact is that the syllable was originally long, and the old quantity as it were comes to life again when the metrical *ictus* falls on the syllable.

Senarii (sc. *versus*) are (iambic) lines consisting each of six feet, or which have *seni pedes*. A Greek trimeter does in fact contain six feet, but it is convenient to reserve the name *senarius* for the Roman type of verse, which does not, like the Greek, show dipodic structure by excluding spondees from the second and fourth places.

σπονδειάζων (sc. στίχος): a hexameter which ends in two spondees: 'me quoque devexi rapidus comes Orionis' (Hor. *Odes* i. 28. 21), 'sententia Phocaeorum' (*Epode* xvi. 17). Homer has such lines, and the atticization of the Homeric text perhaps increased their number, Ατρείδαο becoming 'Ατρείδαο, and ἠόα δῖαν, ἠῶ δῖαν. In Roman poetry this form of line was admitted by Catullus and his contemporaries: 'moenia vexarentur', 'et decus innuptarum'. Cicero rejects it, and thought it an affectation of the νεώτεροι (*Att.* vii. 2. 1). In Augustan poets it is found chiefly when the dispondeus is a Greek proper name (*supra*, p. 23).

σπονδεῖος (πούς), spondee: a foot of two long syllables or a bar of two long notes (𝅗𝅥 𝅗𝅥), so called because it accompanied a libation (σπονδή). The notes were those of a flute, and no doubt they were often slow or protracted (⊔ ⊔ or 𝅗𝅥 𝅗𝅥): Victorinus, 44. 22 K 'dictus a tractu cantus eius qui per longas tibias in templis supplicantibus editur'.

Syllaba anceps. A syllable which is in the peculiar position of standing at the end of a line is regarded as outside ordinary principles of quantity, it is dubious (*anceps*), and if short may count metrically as long (e.g. 'submovere litorā; reducet in sedem vicē', at the end of a κῶλον), or if long as short. Cic. *Orator* 217: 'postrema syllaba brevis an longa sit, ne in versu quidem refert' ('ne in versu quidem', i.e. still less in a closing cadence of prose). A short counting as a long is very common, and Terentianus describes it clearly:

> omnibus in metris hoc iam retinere memento,
> in fine non obesse pro longa brevem.

Reckoning a long as a short is a more difficult and obscure matter (see p. 246 *n.*).

APPENDIX

Synapheia or Synaphea (συνάφεια) : see **Hypermetron**.

Syncope : what happens when a foot is 'cut down' to one syllable, or compressed into one syllable. Gr. τονή: 'protraction' of the syllable, is another name for the same thing. The foot as a rhythmical unit is not really 'cut down'; the syllable becomes longer than an ordinary long, equal to a trochee in trochaic verse ($-\cup = \sqcup$), or to a dactyl in dactylic verse ($-\cup\cup = \sqcup$). The effect belongs chiefly to Greek lyric verse. Roman poets did not use metres in which it occurs in any obvious or certain way. It is doubtful whether Horace anywhere intended it to be felt.

Synizesis (συνίζησις, a 'sinking' or 'settling' together of two vowels) is most conveniently used for what happens when two vowels within a word, which usually are separate syllables, are combined into one long, e.g. when θεός, θεοί is scanned as one syllable (ὑμῖν μὲν θεοὶ δοῖεν, *Il.* i. 18). So too in compounds: a word like *Theodosius* ($\cup\cup\cup\cup\overset{\smile}{-}$, inadmissible in dactylic verse) becomes *Theudosius*. When the vowels are in separate words the term *crasis* is used.

Thesis: see *Arsis*.

(B)

CHRONOLOGIA METRICA

Pre-Homeric lays (Aeolian ?)

EPIC—Homeric hexameter: Ionian : a verse intended for recitation.
ELEGY—Callinus : Tyrtaeus (? date of Tyrtaeus uncertain).
(650) Archilochus of Paros, elegiac verse and iambi. Dactylic and iambic cola combined. Music and poetry at Sparta. Terpander. Alcman.
LYRIC—
Stesichorus, Dorian lyric in Sicily.
 'Epici carminis onera lyra sustinens' (Quint. x, c. 1).
 Metre—many long dactylic cola.

---

600 Alcaeus,
  στασιωτικά and συμποτικά } Lesbos.
 Sappho, ἐρωτικά   } Aeolian yric.

APPENDIX

Mimnermus, erotic elegy. Solon, political verse (elegiac: iambic and trochaic, Archilochian).
Hipponax: scazon or choliambus.
Thespis at Athens: beginning of tragedy: trochaic tetrameter (Ar. *Poet.* c. iv).
Theognis of Megara: elegy, political and social.
Anacreon comes to Athens: Aeschylus gets from him Ἰωνικοὶ ἀνακλώμενοι.

500   Pratinas protests that the words are more important than the music: τὰν ἀοιδὰν κατέστασε Πιερὶς βασίλειαν.

Pindar: elaborate and varied lyric, measures both Dorian and Aeolian.
Bacchylides, a professional verse-maker: simpler and more mechanical style.
Simonides: epigram, θρῆνοι, &c.
TRAGEDY: in metre, dochmii peculiar to it, for a tragic crisis, a moment of tension and suspense.
COMEDY: the ἰαμβικὴ ἰδέα, abusive, personal and political (Ar. *Poet.* c. iv: Crates opened a new vein).
Cratinus, Eupolis, Aristophanes: iambic verse much freer than that of Archilochus.
Gorgias and Thrasymachus begin to study rhythm in oratory.
Euripides: new developments in music (parodied in *Frogs*): music more complex and less subordinate to words. Tragic trimeter freer and more conversational (resolution more frequent).

400   Timotheos: author of a νόμος now known, Πέρσαι. Philoxenus, dithyrambs.

Plutus of Aristophanes: choric parts slight and simple.
RHETORIC:
Rhythm and prose elaborated by Isocrates and others.
Tragedy becomes rhetorical.
Rhetoric invades history (Theopompus and Ephorus).
Decline of the chorus:
   choric part very slight in comedy.
   ἐμβόλιμα in tragedy (Ar. *Poet.* c. xviii ἄρξαντος Ἀγάθωνος).
Isyllus of Epidaurus (hexr., troch. tetr. and Ionics in a paean to Apollo).
Menander: 'New' Comedy (ἠθικὴ ἰδέα) mainly in iambic trimeters (with occasional passages in trochaic tetrameter).
Philetas of Cos, early Alexandrian elegy.

APPENDIX

GREECE	ROME
300 Asclepiades	
Alexandria { lyric metres written κατὰ στίχον / hexameter prevalent Callimachus— scazon for fables elegiac verse in Αἴτια (narrative)	Epitaph of Scipio (L. Corn. Scipio Barbatus—Gnaivod patre prognatus—consul in 298)
Delphic hymn, cretics *Philosophy* again expressed in verse Pure iambi (Stoics—Cleanthes) Scazons (Phoenix — Cynicism and popular moralizing)	Epitaph of L. Scipio, consul in 259
Herondas } Mixed, prose with Μιμίαμβοι verse intermixed in Scazons } (Menippus and Bion)	*Odisia* of Livius Andronicus
Aratus——Lycophron and in Nicander plainer style harsh and obscure	240 plays produced by Livius
	239 birth of Ennius
Rhinthon, ἱλαροτραγῳδία ἱλαρῳδίαι and μαγῳδίαι (Grenfell's Fragment)	235 Comedy of Naevius
	Plautus writing *palliatae*—cantica from ἱλαρῳδίαι? 204 Ennius comes to Rome Naevius's 'Bellum Punicum' in his old age—Saturnians

200

APPENDIX

GREECE	ROME
* [	Ennius flourished
	Annales (hexameter)
	Hedyphagetica (hexam. looser, like Lucilius)
	Saturae (elegiac and other metres, written with considerable finish and precision)
	Tragedies
* [This section (Greece, 200–100) was left by Prof. Hardie unwritten.]	Terence—less canticum than in Plautus (nearer Menander)
	Togata—same metres as palliata
	Lucilius—iambi, troch., then hexam. in Saturae
	Volcatius Sedigitus
	Porcius Licinus—literary matters discussed in verse
	Accius—tragedies
	also Sotadeans
100]	Saturnians (?)

APPENDIX
ROME

	Hexameter	Drama
	Cicero, Aratea	Atellana popular
63 Cicero consul	Lucretius (rather more archaic and more akin to Enn. than his contemporaries)	Tragedy written as a literary composition, not for the stage (Q. Cicero wrote four tragedies in sixteen days)
48 Pharsalus	'Cantores Euphorionis': hexameter smoother and more finished	Mimus popular Laberius
42 Philippi		Syrus
31 Actium	Ciris? Culex?	
	42–38 Eclogues of Virgil Varro Atacinus VIRGIL (70–19)	Varius, Thyestes, 29 B.C.
AUGUSTUS	(Horace: satires and epistles)	
	OVID (poetry invaded by rhetoric)	Ovid, Medea 'Trabeata' written by Melissus
A.D. 14 d. of Augustus TIBERIUS, 14–37	Manilius, Astronomica	
CALIGULA, 37–41 CLAUDIUS, 41–54 NERO, 54–68	Calpurnius, Pastorals Lucan	Seneca, Tragedies (iambic verse, strict: 5th foot always a spondee Lyrics— Horatian verse, usually κατὰ στίχον)
VESPASIAN TITUS	Valerius Flaccus	Octavia, a praetexta
DOMITIAN	Statius Silius	
NERVA, 96–98 TRAJAN, 98–117		
HADRIAN		

APPENDIX

ROME

Other forms of Poetry

Catulus, erotic epigrams
Laevius, Erotopaegnia: metrical experiments
Saturae of Varro: many metres, written with considerable exactness

ELEGY

Catullus	CATULLUS: Hendecas. (Phalaecei κατὰ στίχον): Scazon (5th foot always an iambus): experiments in Sapphics, Glyconics, Asclep., Galliambics
Gallus	
Tibullus	Catalepton? (or some of the pieces in it?)
Propertius	
Ovid	HORACE: metres of Archilochus (Epodes), Alcaeus, and Sappho (Odes)

Phaedrus, Fabulae (in the senarius of comedy)
Caesius Bassus, lyric and iambic poet (and writer on metre?)

Persius, satirist (Stoic)
Petronius, Satyricon (prose, with occasional verse in various metres)
Seneca, Ludus de Morte Claudii (a Varronian or Menippean satire)

Juvenal: satire in regular and sonorous hexameter (rhetoric now invades even satire)
Hadrian: iambic and trochaic dimeters. Epitaph on his horse in Anacreontics
Florus

PRINTED IN ENGLAND
AT THE OXFORD UNIVERSITY PRESS

OXFORD JUNIOR LATIN SERIES

Under the General Editorship of C. E. FREEMAN

Fcap 8vo, in clear type, with introductions, indexes of proper names, notes, and vocabularies. Cloth, 2s. net

June 1920

'We extend a hearty welcome to this new series, which is assured of success if the future authors to be included in it find editors with the powers of lucid exposition and understanding of boys' needs which are possessed by Mr. Freeman. The introductions are admirably adapted for young readers, and Mr. Freeman is to be heartily congratulated upon what he has achieved, both in these and in the notes, and it is all done simply by taking to heart the old injunction of Marcus Aurelius, ἅπλωσον σεαυτόν!'—*The School World*.

(Of *Horace, Select Odes*) 'This delightful edition ... It would be absurd to deny that the selection has been made with great discrimination. The notes are simplicity itself, and deserve the attention of all teachers of the subject. The introduction, too, is all that is required, as well as the brief, but clear, explanation of Horatian metres. We heartily congratulate Mr. Jackson on his success as an editor and commentator.'—*Secondary Education*.

Virgil, Aeneid I, edited by J. JACKSON. 1920. Pp. 134.

Virgil, Aeneid II, edited by J. JACKSON. 1920. Pp. 140.

Virgil, Aeneid IV, edited by C. E. FREEMAN. 1917. Pp. 108.

Virgil, Aeneid V, edited by C. E. FREEMAN. 1918. Pp. 144.

Virgil, Aeneid VI, edited by C. E. FREEMAN. 1918. Pp. 160.

Horace, Select Odes, edited by J. JACKSON. 1919. Pp. 138.

Selections from Ovid, edited by C. E. FREEMAN. 1917. Pp. 128.

Livy I, edited by C. E. FREEMAN. 1917. With a map. Pp. 198.

Dr. Lowe's Readers

Fcap 8vo, with notes, maps, vocabularies, and exercises. 2s.

Rome and Her Kings: Selections from Livy, Book I, by W. D. LOWE and C. E. FREEMAN. 1916. Pp. 110, with a map and frontispiece.

Tales of the Civil War, from the third book of Caesar's Civil War. Pp. 100, with three maps.

Scenes from the Life of Hannibal: Selections from Livy. Pp. 127, with five maps.

Caesar in Britain: Selections from the fourth and fifth books of the Gallic War. Pp. 96, with a map and six illustrations.

Selections from Ovid. Pp. 96, with five illustrations.

Selections from Cicero. Pp. 96, with a frontispiece.

Tales of Great Generals: Selections from Cornelius Nepos. Pp. 96.

Anecdotes from Pliny's Letters. Pp. 96, with two illustrations.

The Fall of Troy, adapted from Vergil's *Aeneid*. Pp. 96, with five illustrations.